i-Net+

10 Steps To Certification

i-Net+

10 Steps To Certification

LightPoint Learning Solutions

iUniverse.com, Inc.

San Jose   New York   Lincoln   Shanghai

i-Net+ 10 Steps To Certification

Published by iUniverse.com, Inc.

For information address:
iUniverse.com, Inc.
5220 S 16th, Ste. 200
Lincoln, NE 68512
www.iuniverse.com

Cover Creation by Shay Jones

Graphic Production by Matt Bromley, Associate Consultant

ISBN: 0-595-16785-3

Printed in the United States of America

Acknowledgments

We are pleased to acknowledge the following people for their important contributions in the creation of this study guide.

Technical Writer—Caleb Thompson, MS, MCT, MCSE, MCP+I, A+, Network+

Technical Writer—Carl A. Scharpf, i-Net+, MSCE, CNI, CCNA

Technical Writer—Eric Clise

Technical Writer—Patrick Pritchett

Supplemental Content—Loral Pritchett

Editors—Anita Crocus and Nina Gettler

Proofreader—Nina Gettler

Cover Creation—Shay Jones, AA, MCSE, MCP

Technical Reviewers—Cathe Reed and Shay Jones, MCSE

Graphic Designer—Matt Bromley

V.P. of Publishing and Courseware Development—Candace Sinclair

Course Prerequisites

The i-Net+ study guide targets individuals interested in demonstrating baseline technical knowledge that would allow him or her to pursue a variety of Internet-related careers. The certification exam offered by CompTIA validates entry-level knowledge of Internet technology.

The i-Net+ exam tests Internet technical professionals who are hands-on specialists responsible for implementing and maintaining Internet, intranet and extranet infrastructure and services as well as development of related applications.

In addition, we recommend that you have a working knowledge of the English language, so that you are able to understand the technical words and concepts this study guide presents.

To feel confident about using this study guide, you should have the following knowledge or ability:

■ The desire and drive to become an i-Net+ certified technician through our instructions, terminology, activities, quizzes, and study guide content

■ Basic computer skills, which include using a mouse, keyboard, and viewing a monitor

■ Basic networking knowledge including the fundamentals of working with Internet browsers, e-mail functionality, and search engines

■ IP, remote connectivity and security

Hardware and Software Requirements

To apply the knowledge presented in this study guide, you will need the following minimum hardware:

- Intel-based computer 486/66 MHz processor

- 16 MB RAM

- 500 MB of available hard disk space

- CD-ROM drive

- Mouse

- VGA monitor and graphics card

- Internet connectivity

To apply the knowledge presented in this study guide, you will need the following minimum software installed on your computer:

- Microsoft Windows 95/98

- Microsoft DOS 6.0 or higher

- Microsoft Internet Explorer or Netscape Communicator

Symbols Used in This Study Guide

To call your attention to various facts within our study guide content, we have included the following three symbols to help you prepare for the i-Net+ exam.

 Tip: The Tip identifies important information that you might see referenced in the certification exam.

 Note: The Note enhances your understanding of the topic content.

 Warning: The Warning describes circumstances that could be harmful to you and your computer system or network.

How to Use This Study Guide

Although you will develop and implement your own personal style of studying and preparing for the i-Net+ exam, we've taken the strategy of presenting the exam information in an easy-to-follow, ten-lesson format. Each lesson conforms to CompTIA's model for exam content preparation.

At the beginning of each lesson, we summarize the information that will be covered. At the end of each lesson we round out your studying experience by providing the following four ways to test and challenge what you've learned.

Vocabulary—Helps you review all the important terms discussed in the lesson.

In Brief—Reinforces your knowledge by presenting you with a problem and a possible solution.

Activities—Further tests what you have learned in the lesson by presenting ten activities that often require you to do more reading or research to understand the activity. In addition, we have provided the answers to each activity.

Lesson Quiz—To round out the knowledge you will gain after completing each lesson in this study guide, we have included ten sample exam questions and answers. This allows you to test your knowledge, and gives you the reasons why the "answers" were either correct or incorrect. This, in itself, enhances your power to pass the exam.

You can also refer to the Glossary at the back of the book to review terminology. Furthermore, you can view the Index to find more content for individual terms and concepts.

Introduction to i-Net+ Certification

The i-Net+ certification exam is a testing program sponsored by the Computing Technology Industry Association (CompTIA) that certifies the competency of entry-level Internet technical professionals.

When you receive your i-Net+ certification, it proves your competence by having earned a nationally recognized credential as an Internet technical professional. In addition, major vendors, distributors, resellers, and publications back the Computing Technology Industry Association program, which gives this exam the credibility it deserves.

The i-Net+ exam covers a vast range of vendor-independent hardware and software technologies, as well as basic Internet and Web page design knowledge, technical skills and practices, as defined by over 45 organizations in the information technology industry.

To help you bridge the gap between needing the knowledge and knowing the facts, this study guide presents Internet technology and networking practices essential for passing the i-Net+ certification exam by CompTIA.

Note: This study guide presents technical content that should enable you to pass the i-Net+ certification exam on the first try.

To become a certified i-Net+ Technician, you will need a 68% score to pass the i-Net+ exam. Ninety minutes is the allotted time to take the test, which consists of 65 questions.

Tip: According to CompTIA, the i-Net+ certification is a lifetime certification. Once you pass the exam, you will not be required to ever take it again.

Certification Skill Measurements

To help you prepare for the i-Net+ certification exam, CompTIA has weighted the test objectives according to category, as shown in the following table.

Test Objectives	Weighted Exam Percentage
Internet Basics	10%
Internet Clients	20%
Development	20%
Networking and Infrastructure	25%
Internet Security	15%
Business Concepts	10%

i-Net+ Study Guide Objectives

Successful completion of this study guide is realized when you can competently understand, explain and implement Internet technology and its recommended practices. You must fully comprehend each of the following objectives and their related tasks to prepare for the i-Net+ certification.

Internet Basics

- Describe a URL, its functions and components, different types of URLs and use the appropriate type of URL to access a given type of server

- Identify the issues that affect Internet site functionality, such as performance, security and reliability

- Describe the concept of caching and its implications

- Describe various types of search indexes, such as a static index/site map, keyword index, and a full text index

Internet Clients

- Describe the infrastructure for supporting an Internet client

- Describe the use of Web browsers and various clients, such as FTP clients, Telnet clients, e-mail clients, all-in-one clients/universal clients, within a given context of use

- Explain the issues to consider when configuring the desktop

- Describe MIME types and their components

- Identify problems related to legacy clients, such as TCP/IP sockets and their implications on the operation system

- Explain the function of patches and updates to client software and associated problems

- Describe the advantages and disadvantages of using a cookie and how to set cookies

Development

- Define programming-related terms as they relate to Internet application development

- Describe the differences between popular client-side and server-side programming languages

- Describe the differences between a relational database and a non-relational database

- Identify when to integrate a database with a Web site and the technologies used to connect the two

- Demonstrate the ability to create HTML pages

- Identify popular multimedia extensions or plug-ins

- Describe the uses and benefits of various multimedia file formats

- Describe the process of pre-launch site and application functionality testing

Networking and Infrastructure

- Describe the core components of the current Internet infrastructure and how they relate to each other

- Identify problems with Internet connectivity from source to destination for various types of servers

- Describe internet domain names and DNS

- Describe the nature, purpose, and operational essential of TCP/IP

- Describe the purpose of remote access protocols

- Describe how various protocols or services apply to the function of a mail system, Web system, and file transfer system

- Describe when to use various diagnostic tools for identifying and resolving Internet problems

- Describe hardware and software connection devices and their uses

- Describe various types of Internet bandwidth technologies (link types)

- Describe the purpose of various services, specifically what they are, their functionality, and features

Internet Security

- Define the following Internet security concepts: access control, encryption, auditing ad authentication, and provide appropriate types of technologies currently available for each

- Describe VPN and its functions

- Describe various types of suspicious security-breach activities

- Describe access security features for an Internet server, such as e-mail server, and Web server

- Describe the purpose of anti-virus software and when to use it

- Describe the difference between the following as they relate to security requirements: intranet, extranet and Internet

Business Concepts

- Explain the issues involved in copyrighting, trademarking, and licensing
- Identify the issues related to working in a global environment
- Define the following Web-related mechanisms for audience development, such as attracting and retaining an audience: Push vs. Pull technology
- Describe the differences between the following from a business standpoint: intranet, extranet, and Internet
- Define E-commerce terms and concepts

Figures

List of Tables

Table of Contents

Lesson 1: Internet Basics

Digital transmissions have been around for several thousand years. According to the epic poet Homer, around 1200 B.C. the Greeks announced their victory over the Trojans by sending an overnight message nearly 400 miles across the sea from Troy to Greece. A string of ships lit torch beacons that transmitted the prearranged signals. A beam of light indicated triumph. An absence of light indicated that the struggle continued.

The world has changed drastically since the Greeks sent their 1-bit signal. The light of victory is easy to understand, but how do we derive meaning from the light that travels through fiber-optic cables? This lesson will provide you with a good foundation for understanding and using the Internet and set you on the right course for passing CompTIA's i-Net+ exam.

After completing this lesson, you should have a better understanding of the following topics:

■ Internet Overview

■ Network Types

■ Data Access and Retrieval

■ Internet Infrastructure

■ Connection Methods

■ Specialized Internet Servers

■ In Summary

Internet Overview

Although the World Wide Web (WWW) seems to have burst out of nowhere in the 1990s, the history of the Internet can be traced back to the late 1950s, when the Soviet Union launched the first artificial satellite, Sputnik, in 1957. Soviet technological advances in space and nuclear weapons thrust the United States (U.S.) Government into action with many new science and technology initiatives, including the Advanced Projects Research Agency (ARPA). Soon ARPA saw the need for a communication infrastructure to link scientists and share valuable computer resources. This project eventually evolved into the Internet.

ARPANet Connectivity

ARPANet, established in 1969, initially connected four universities, including the University of California at Los Angeles (UCLA), the Stanford Research Institute, (SRI), the University of California at Santa Barbara (UCSB), and the University of Utah in Salt Lake City. By 1971, 15 sites and 23 host computers had joined the network. In 1973, ARPANet saw the first international sites established at the University College of London and the Royal Radar Establishment in Norway.

While working at a government organization in the early 1960s, the RAND (Research and Development) Corporation, Paul Baran, whom many consider the father of computer networking, developed the idea of packet switching. This technology was adopted by ARPANet. His idea was to divide messages into packets, each labeled with a destination address. The packets would wind their way through a nation-wide network and then regenerate into the original message at their final destination. The theory was that if one route were destroyed—nuclear destruction being a major threat during the cold war—the message could still be sent through an alternate route to its destination.

 Note: The Internet still reflects the original designs of its pioneers—there is no central computer through which all Internet traffic flows. Instead, numerous routes typically connect any two computers on the Internet.

NSFNet Connectivity

In the 1980s, ARPANet evolved into NSFNet, a project funded by the National Science Foundation (NSF). The main constituents of the network remained universities, government agencies, and organizations involved in research. In the mid-1980s, the National Science Foundation funded several national supercomputer centers including the National Center for Supercomputing Applications (NCSA) at the University of Illinois at Urbana-Champaign. From these research centers emerged many of the Internet technologies that we use today.

Internet Creation

In February 1994, the NSF announced that it would build four huge exchange points for Internet traffic called Network Access Points (NAPs): one in San Francisco, one in Chicago, one in New Jersey, and one in Washington, D.C. Private telephone companies, including PacBell and Sprint, were given the responsibility of operating these NAPs. On April 30, 1995, the NSFNet was essentially shut down and the NAP architecture became the Internet.

Today, the Internet has become one of the most important conduits for business activity and has experienced exponential growth in both the number of users and the number of connections. Several large companies, including IBM, PSINet, and UUNet, maintain the main transmission lines of the Internet, which are the Internet backbone. In addition to the original four NAPs, hundreds of private exchanges have appeared.

Descriptions of Internet architecture, policies, history, and more can be found in a series of documents called Request For Comments (RFC). Some RFCs are funny, such as one called "Twas the Night Before Start-up" (RFC968); some are highly informative, such as "Requirements for Internet Hosts" (RFC1122 and RFC1123); and some are just downright interesting such as "Request For Comments Reference Guide" (RFC1000). The introduction to RFC1000 offers a good perspective of the early days of the Internet. For more information on RFCs, refer to the RFC Editor's archive site at www.rfc-editor.org.

World Wide Web Establishment

Tim Berners-Lee is arguably the main person responsible for the Internet becoming the defining technology as we enter a new millennium. He made the Internet easy to use. Working in a particle physics laboratory in Geneva, Switzerland, Dr. Berners-Lee added an important item to his resume—he invented the World Wide Web (WWW), or more simply, the Web.

Dr. Berners-Lee envisioned a cyber world in which a physics researcher could easily access information on another colleague's computer. By selecting links in the current document, a person could pull up related documents on the same computer, a computer down the hall, or a computer across the world. These special documents, each of which has a unique address, became known as Web pages.

The idea of links that allow you to jump from one document to the next is based on the work of Ted Nelson. In the 1960s, he developed HyperText, a system in which different objects are interconnected by hotspots on the screen called hyperlinks. Figure 1.1 displays a Web page in the Netscape browser. Many of the objects that you see on the screen are hyperlinks: the underlined text, the Dow Jones Industrial Average chart, the tabs Getting Started, Planning, and so on; everywhere you see the word "Go." If you choose one of these hotspots, you are taken to a different Web page. For example, if you choose the chart, you go to a page that displays a blown up view of the chart.

Hyperlinks on a page are usually easy to identify. Text links are often underlined and a different color from the main body of text. Graphical images are potential links, and the only way to know for sure is to move the pointer over the image. If the pointer changes into a hand with a pointed index finger, you have a link.

Figure 1.1 Netscape Browser Web Page

Web Browser Invention

To view a Web page, you need a special piece of software called a Web browser. Marc Andreessen was a graduate student at the University of Illinois at Urbana-Champaign, a national supercomputer center, where, in 1993, he led a team that invented the first graphical browser entitled Mosaic. Andreessen saw the terrific potential for Mosaic—it had spread like wildfire through university communities across the U.S. He left the university to help establish Netscape. Netscape became one of the Internet's early success stories when its Web browser called Navigator captured an overwhelming market share. Many other companies soon joined the browser war, including Microsoft with its Internet Explorer. Today, Netscape and Microsoft battle for dominance in the browser market.

Network Types

A network is an interconnected collection of computers that share hardware, software, and data. A network can be as simple as two computers cabled together to share a printer or as complex as the Internet—a vast collection of local, regional, and national networks. Although it is difficult to wrap up the definition of a network into a neat package, this section gives you a good idea of where we are and where we are going.

Local Area Network (LAN)

As the name implies, a LAN covers a small area such as an office, one floor of a building, or one department of a large organization. One or more cables connect personal computers together to share resources such as printers and databases.

Internetworks

When you start linking computers located on several floors of a large building or connecting small buildings in a common location, you have a collection of LANs called an internetwork. Like a LAN, defining the exact limits of an internetwork is challenging, but they are both located in a small area where no interaction is required with a cabling system from a third party, such as the telephone company.

Tip: You can distinguish an internetwork from a LAN by looking for a router or switches. A router is a device that connects two separate networks and then routes data between them, which allows data exchange between the networks.

Wide Area Networks (WANs)

A WAN is a collection of LANs or internetworks that covers a large geographic area, such as multiple branches of a large company. WANs often use a commercial carrier, such as a long-distance telephone company, to link sites that can extend hundreds or thousands of miles.

Metropolitan Area Networks (MANs)

MAN refers to a small WAN that covers a city or metropolitan area. It is not uncommon for large organizations to have networks that work on many levels. For example, a university will have LANs and internetworks for local access on the main campus, a MAN could connect the main campus with one or more branch campuses, a medical school, or perhaps a research center, and a WAN might provide communication with other universities in the state or country.

Internet

The Internet is the ultimate expression of a WAN. This Byzantine "network of networks" connects millions of computers and users worldwide. The complexity is so great that an in-depth definition tends to describe chaos rather than order. A subset of the Internet, the hugely successful World Wide Web, uses simple point-and-click technology that enables the average computer user to effortlessly browse myriad sources of data.

Intranets and Extranets

Many organizations have realized the usefulness of World Wide Web technologies and have implemented them on a smaller scale. An intranet is a self-contained, Internet-like network that organizes internal communication. For example, a personnel department could post information about medical insurance plans, which internal employees may access, but external non-employees cannot access. Intranets have proven so successful that they have expanded into extranets—intranets that can be accessed by authorized users outside of the intranet. Extranets allow businesses such as a company and its supplier, to connect with one another on an authorized basis.

Data Access and Retrieval

If you ask four different people how they access data on the Web, you will likely get four different answers. Basic navigation techniques that are common to most Web users include using portals, doing Web searches, typing in the desired address, and using bookmarks.

Entering through Portals

When you launch your browser, the initial page, or home page, appears on the screen. Often the company that has provided you with Internet access configures this page for you. For example, the company America Online (AOL) has a standard initial page that they display when a customer uses their services to access the Internet. The page can be configured to a certain degree so that it displays links to your liking. A handful of sites have become very popular in providing the initial page that many users see.

 Note: The term home page also refers to a Web page that people create to publish information about themselves.

These portals to the Web have links to news, sports, weather, electronic mail, and many other places that would be of interest to a Web user. Today, some of the most popular portals are found at America Online, Netscape, the Microsoft Network, and Yahoo!

You can easily use Netscape Netcenter or any other portal as your browser's initial page. The Netscape Netcenter (Figure 1.2) is an extremely popular portal at www.netscape.com, and it is full of valuable links.

To set the home page in Netscape's browser, from the View menu, choose Preferences. When using Microsoft Internet Explorer, from the Tools menu, choose Internet Options to set the home page preferences.

Figure 1.2 Netscape Netcenter Portal

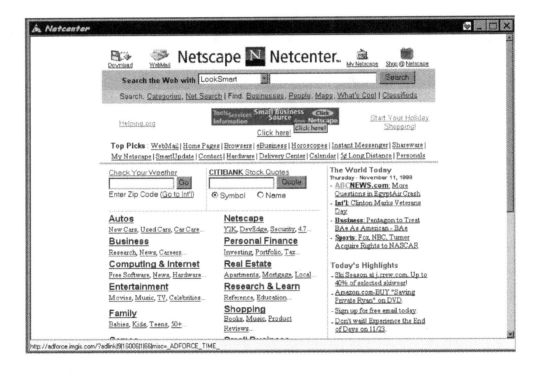

Navigating with Search Engines

Portals are great starting points for navigating the Web, but often they do not have direct links to the information that you desire. Search engines such as AltaVista, InfoSeek, Excite, Lycos, and Yahoo!, use many methods to try to keep track of the content of pages on the Internet. You simply type in the title of a topic in which you are interested, and then the search engine returns a list of related Web pages. Often the number of links found by a search engine overwhelms users. Hundreds, thousands, or even hundreds of thousands of links are common. An AltaVista search for basketball finds over 4 million pages (Figure 1.3).

Figure 1.3 AltaVista Search Results

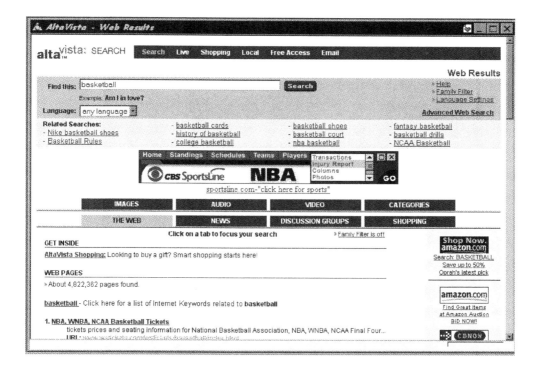

Search engines have advanced features to assist in narrowing your search. For example, an AltaVista search for: **basketball+women+ucla** reduces the number of pages to around 16,000, which is still a lot, but more manageable. If you are lucky, the most relevant pages are listed first. The plus sign (+) indicates that you want pages that include the words "basketball" and "women" and "ucla." Plus signs perform an And operation.

Minus signs (-) indicate a Not operation. For example, assume that you want information about radio stations on the Island of Jersey in the English Channel. A search for: **jersey+radio** lists radio stations from New Jersey in addition to the Island of Jersey. If you enter: **jersey–new+radio** you obtain better results because this search specifies that you do not want pages with the word "new."

In addition to And and Not operations, you can create queries with Or operations. Or operations do not have plus or minus signs. For example, if you are interested in information on the gnarled trunks of olive trees, a search for: **olive tree trunk** returns pages that describe olives or trees or trunks. This could include olive oil, genealogy trees, and elephant trunks. A good way to narrow this down is with double-quote marks ("). For example: **"olive tree"+trunk** finds pages with the words "olive tree" and "trunk." The two words "olive tree" must appear right next to each other, otherwise, the page is ignored.

Tip: To link to many search engines, see www.search.com. In addition, the site www.monash.com/spidap4.html provides a helpful guide for searching.

Visiting Sites via Uniform Resource Locators (URLs)

Of course, if you know the address of a desired page, you can simply enter it into the browser. Internet addresses have a very precise format. A URL is a highly structured string of letters and symbols that points to a document on a computer. No two Internet documents have the same URL. A Web site usually has many pages that are categorized into different folders. Figure 1.4 shows the default.htm file is located in the folder called columns. Any file ending with .htm or .html is a Web page.

Figure 1.4 A URL

http://www.winmag.com/columns/default.htm

Protocol   Computer Name   Folder Name   File Name

Protocols define, among other things, how to package data that travels over communication media. Often, different types of data use different protocols. HyperText Transfer Protocol (HTTP) refers to the protocol used to package Web pages. When you type a URL into the address box in a modern Web browser and leave off the letters HTTP, the browser will insert them.

Understanding Domain Names

Most computer names in a URL consist of a prefix, typically **www**, and a domain name, typically a combination of an organization's name and Internet category. For example, in the domain name **winmag.com**, Winmag stands for Windows Magazine and **.com** represents a top-level domain. When you acquire a domain name, you request the first part of the domain name (winmag in this example). You can choose the second part, or extension, based upon what type of entity your site is (.com in this example represents a commercial site). Table 1.1 lists six of the most common top-level domains.

Table 1.1 Top Level Domains

Top-Level Domain	Description
.com	Commercial site
.org	Non-profit organization
.gov	U.S. government agency
.net	Networking site, often Internet related
.mil	U.S. military site
.edu	School, such as a college or university

During most of the 1990s, InterNIC, a cooperative endeavor between the U.S. Government and Network Solutions, Inc. was the sole provider of domain name registration services for .com, .net, and .org top-level domains. InterNIC decided who received a particular domain name. In the late 1990s, the United States Government privatized the management of domain names to increase competition for domain name registration services. The Internet Corporation for Assigned Names and Numbers (ICANN), a non-profit corporation, has responsibility for the accreditation of new domain registrars for the top-level domains of .com, .net, and .org. Many companies have been accredited as registrars and are currently operational, including America Online in the United States, France Telecom/Oléane in France, and interQ Incorporated in Japan.

Other types of top-level domains exist. Country domains use two letters, such as .ca for Canada, .us for the United States, .mx for Mexico, and .ch for Switzerland. The URL www.cern.ch is the address of the Web site for the particle research laboratory that Tim Berners-Lee worked at when he invented the World Wide Web. See www.iana.org/cctld.html for more information on country domains.

 Note: In recent years, Web site owners have requested new generic top-level domains, such as .firm, .store, .nom, and .arts to distinguish their business classification. These domains would not be difficult to create and would help relieve shortages in existing names.

Understanding Port Numbers

Each application running on a computer has a port number associated with it. Many people think the application port is a physical device, but it is just a number that identifies a program running on a computer. There are physical ports on the back of your computer, but those are different.

Each packet has a destination application port and a source application port. When a computer receives a packet of data, it looks at the destination port number and then forwards the packet to the corresponding application. When a packet leaves a computer, the computer inserts the port number of the destination application.

Many application port numbers are standard. Port 80 represents the HTTP protocol. In the early days of the Web, some URLs contained port numbers, for example, www.usc.edu:80. Port numbers are still inserted into packets, but they are not necessary in URLs. The underlying software takes care of this for you.

 Note: Port numbers are located in TCP and UDP headers.

Creating Bookmarks

When you find a site that you would like to revisit, create a bookmark. A bookmark is an entry in a list of favorite sites that is maintained by your browser. For example, to bookmark a site in Internet Explorer, from the Favorites menu, choose Add to Favorites. Next time that you want to go back to the site, simply choose its name from the Favorites menu instead of re-entering the site's URL.

Internet Infrastructure

The paramount concern of most Internet users seems to be the speed at which they can access data. The World Wide Web's nickname "The World Wide Wait" is sometimes well deserved. To understand why some connections seem as fast as light, while others seem to crawl, it helps to understand the basic infrastructure of the Internet.

Transmitting Data on Bandwidth

Bandwidth measures the data carrying capacity of a transmission system. Just as a thicker hose can carry more water, the greater the bandwidth of a transmission line, the greater the flow of data. Typically, bandwidth is measured in Bits Per Second (BPS). A bit, usually described as a 0 or 1, is the most basic building block of data. A character that you see on a computer screen is made up of 8 bits and is referred to as a byte. Each character uses a different combination of 0s and 1s. For example, the letter A is represented in the computer as 01000001. No other character uses this combination of 0s and 1s.

The average personal computer that you use at home has the ability to receive data over phone lines at 56 Kbps. The letter K, or kilo, comes from the Greek word for 1,000. In reality, 1 K is 2^{10} or 1,024. A bandwidth of 56 Kbps actually carries 57,344 Bits Per Second (BPS), which sounds fast but is usually the main bottleneck of data transmission for home Internet users.

The connection between your house and the local phone company is exceedingly slow compared to the rest of the connections that make up the Internet's infrastructure.

In the U.S., telephone companies began experimenting with digital circuits in the early 60s. Digital circuits carry data in the form of 0s and 1s. The phone companies' main motivation was not the transmission of computer data, but the desire to carry large quantities of high-quality voice signals over long distances.

Analog signals, the transmission method used in early phone systems, had problems in long-distance environments. Today, the connection between your home and the telephone company's central office is typically an old analog line that was designed for voice transmissions; all other interconnections are digital.

The U.S. Public Switched Telephone Network (PSTN) consists of the following component categories:

Subscriber wiring and equipment—Designed for analog telephones, it consists of telephones, cables within walls, and any other devices located at a residence or business.

Local loop—Connects a local telephone company's central office to a business or residence.

Groups of Central Offices—Interconnects high capacity trunk lines to each other and to switching offices that provide interconnectivity access.

In the U.S., digital telephone circuits are identified by the letter T followed by a number. In Europe, digital circuits start with an E and then a number. The highest capacity digital lines consist of an OC followed by a number. OC stands for optical carrier and requires fiber-optic cable. Table 1.2 lists the most common types of digital circuits. The letter M stands for mega and represents a value of approximately one million. For example, 1.544 Mbps is equivalent to approximately 1,544,000 bps.

Table 1.2 Digital Circuits Data Rates

Name	Bit Rate (Mbps)	Voice Circuit Capacity
T1	1.544	24
T3	44.736	672
E1	2.048	30
E3	34.368	480
OC-1	51.840	810
OC-3	155.520	2,430
OC-12	622.080	9,720
OC-48	2,488.320	38,880

Fiber-optic cable carries ten times more long-distance digital traffic than satellites.

A good example of a long-distance carrier is UUNet, a division of MCI WorldCom. UUNet's U.S. network consists of DS-3 (similar to T3), OC-12, and OC-48 trunks, which are augmented with

OC-12 "metro rings" in 10 metropolitan areas   (Figure 1.5). The Canadian and U.S. networks are linked with more than 380 Mbps of aggregate bandwidth.

Linking Communications with Internet Service Providers

In the U.S., several companies called Network Service Providers (NSP) maintain the nationwide communications links that make up the Internet backbone. Good examples are PSINet and UUNet, both of which have engineered their infrastructures for optimal Internet performance.

Figure 1.5 UUNet's U.S. Network

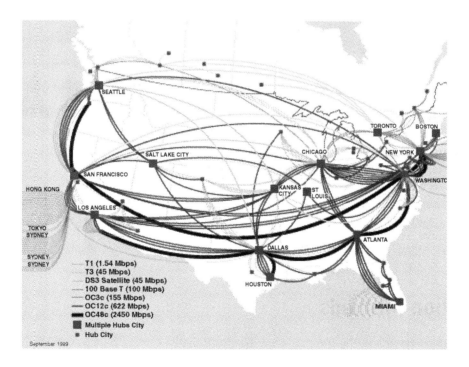

Unfortunately, you cannot directly connect your computer to the backbone. An Internet Service Provider (ISP) provides Internet access to businesses, large and small organizations, and individual users. From your home, for example, you would use a telephone line to connect to an ISP and the ISP connects to a National Attachment Point (NAP), known as an Internet traffic exchange point. The NAPs and the Internet backbone links are maintained by NSPs (Figure 1.6).

Figure 1.6 ISPs and NAPs

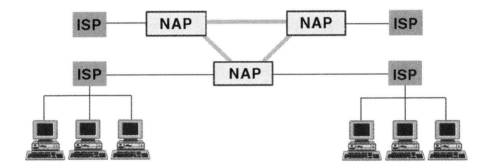

ISPs range from small companies servicing a few hundred users to huge enterprises, such as America Online, which service millions. For an extensive list of U.S. and Canadian ISPs, check out www.board-watch.internet.com/isp/ac/index.html which is Boardwatch Magazine's Directory of Internet Service Providers. You can use the list to look up details regarding ISP connection services. For example, if you want to know which ISPs in your area provide Digital Subscriber Line (DSL) service, Integrated Services Digital Network (ISDN) service, or cable modem access, you can find it on this list.

Connection Methods

For years, the slowest link in the Internet chain has been the local loop, the connection from your residence to the local telephone company's central office. Large businesses and organizations have the financial resources to lease very expensive, high-speed digital lines from the telephone company to overcome slow-speed link limitations.

A large university might have several T1 lines or even a T3 line connecting it to the outside world. On the other hand, residences and small businesses have been stuck with 28 to 56 Kbps connections that can make the Internet exceedingly frustrating to use.

What if you could replace the local loop between your house and the telephone company with an affordable, high-speed digital connection? In recent years, phone companies have made great strides in getting digital lines out to residences and small businesses. Some people have even bypassed the telephone company for their cable T.V. company and are now receiving Internet access through their cable TV system.

Standard Modems

A modem is a device that converts digital signals used in a computer into analog signals that can travel over standard phone lines. Essentially, your modem changes the computer's 0s and 1s into different sounds so that they can travel over copper wires from your residence to the central telephone office.

This process also works in reverse. When analog sounds come in over the phone line, the modem converts them into digital 0s and 1s that the computer understands. In more technical terms, the conversion process involves modulating and demodulating a signal. Modem is short for MOdulate/DEModulate.

Standard modem speeds have achieved a maximum rate of to 56 Kbps. This speed is for downstream transmissions only, which fit nicely with what most want to do—receive data from the Internet. The slowest modem that seems tolerable to most people these days is 28.8 Kbps. Anything slower is just not fast enough to handle the loading of intensive graphics from the Web.

Integrated Services Digital Network (ISDN)

ISDN is an industry standard for sending voice, video, and data over digital telephone lines. Most ISDN lines offered by telephone companies give you two lines at once. These lines are referred to as B channels, and each can support data transmission rates of 64 Kbps. You can use one line for voice and one for data, or you can combine the two to create a wide data channel capable of achieving speeds of up to 128 Kbps.

Besides speed, one of the main advantages when using ISDN is that you can change an existing analog phone line into an ISDN line. The phone company will have to perform the conversion and provide you with a special ISDN adapter. Although ISDN prices are coming down, consumers are now opting for faster digital technologies such as DSL and cable modems.

Digital Subscriber Line (DSL)

DSL refers to two main types of digital connections: Asymmetric Digital Subscriber Line (ADSL) and Symmetric Digital Subscriber Line (SDSL). Since there also exists HDSL, VDSL and more, the acronym xDSL is becoming a catch-all term. All DSL, regardless of type, requires special high-frequency modems and the service is available in only limited areas.

DSL and ISDN are similar because they both operate over existing telephone lines and both require that a residence be relatively close to a central office, usually less then 20,000 feet. The speed difference, however, is striking. DSL uses advanced modulation techniques to achieve downstream data rates that are measured in megabits per second.

ADSL supports downstream transmission rates of up to several Mbps and upstream rates of up to 640 Kbps. The term asymmetric points to the fact that there is a significant difference between downstream and upstream transmission rates. SDSL is a European DSL standard that supports symmetric traffic and equivalent data transmission rates in each direction, up to 3 Mbps.

Cable Modems

The nature of cable TV lines theoretically permits the transmission of enormous amounts of data. Sounds like a great idea, right? Except for the fact that the entire cable TV system was designed to send data in one direction—into your home. The technological hurdles of sending data in the opposite direction proved to be quite formidable. Cable modems, however, achieve data transfer rates similar to and perhaps in excess of those achieved through DSL connections.

To access the Internet through cable, a cable modem is required. The computer connects to the cable TV system and receives data transmission rates measured in megabits per second.

 Note: Now that AT&T has bought TCI cable, the number of cable modems in use in the U.S. should increase dramatically.

DirecPC

Every system described so far connects your PC to the Internet through cables: analog or digital telephone cables or high-speed cable TV lines. However, wireless alternatives exist.

Hughes Network Systems has developed DirecPC, a system that connects your PC to a Hughes satellite orbiting at about 22,500 miles above the earth. For this technology to work, you need the following:

■   A DirecPC satellite dish

■   A DirecPC external modem

■   Satellite access software

■   A 28.8 Kbps or faster modem

A modem is required because all upstream data travels over telephone lines. The satellite provides only downstream data. Most consumers are satisfied with this arrangement since the primary use of the Internet is to receive data. They are even more satisfied when they learn that downstream transmission rates from the satellite can be as high as 400 Kbps. Of course, this is not as high as DSL or cable modems, but the availability is much greater.

You need one more thing with DirecPC—an unobstructed line of sight to the south. The satellite dish must point to the Hughes' satellite located in the southern sky.

Processing DirecPC Requests

When a URL is requested, the analog modem sends the request over regular phone lines to the user's ISP. The ISP redirects the request to the DirecPC Network Operations Center (NOC). The NOC then sends the request to the Web site that actually contains the desired Web page. After the NOC receives the page, it uploads it to the DirecPC satellite, which beams it down to the user's PC (Figure 1.7).

Figure 1.7 Hughes Network Systems DirecPC

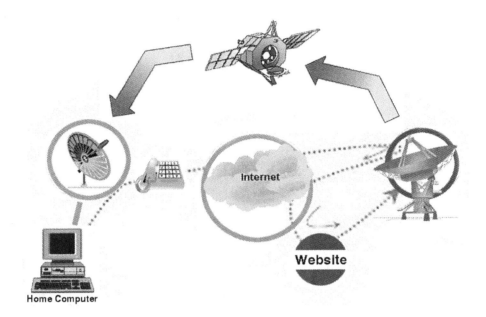

Home Computer

Internet

Website

 Note: Although DirecPC has a relatively small user base, a new system of 288 satellites called Teledesic could revolutionize the way many people access the Internet. Teledesic, which has several high-profile backers such as Bill Gates, Motorola, and Boeing is scheduled to go into service by 2004. For more information, see www.teledesic.com.

Cellular Connections

A wireless connection does not always require that your signals travel into outer space. More down-to-earth alternatives are available. Cell phones, for example, send transmissions that travel through the air to a local transmitter and are relayed to their destination through one of the phone companies. Computers accessing the Internet can also use this well-established technology.

Among the many alternates, the Sprint PCS Wireless Web Connection is one of the most popular. Instead of using a standard modem, you connect your computer to a wireless Sprint PCS phone. Data travels from your computer, through your cell phone and then out to the rest of the world (Figure 1.8). The connection speed is relatively slow, 14.4 Kbps, but the freedom of mobility is unparalleled. Anywhere that you can use a cell phone, you can connect to the Web.

Figure 1.8 Sprint PCS Wireless Web

Handheld PCs (HPCs)

After making a couple of false starts, HPCs are finally making their mark, but mainly along two different paths: one based upon 3Com's Palm line of computers and the other centered around Microsoft Windows CE.

Palm Computing

Palm computing leads the first wave of HPCs that can run Web-based applications. The Palm OS has a proprietary operating system from 3COM, and has a small footprint, the area of space needed to sit on a flat surface or desk, which is essential for small computers. Although Web access is limited—Palm computers have tiny screens—wireless e-mail availability through a palm-sized computer can be indispensable to people with busy schedules (Figure 1.9).

Figure 1.9 Palm Computing

HPCs with Microsoft Windows CE

Companies such as Casio and Hewlett-Packard are leading the way in Windows CE-based HPCs. Microsoft designed Windows CE specifically for consumer electronic devices, such as small PCs. Although there have been complaints about it being unwieldy because it is Windows 98 shoehorned into a small package, the wide range of applications makes it worth a look. There is even a special version of Microsoft Office for Windows CE.

WebTV

We have seen many ways to connect a computer to the Internet: through standard phone lines, via the cable company, by cell phone, and by satellite. What do you do, however, if you don't have a computer? WebTV by Microsoft might be the answer.

As the names implies, WebTV uses your TV to display Web pages. A WebTV Internet unit, a device about the size of a VCR, sits on top of your TV and acts as doorway to the Internet. You simply connect it to both your TV and to a telephone jack and presto, you have Web access. In addition to Web pages, you can send and receive e-mail, have real-time chats with friends and do just about anything you could do with a PC-based Internet connection.

Both Sony and Phillips make WebTV Internet units (Figure 1.10). They come with standard features such as a built-in 56-Kbps modem and a remote control device.

Figure 1.10 Sony's WebTV Internet Unit

Specialized Internet Servers

When you travel across the Internet, you are connecting to a succession of computers called servers, computers whose main role is to serve up information.

A server can perform many tasks, however, in large organizations and especially on the Internet it is a good idea to set up a server to perform just one or two roles. If a server is stretched too thin, it will not perform anything very well.

A combination of hardware and software determines the role a server plays. For example, a fax server has special fax hardware and software for managing heavy fax traffic. Below are descriptions of the types of servers you may come across while using the Internet.

Web Servers

Web servers are by far the most well known type of server, providing data in the form of Web pages. Web servers accept requests from a browser, such as Netscape or Internet Explorer and then send back the corresponding Web page. The traditional language for creating Web pages is the Hypertext Markup Language (HTML).

Apache, developed by the Apache group, is by far the most widely used Web server on the Internet. ISPs like Apache's stability because it rarely crashes, and it is free. Apache is also available in several different versions: UNIX, Linux, and Windows NT.

Microsoft Internet Information Server (IIS) and Netscape Enterprise Server are two other mainstream Web servers. Like many modern Web servers, both do more than just serve up Web pages. For example, IIS which, like Apache, is free, ships with many built-in components, including a File Transfer Protocol (FTP) server and a general-purpose certificate server.

You can increase the power of a Web server beyond its ability to deliver standard HTML-based Web pages. Some of the ever-expanding numbers of tools that can be used are as follows:

- CGI scripts
- Server-Side Includes (SSI)
- Secure Socket Layer (SSL) security
- Active Server Pages (ASPs)

Since Web pages have become such an effective means for distributing information, many organizations create intranets and extranets that revolve around Web server technologies. Even small organizations can create an intranet by setting up Microsoft Personal Web Server (PWS) on a Windows 95/98 computer.

Cache Servers

Cache servers store frequently used Web pages and their components, graphical images, small programs and more. When you request a Web page over the Internet, there is a good chance that in addition to sending you the desired page, your ISP will keep a copy on a cache server. By doing this, when you or someone else requests the same page, the ISP does not have to scour the Internet for the page; it can simply send out the one stored on the cache server.

The word cache refers to a place in memory where data is stored enabling rapid data access. You might have heard of RAM caches, hard disk caches, CD-ROM caches and so on. The main idea is to store frequently used data in a location that you can access more quickly than the original location.

ISPs and companies with intranets and extranets use cache servers to improve response times and to make better use of bandwidth. If requested Web objects are in the cache server, they are sent out immediately. There is no need to go out on the Internet and retrieve the objects from the original server.

The hit rate, or the rate at which requested Web objects are found on the cache server, depends on many factors including the following:

The size of the community that is requesting Web pages—Is the cache server supporting a large or small group of people?

The diversity of the user community—Are people requesting vastly different pages?

The size of the cache—How much data can fit in the cache?

Algorithms used for caching—Sophisticated methods for deciding which pages stay in the cache and which do not.

A well-designed cache can achieve hit rates of 30% to 60%, which can save ISPs money by drastically reducing bandwidth costs.

Communications Servers

A communications server provides a means for users to remotely connect to a network. A company sets up a communications server so that users who are at home or on the road can use a modem to dial in to the server and then have access to the company's network resources. The full security system of the network still applies to those users who dial in remotely.

Windows NT Server and Windows 2000 Server both include a powerful communications program called Remote Access Service (RAS). Ideally, you set up RAS on a separate computer that has several modems that do nothing but receive calls from remote employees who want to access network resources such as the company's e-mail system. Remote users could even access the Internet through connections to a RAS computer.

Microsoft RAS has a feature found in most communications servers—the ability to call back a remote user. You call up an RAS server, and, if configured to do so, it will call you back at a predefined phone number. This is great for a couple of reasons. First, the company pays for the phone call rather than the remote user. Second, callback options add an extra layer of security. If a hacker tries to dial into a network, the RAS server will call back a predefined phone number and not the hacker's phone number.

ISPs use communications servers to enable their customers to dial in and access the Internet. To handle large numbers of calls, an ISP has special remote-access devices that can simultaneously accept multiple 56-Kbps calls. An example of such a device is the Shiva LanRover, which supports over 20 concurrent 56-Kbps sessions from the outside and then sends them down a T1 connection. Typically, there are no callback services set up for this type of communications server.

Regardless of the type of communications server that you choose, it must support the Point-to-Point Protocol (PPP). A protocol specifies, among other things, how to package data that travels across a communications medium. PPP controls communications from a user's residence over telephone lines to the ISP.

Database Servers

A database is a highly structured repository of data that provides easy data access and retrieval. Database servers maintain vast databases. For example, the inventory of a company that sells computer supplies could fit well into a database. Libraries store their card catalog systems as databases, colleges place registration information into databases.

Since database services can be separated into a client part and a server part, these types of systems are often called client/server systems. The client component, or front-end, is often a Web browser such as Netscape or Internet Explorer; the server component, or back-end, consists of the management tools that you need for a Database Management System (DBMS). Examples of the back-end component are Oracle and Microsoft SQL Server.

Mail Servers

When you send an e-mail message across the world, it does not travel directly from your computer to the recipient's computer. Intermediary servers called mail servers handle your message. Your message hops across the Internet until it reaches the recipient's mailbox, a location on a mail server where e-mail is delivered. The message stays in the mailbox until the user checks his or her mail, at which time the message downloads from the local mail server to the user's computer. The recipient can then read the message.

Microsoft Mail (MS Mail) was an early Microsoft e-mail server. MS Mail suffered from a number of deficiencies, including weak security, incompatibility with other mail systems, and inadequate administrative tools. Microsoft scrapped MS Mail and created Microsoft Exchange Server from the ground up. Today Exchange Server is one of the most sophisticated mail servers available. Many other good mail servers exist for UNIX, Linux, and Windows NT.

The primary function of a mail server is to forward a message from sender to recipient. A sender uses an e-mail client program such as Eudora or Microsoft Outlook to compose the message and address it to the recipient. The address looks similar to a URL, such as mike@lightpointlearning.net. The recipient's name, Mike in this example, is to the left of the @ symbol. The domain name, light-pointlearning.net in this example, is to the right.

Outgoing messages are packaged with the Simple Mail Transport Protocol (SMTP) and then transferred to the sender's mail server. The sender's mail server uses the domain name part of the e-mail address and the SMTP protocol to forward the message to the recipient's mail server. If the sender and recipient have the same mail server, the message does not travel far. If the recipient's mail server is across the country, then multiple computers could be involved in storing and forwarding the message.

When the message reaches the destination mail server, it is placed into an electronic mailbox. The recipient uses e-mail client software to check for mail. Any mail that is in the mailbox can be downloaded to the recipient's computer. Either one of two protocols are used in this last step of e-mail delivery: the Post Office Protocol (POP) or the Interactive Mail Access Protocol (IMAP).

SMTP sends and forwards mail, and the POP and IMAP protocols download mail. ISPs can use the same computer as both an SMTP server and POP/IMAP server, or they can separate the two functions into different computers for better access times.

Note: Free e-mail services such as Hotmail or Lycos let you use your Web browser to easily check your mail. Many people like these services because they can access e-mail from any computer that has a Web connection, and besides, it is free.

Mailing Lists

Mail servers provide many services such as public folders for distributing company information and address books for managing frequently used addresses. Additionally, in a comprehensive mail service environment, users are able to create and manage mailing lists. Mailing lists are lists of users who all wish to receive a common set of mail.

To use a mailing list, a user first subscribes to a list of interest such as one devoted to fly-fishing or scrapbooking. When a user sends a message to the list, everyone in the list receives the message. If there are 20 people on the list, all 20 are sent the message. When a mailing list user checks his or her e-mail, the message appears in the e-mail client software, along with any other e-mail messages.

Lightweight Directory Access Protocol (LDAP) Servers

LDAP is an Internet protocol that accesses network directories. It is implemented in many different environments. UNIX networks use a stand-alone LDAP daemon (SLAPD), Novell Networks use Novell Directory Services (NDS), and Windows 2000 uses Active Directory (AD). Each computer environment supports distributed databases that can be spread across multiple computers.

A network directory is a database of objects that represent users, groups, printers, and other network resources. Network directory databases are designed to give quick replies to large numbers of queries. A query might ask, "What is Mike's e-mail address?" Alternatively, "Does the marketing group have permission to print to the color laser printer?"

 Note: The details of LDAP are located in RFC 1777, The Lightweight Directory Access Protocol and in RFC 1779, A String Definition of Distinguished Names.

Proxy Servers

A proxy server is a server that sits between a client application, such as a Web browser, and a remote server. The primary function of a proxy server is to allow many computers to share a single Internet connection for a variety of purposes. You can use a proxy server as a cache server. Proxy servers store frequently accessed files so that clients, for instance Web users, get considerably better response time when they access a Web page that is already in the proxy server's cache.

A proxy server can prevent an organization's employees from accessing certain Web sites, and it can set restrictions based on protocols. For example, employees could make FTP requests but not HTTP requests.

You can use a proxy server as a firewall and added security to prevent outside intruders from penetrating your network. Proxy servers can block outside users with specific Internet addresses that prevent the intruder from accessing the network. In addition, proxy servers can support hundreds or thousands of users. Major online services such as America Online or the Microsoft Network use scores of proxy servers.

Certificate Servers

Whether you are involved in physical or electronic transactions, security is of paramount importance. In physical transactions, such as those at a department store, you receive many cues that make you feel confident that your personal and financial information is protected. When you hand your credit card to a clerk, you visually track how the clerk handles your card number, and then you immediately receive the merchandise.

On the Internet, you do not have any of these visual or physical cues. How do you know that your card number will not be given to a third party? How do you know that you are dealing with a legitimate company that will send you your merchandise? Today, digital certificates can secure online transactions.

A digital certificate is the electronic version of a business license. After exhaustively reviewing an applicant's credentials, a trusted third party called a Certificate Authority (CA) issues a digital certificate. For example, VeriSign, a well-known CA, investigates such things as Dun and Bradstreet numbers, Articles of Incorporation, and credit histories before issuing digital certificates.

CAs use certificate servers to manage the issuance, revocation, and renewal of digital certificates. In addition to commercial CAs, corporations can purchase certificate servers from vendors that have been certified by a CA. A corporation could then issue certificates to employees to do business either within the company or with other companies.

A sophisticated system of encryption, digital keys, and other mechanisms ensure that your transactions with a certified site are safe.

E-Commerce Servers

Electronic commerce, or E-commerce, has its roots in business-to-business transactions, which originated more than 20 years ago. Since then, E-commerce has evolved into the conduct of commerce in goods and services over the Internet. Companies such as amazon.com and e-bay, which do business exclusively over the Internet, have become multibillion-dollar enterprises and, in the process, have become household words.

Many people look at E-commerce merely as business transactions that take place over the Internet. Using this narrow definition, a program such as Microsoft Site Server, Commerce Edition, is an example of an E-commerce server. Although Site Server allows companies to transact business online with secure order capture, management, and routing, it must be combined with other tools for operations such as accounting and inventory maintenance.

A broader definition of E-commerce includes the following:

- Electronic goods and services presentation

- Online order taking

- Online customer bill presentation

- Automated customer account inquiries

- Online goods and services payments

- Automated inventory management

- Automated supply chain management

Companies such as IBM sell packaged sets of specially designed, integrated software components for establishing a complete E-commerce site. Red Hat, one of the leading providers of Linux software, has a turnkey E-commerce server that is said to include everything necessary to set up an E-commerce site. Of course, you could also acquire Site Server and combine it with other Microsoft products, such as their database server software, SQL server, their Web server software, Internet Information Server (IIS) and so on to put together a complete E-commerce solution.

Older Server Types

The following servers have been around for a long time but have gotten somewhat lost in the shuffle since the Web hit the scene. While Telnet, FTP, and news servers still have roles to play, Gopher servers may have outlived their usefulness.

Telnet Servers

Telnet, one of the oldest applications on the Internet, permits a computer to act as a terminal for another computer. This means that once a Telnet session is established, a user can run applications that use the Central Processing Unit (CPU) of the remote computer. This is important if the remote computer is a large, powerful mainframe computer that is capable of running applications that cannot run on your local PC.

A Telnet server is a server that can run the Telnet program. Once Telnet is launched on a computer, a remote user can log on to the Telnet server and run programs on the Telnet computer's CPU. Nowadays, one of the primary uses for Telnet is the remote administration of computers and the remote configuration of network devices such as routers and switches.

FTP Servers

The File Transfer Protocol (FTP) is one of the oldest application protocols on the Internet, and for a long time it was one of the most popular. Until 1995 when the Web surpassed it, FTP carried more Internet traffic than any other protocol.

As the name indicates, FTP transfers files between computers. The two computers do not need the same operating system. For example, the FTP server can be running UNIX and the FTP client computer can be running Windows. You do not even need a user account on the FTP server from which you are transferring data. A standard logon account called Anonymous is used, and often you do not even need to type in this account name, since logging on is automatically done for you.

Companies use FTP servers to post software drivers and updates. For example, a company called Symantec posts virus definition files so that their customers always have access to the most up-to-date information on viruses. You use an FTP client program, such as the Web browser shown in Figure 1.11, to connect to Symantec's FTP site. The address is ftp://symantec.com. Other FTP clients exist, including WS_FTP and the text-based FTP client built into most versions of Windows.

Figure 1.11 FTP

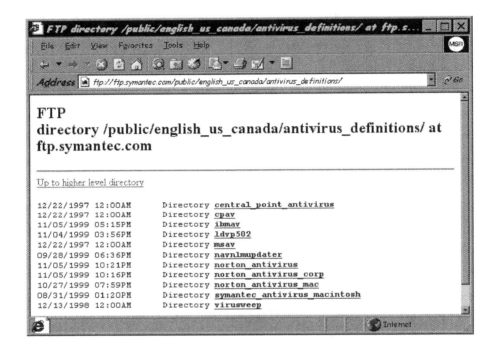

Although it is a great tool for transferring data, FTP servers are slipping in popularity. The ubiquitous Web server can now perform many of the file transferring functions of an FTP server.

News Servers

Mailing lists are a very inefficient way of distributing a message, especially to a large group of users. Since each message is replicated and sent to each member of the list, an explosion of e-mail can result. It is possible for one message to be copied and sent to thousands of users.

News servers try to solve this problem by placing a message into a news database, which users can browse at their own leisure. These news databases are divided into newsgroups—sets of related messages.

The Usenet newsgroup system is the most popular implementation of news servers. You can create a message using any e-mail client and then post the message into a newsgroup. The Network News Transfer Protocol (NNTP) relays the message to other news databases throughout the Usenet server network. NNTP handles the posting, distribution, and retrieval of news articles.

Tens of thousands of newsgroups exist and often with no restrictions on what can be posted. This permits a free exchange of ideas, but it can also lead to chaos. When you find the right newsgroup, the news can be invaluable. For example, one source of Windows NT peer-level technical support is Windows NT newsgroups. An administrator can describe a difficult problem that he or she has been experiencing, and often within 24 hours another administrator has posted a viable solution.

 Note: The Web site www.deja.com is a great place for exploring newsgroups. Look for newsgroups listed under the Discussions section.

When you want to see what is new in a newsgroup, you connect to the news server at your ISP. You open a newsgroup, for example one on dinosaurs or photography, and then download the current list of messages. The actual messages are not immediately downloaded, just a list of subject titles that provide a short description of each message. When you see something of interest, you can download the message contents. Figure 1.12 lists newsgroups found on America Online.

Figure 1.12 Newsgroups

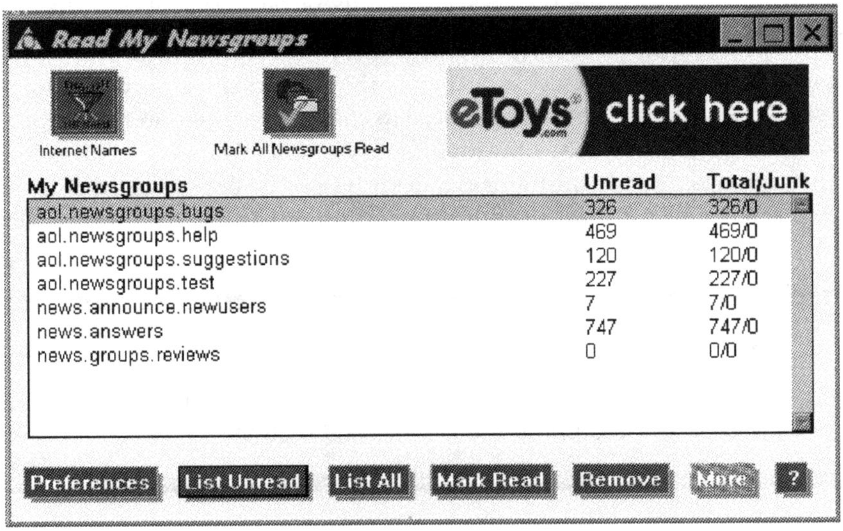

Gopher Servers

Before the introduction of the Web, Gopher was the primary tool for browsing the Internet. Gopher servers excel at providing text-based information in the form of menus. Menu items represent either files or submenus, which are located on the same computer or any other computer in "Gopherspace." When you select a file in a Gopher menu, you see its text-based contents on the screen. Interest in Gopher has diminished significantly since the advent of the Web.

In Summary

The ancient Greeks who sent messages by torchlight could never have imagined the speed and ease of use of today's communications systems. They would also have a hard time understanding how the World Wide Web could appear almost overnight, but it really did not. It does, however, seem that way and within ten years, it has become one of the main technologies of a new millennium.

One of the main reasons behind the Web's success has been the multi-purpose Web browser. Not only can you view Web pages with Netscape or Internet Explorer, but you can also use them as e-mail clients, database front-ends, newsgroup readers, FTP clients and more. As the Internet continues to evolve, the Web browser will continue to mature as the universal front-end for most applications.

Data transfer rates will continue to increase. Bandwidth hungry content such as audio and video will become standard denizens in our Web browsers. Wide data paths will enable the development of applications that we have yet to imagine. Maybe we will even be able to virtually feel the products that everybody will be buying through E-commerce.

Vocabulary

Review the following terms in preparation for the certification exam.

Term	Description
ADSL	Asymmetric Digital Subscriber Line is a type of DSL that supports downstream transmissions rates of up to several Mbps and upstream rates of up to 640 Kbps.
Apache	A popular Web server made by the Apache group.
ARPA	Advanced Projects Research Agency is a Department of Defense agency responsible for new scientific and research initiatives.
ARPANet	An early ARPA research network that evolved into the Internet.
bandwidth	The measure of the data carrying capacity of a transmission system.
bit	The basic building block of data, usually described as a 0 or 1.
bookmark	An entry in a list of favorite sites that is maintained by your browser.
BPS	Bits Per Second. Used to measure the data rate of a transmission medium.
byte	A combination of 8 bits, used, among other things, to represent characters such as letters of the alphabet or numbers.

Term	Description
CA	Certificate Authority is a trusted third party, which after exhaustive background checks, issues digital certificates.
cable modem	A device that enables you to access the Internet through your cable TV system.
cache server	Servers that store frequently used Web pages and their components to speed client Web page access.
certificate servers	Servers that manage the issuance, revocation, and renewal of digital certificates.
communications server	Servers that provide a means for users to remotely connect to a network.
database	A highly structured collection of data.
database servers	Servers that maintain databases.
DBMS	Database Management System is a program used to manage a database.
digital certificate	The electronic version of a business license, issued by a Certificate Authority.
DirecPC	A system developed by Hughes Network Systems that provides Internet access by connecting a PC to a satellite orbiting the earth.
domain name	The part of a URL that is typically a combination of an organization's name and top-level domain.
domain registrar	A company accredited to register domain names.
DSL	Digital Subscriber Line is a digital transmission system, which is faster than ISDN. It is in use in some residences.

Term	Description
E-commerce server	Servers used for E-commerce.
e-mail	Electronic mail.
extranet	Intranets which are accessed by authorized users outside of the intranet, and allow businesses such as a company and its supplier, to connect.
FTP	File Transfer Protocol—an Internet protocol used for transferring files among diverse computers.
FTP server	Servers used for sending out and receiving FTP file transfers.
Gopher server	Servers used to display distributed text files by listing them in menus.
home page	The initial page a user sees in a browser. A Web page that users create to publish information about themselves.
HPC	Handheld Personal Computer. A computer that fits in the palm of your hand.
HTML	HyperText Markup Language. A computer language used for creating Web pages.
HTTP	HyperText Transfer Protocol. A protocol used to package and transfer Web pages.
ICANN	Internet Corporation for Assigned Names and Numbers. A non-profit corporation that has responsibility for the accreditation of new domain registrars for the top-level domains of .com, .net, and .org.
IIS	Internet Information Server is a popular Web server made by Microsoft.

Term	Description
IMAP	Interactive Mail Access Protocol is a protocol used for incoming mail messages.
Internet	A network of networks connecting millions of computers in local, regional, national networks.
internetwork	A collection of LANs connected via routers.
InterNIC	A cooperative activity between the U.S. Government and Network Solutions, Inc. For many years, it was the sole provider of domain name registration services for .com, .net, and .org top-level domains.
intranet	A self-contained, Internet-like network used for internal communications within a business.
ISDN	Integrated Digital Subscriber Line is a digital transmission system used in some residences.
ISP	Internet Service Provider is a company or organization that provides Internet access to businesses, large and small organizations, and individual users.
K	A kilo or kilobyte is 1,024 bytes of data storage.
LAN	Local Area Network is a small network that covers a small area such as an office, one floor of a building, or one department of a large organization.
link	A spot in a Web page that transfers you to another Web page.
local loop	Connects the subscriber wiring at a business or residence to the telephone company's local central office.
M	Mega or megabyte is 1,048,576 bytes of data storage.

Term	Description
mail server	Servers that manage e-mail.
mailing list	A list of users who all wish to receive a common set of mail.
MAN	Metropolitan Area Network is a small WAN that covers a city or metropolitan area.
modem	It modulates and demodulates signals. It changes digital signals found in a computer into analog signals that can travel over an analog phone line and also performs the reverse process.
NAP	Network Access Point is a large exchange point for Internet traffic. Established by the NSF.
Navigator	Netscape's first browser.
Netscape Enterprise Server	A popular Web server made by Netscape.
news server	A server that maintains a database of newsgroups.
newsgroup	A collection of messages with a related theme, located on a news server.
NOC	Network Operations Center, main operations center for DirecPC.
NSFNet	Funded by the National Science Foundation, this network's main constituents were universities, government agencies, and organizations involved in research. ARPANet was its foundation and it later evolved into the Internet.

Term	Description
NSP	Network Service Providers are companies such as PSINet and UUNET which maintain the nationwide communications links that make up the Internet backbone.
packet switching	A networking technology that divides a message into packets, each labeled with a destination address. The packets travel through a network and are reassembled at the destination.
POP	Post Office Protocol is a protocol used for incoming messages.
port number	The number associated with an application.
portal	An all-purpose link to the Web. It contains news, sports, weather, electronic mail and more.
PPP	Point-to-Point Protocol is a protocol that controls communications from a user's residence over telephone lines to an ISP.
proxy server	A server located between a client application and remote servers which provides, among other things, security into and out of your network.
PWS	Personal Web Server is a popular Web server made by the Microsoft for PCs running Windows 95/98.
RAS	Remote Access Server. A Microsoft communications server.
SDSL	Symmetric Digital Subscriber Line. A European DSL standard that supports symmetric traffic, equivalent data transmission rates in each direction, of up to 3 Mbps

Term	Description
search engine	A site such as AltaVista or InfoSeek that helps you search for information on the Internet.
SMTP	Simple Mail Transport Protocol is a protocol used for outgoing messages and communications between mail servers.
SQL Server	A Microsoft database management system.
Telnet server	Servers which permit a computer to act as a terminal for another computer.
URL	Uniform Resource Locator is an address that points to a document on the World Wide Web.
Usenet	The most popular newsgroup system.
WAN	Wide Area Network is a collection of LANs or internetworks that covers a large geographic area such as multiple branches of a large company.
Web browser	A program used to display Web pages.
Web page	A page displayable in a Web browser, containing hot links, text, graphics, video, audio and more.
Web server	A server that provides data in the form of Web pages.
WebTV	A system that displays Internet content on your TV screen.
WWW	World Wide Web is a subset of the Internet characterized by easy-to-navigate Web pages.

In Brief

If you want to...	Then do this...
Create an internetwork	Connect LANs with a router.
Create an Internet-like network for internal communications within a business	Set up an intranet.
Connect two or more organizations to create an Internet-like network	Set up an extranet.
Use a hyperlink	Choose its hotspot.
View Web pages	Use a browser.
Look up details on an Internet standard	Search through the RFCs.
Have quick access to popular sources of Web data	Use a portal.
Search for data	Use a search engine.
Revisit a favorite site on the Web	Bookmark the site in your browser.
Connect an ISP to the Internet	Make a connection between the ISP and an NAP.
Connect your computer to the Internet using standard analog phone lines	Get a modem.
Communicate digitally from your home to the local telephone office	Get an ISDN or DSL line.
Access the Internet through the cable TV system	Get a cable modem.

If you want to...	Then do this...
Use your TV to display Internet content	Get WebTV.
Display Web pages to the Internet community	Set up a Web server.
Increase retrieval rates to frequently accessed Web pages	Set up a cache server.
Enable users to have remote, dial-in access to a network	Set up a communications server.
Allow e-mail access to end users	Establish a mail server.
Add some filtering of outgoing and incoming messages	Place a proxy server between your network and the outside world.
Verify the legitimacy of an organization and its products or services	Set up a certificate server or use one from a CA.
Run programs on a remote server	Use Telnet.
Copy files from a remote server, even in a heterogeneous operating system environment	Use FTP.
Access newsgroups	Use a news server.

Lesson 1 Activities

Complete the following activities to prepare for the certification exam.

1. Describe how a company could make a large library of graphical images available to the public.

2. Explain how a residence is connected to the central telephone office.

3. Describe how a computer uses a destination port address.

4. Describe the meaning of bps.

5. Explain how to search for information about gray chinchillas on the Internet.

6. Describe how Soviet satellite and weapon advances led to the development of the Internet.

7. Describe RFCs.

8. Explain what the letters .com represent in the URL www.novell.com.

9. Describe a NAP.

10. Explain what bandwidth means to you as a user.

Answers to Lesson 1 Activities

1. By setting up an FTP server, a company could supply lists of file names to the public. Users could then transfer files in which they were interested.

2. A residence contains subscriber equipment: telephones, wiring and so on. A local loop connects the residence to the telephone company's local central office (CO). The local loop consists of copper lines.

3. Every application running on a computer has a port number associated with it. Data packets have destination port addresses in their TCP header. When a computer receives a packet of data, it looks at the destination port number and then forwards the packet to the corresponding application.

4. The letters bps stands for bits per second. Data transfer rates are measured in bps.

5. First, connect to an Internet search engine like AltaVista. Next, enter the search string chinchilla+gray.

6. Soviet technological advances in space and nuclear weapons prompted the U.S. Government to create the Advanced Projects Research Agency (ARPA). Soon ARPA saw the need for a communications infrastructure to link scientists and share valuable computer resources. This project, called ARPANet, would eventually evolve into the Internet.

7. Descriptions of Internet architecture, policies, protocols, history and more can be found in a series of documents called Request For Comments (RFC).

8. The letters .com represent a top-level domain for commercial sites.

9. NAPs are exchange points for Internet traffic. ISPs connect to NAPs in order to get Internet backbone access.

10. Bandwidth is the measure of the data carrying capacity of a transmission system. The more bandwidth you have, the faster data will travel to and from your computer.

Lesson 1 Quiz

These questions test your knowledge of features, vocabulary, procedures, and syntax.

1. What can you use to speed up access to Web pages?

    A. A database server

    B. An FTP server

    C. A cache server

    D. A communications server

2. Which of the following protocols is used for downloading e-mail?

    A. FTP

    B. SMTP

    C. POP

    D. SNMP

3. Which of the following is a self-contained network that uses Web technologies to connect one business with another?

    A. A MAN

    B. An intranet

    C. An internetwork

    D. An extranet

4. What language is used to create Web pages?

    A. HTML

    B. HPC

    C. HTTP

    D. Netscape

5. Which of the following transmits data the fastest?

   A. T1

   B. T3

   C. E3

   D. OC-1

6. What is the acronym of an Internet traffic exchange point?

   A. NSP

   B. NAP

   C. ISP

   D. FTP

7. What is the fastest speed available for analog modems?

   A. 28.8 Kbps

   B. 33.6 Kbps

   C. 56 Kbps

   D. 56 Mbps

8. What type of connection does WebTV use?

   A. Analog phone connection

   B. DSL

   C. ISDN

   D. Cable modem

9. Which of the following is a valid FTP address?

   A. ftp\\ftp.symantec.com

   B. ftp:/ftp.symantec.com

   C. ftp:symantec.com

   D. ftp://ftp.symantec.com

10. What is the name of a hotspot in a Web page that is linked to a different point on the same page or is linked to a totally different page?

    A. A Web browser

    B. A port

    C. A local loop

    D. A hyperlink

Answers to Lesson 1 Quiz

1. Answer C is correct. Cache servers maintain copies of frequently accessed Web pages in RAM.

    Answer A is incorrect. Database servers are repositories of data.

    Answer B is incorrect. FTP servers store files that users can download.

    Answer D is incorrect. Communications servers accept connections over phone lines from remote computers.

2. Answer C is correct. POP stands for post office protocol and is used to download e-mail.

    Answer A is incorrect. FTP is not used for transferring e-mail; it is used for downloading and uploading files.

    Answer B is incorrect. It is true that the SMTP is an e-mail protocol, but it is not used to download e-mail. It is used, among other things, to upload   e-mail.

    Answer D is incorrect. SNMP is the Simple Network Management Protocol.

3. Answer D is correct. An extranet uses Web technologies to connect the networks of two separate businesses.

    Answer A is incorrect. A MAN could be the infrastructure of an extranet but it does not necessarily use Web technologies.

    Answer B is incorrect. An intranet is used for internal communications within a business.

    Answer C is incorrect. An internetwork could be the infrastructure of an extranet but it does not necessarily use Web technologies.

4. Answer A is correct. HTML stands for HyperText Markup Language, the language used to create web pages.

    Answer B is incorrect. HPC stands for Handheld PC.

    Answer C is incorrect. HTTP is a protocol not a language.

    Answer D is incorrect. Netscape is a company that makes browsers and other Web software.

5. Answer D is correct. OC-1 transmits data at 51.840 Mbps.

    Answer A is incorrect. T1 transmits data at 1.544 Mbps.

    Answer B is incorrect. T3 transmits data at 44.736 Mbps.

    Answer C is incorrect. E3 transmits data at 34.368 Mbps.

6. Answer B is correct. NAP stands for Network Access Point.

    Answer A is incorrect. NSP stands for Network Service Point.

    Answer C is incorrect. ISP stands for Internet Service Provider.

    Answer D is incorrect. FTP is a protocol.

7. Answer C is correct. 56 Kbps is the fastest analog modem available.

    Answer A is incorrect. 28.8 Kbps is an old standard.

    Answer B is incorrect. 33.6 Kbps is an old standard.

    Answer D is incorrect. 56 Mbps does not exist.

8. Answer A is correct. WebTV connects to a standard phone line.

    Answer B is incorrect. WebTV does not use DSL.

    Answer C is incorrect. WebTV does not use ISDN.

    Answer D is incorrect. Although WebTV connects to your TV, it does not use the cable TV system to transmit data.

9. Answer D is correct. You need the name of the protocol, a colon, two forward slashes, and then the URL.

    Answer A is incorrect. You cannot use backslashes and the colon is missing.

    Answer B is incorrect. Only one forward slash is shown.

    Answer C is incorrect. No slashes shown.

10. Answer D is correct. Hyperlinks connect you to other points on the same page or to other pages.

Answer A is incorrect. A Web browser contains Web pages that contain hotspots.

Answer B is incorrect. A port is a reference number for processes running on a server.

Answer C is incorrect. A local loop connects a residence to the central phone office.

Lesson 2: OSI Model and Protocols

The Open Systems Interconnection (OSI) model is industry-accepted network architecture for dividing the task of moving data across a network into seven sequential processes or layers. Each layer handles a specific piece of the process by using a standardized set of rules known as protocols. By adhering to accepted protocols for defining the functionality of each layer, hardware manufacturers and software developers create products that communicate with each other.

After completing this lesson, you should have a better understanding of the following topics:

- OSI Model

- IEEE 802 Specifications

- Protocol Suites and Protocols

OSI Model

Several organizations, prominent among them International Standards Organization (ISO) and the Institute of Electrical and Electronic Engineers (IEEE), have been very influential in creating open networking standards for the computer industry. By focusing on open standards (system architecture that is freely available to everyone), these organizations have played a major role in promoting network compatibility in the computer industry.

In 1978, ISO published a set of standards that describes the seven layers of the OSI model. The purpose of the project was to create a set of protocols with an open standard. This allows different and sometimes incompatible devices to communicate on a network.

Each layer handles a specific portion of the communication process. Furthermore, each layer functions independently of the other layers. This modular concept makes it possible to modify one layer without affecting the function of another layer. The OSI model is shown in Figure 2.1.

Seven Layers

When thinking about the function of each layer in the OSI model, remember that each layer performs its tasks in two directions. Incoming data is processed and handed off to the layer above until it is processed by an application such as an

e-mail program. Outgoing data is processed and sent down the OSI model until it reaches the Physical Layer. Here it converts to voltage variations that transmit along the network cable. These voltage variations represent the 1s and 0s of the binary information sent on the network.

Each layer in the OSI model is conceptually independent of the other layers in the model. A layer processes incoming or outgoing data in synchronization with the corresponding layer in the remote device with which it is communicating.

Figure 2.1 OSI Model

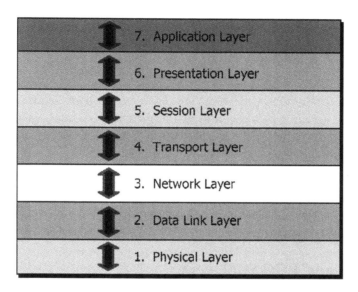

The following paragraphs describe the seven layers in the OSI model.

Physical Layer

The first layer in the OSI model is the Physical Layer. This layer describes the standards for the physical connection to the network. The design of the connection receptacle, the number and placement of connecting pins, and the function of each circuit in the Network Interface Card (NIC) are all Physical Layer considerations. The standards for the Physical Layer also define the acceptable voltage levels and voltage variations on a network cable and how that translates into binary information.

Tip: The first layer in the OSI model is the bottom layer. The top layer is the seventh layer. This makes sense if you think of how data progresses from a network to an application. A NIC first senses the data (Physical Layer), and from there it is processed until your e-mail program informs you that you have mail.

Data Link Layer

The Data Link Layer is the second layer in the OSI model. The primary purpose of this layer is to facilitate reliable communication between two points on a network. In this layer, the binary information detected by the Physical Layer is assembled into units of data called frames. The Data Link Layer places header and trailer information (data at the beginning and end of each frame) so that each device can determine the beginning and ending of each frame.

The header information also allows the receiving device to properly sequence the frames as they arrive. The Data Link Layer is subdivided into two more sublayers, the Logical Link Control (LLC) and the Media Access Control (MAC). This subdivision of protocols allows clear process assignment within the layer. The LLC and MAC are shown in Figure 2.2.

The MAC sublayer has two functions. First, the MAC is responsible for the physical address of the network device. This is referred to as the MAC address of a device. Typically this address is hard coded into the NIC.

Figure 2.2 MAC and LCC Sublayers

| Application Layer |
| Presentation Layer |
| Session Layer |
| Transport Layer |
| Network Layer |

| Data Link Layer | Logical Link Control (LLC) Sublayer |
| | Media Access Control (MAC) Sublayer |

| Physical Layer |

Note: If you remove a NIC from one computer and install it in another, the MAC address moves with the NIC.

Second, the MAC controls access to the network. The MAC listens to the network for pauses in network traffic before sending data. If data is simultaneously transmitted from more than one device on a network, the data signals will collide and scramble, which causes lost or undeliverable data. The MAC sublayer is responsible for minimizing these signal collisions.

The LLC sublayer establishes connections between network devices. The LLC handles error correction and flow control. Error control is accomplished by using an algorithm to run a calculation on the data. The results of the calculation are compared to an expected result. If the two numbers match, the data is determined to be error-free. The calculation result is called a checksum. Networks can have devices capable of transmitting data at different speeds. The LLC regulates the speed of the data being sent so that it is compatible with other devices on the network.

Network Layer

The Network Layer performs addressing and routing functions. Networked computers have both a physical identity (the MAC address) and a logical address. The logical address is configured in software and describes the location of a network device. An Internet Protocol (IP) address is a logical address. One function of the Network Layer is the translation between MAC addresses and logical addresses.

The path, or route, a signal takes on a network is controlled by the Network Layer. The Network Layer determines the path based on the logical address of the network devices. Devices, such as routers, redirect network traffic based on this information. Routers are referred to as layer three devices.

Transport Layer

This layer manages the efficient and reliable transmission of data on a network. One task of the Transport Layer is to repackage data into network-efficient packets. A large block of data is broken into smaller packets for transmission efficiency. Packets also have header information specific to them, including the total number of packets associated with a data block and the assembly sequence. The

Transport Layer in the receiving device uses this information to determine that all packets have been received and then reconstructs the data properly, even if the packets are received out of order.

Session Layer

A session is the period of time when the computers are connected with each other. The Session Layer handles the initial contact, the session, and the termination of the session. NetBIOS is a standard interface used by Microsoft and others for handling sessions between computers.

Presentation Layer

The Presentation Layer transforms the data from a format used by computer applications to a format that streams data over a network. Data compression and encryption also occur in this layer.

Application Layer

The seventh layer of the OSI model is the interface between the computer application and the data transmitted or received across a network. By standardizing this layer, programmers can design their e-mail, file server, file transfer, and other computer programs with a consistent network interface.

IEEE 802 Specifications

Just as the ISO was responsible for developing the OSI model for layered protocols, the IEEE published a set of standards for devices associated with moving data on a Local Area Network (LAN). The project, IEEE 802, is named after the year, 1980, and the month (2 for February) it started. Eventually the project yielded twelve standards labeled 802.1 through 802.12. (Table 2.1).

Table 2.1 Twelve 802 Standards

IEEE Standard Number	IEEE Standard Name
802.1	Spanning Tree Algorithm
802.2	Logical Link Control (LLC) Portion of the Data Link Layer
802.3	Ethernet
802.4	Token Bus
802.5	Token Ring
802.6	Distributed Queue Dual Bus (DQBD)
802.7	Broadband Technology
802.8	Fiber-Optic Technology
802.9	Integrated Data and Voice
802.10	Network Security
802.11	Wireless Networks
802.12	100VG-AnyLAN

802.1 Spanning Tree Algorithm

Formerly called Internetworking (high-level interface group), this standard describes how transparent bridges use the Spanning Tree Algorithm. Bridges are network hardware devices that connect network segments into one logical network. One type of bridge, a transparent bridge, uses the Spanning Tree Algorithm to detect other bridges on the network. The algorithm also detects when another bridge fails and removes network loops.

Note: Removal of network loops stops perpetuating broadcast cycles called a broadcast storm. An important function of bridges is to prevent broadcast storms.

802.2 Data Link Layer's LLCPortion

The LLC is a sublayer of the Data Link Layer in the OSI model. This standard defines the protocols for the LLC. LLC manages data-link communication and defines usage of logical interface points. Other computers can use these points called Service Advertising Protocols (SAPs) to transfer information from the LLC sublayer to upper layers in the OSI model.

802.3 Ethernet

This protocol defines standards for the MAC sublayer of the Data Link Layer and the Physical Layer in the OSI model, as well as defining the original specifications for Ethernet. The protocol is also known as Carrier-Sense Multiple Access with Collision Detection (CSMA/CD) LAN (Ethernet).

 Note: The most common network protocol in use today is Ethernet II, which has slightly different specifications than 802.3.

This standard enables devices to detect a collision and allows computers to transmit data if no other computer is transmitting. It is a type of contention protocol that allows nodes to contend for network access.

802.4 Token-Bus LAN

This protocol defines standards for token-bus LANs, including the token-passing mechanism for traffic regulation of the bus at the Data Link Layer's MAC sublayer and at the Physical Layer. A token-bus network is very similar to a token-ring network, but the endpoints of the bus do not meet to form a logical ring. This architecture was not widely adopted, however, and today, virtually all token-type network systems are token rings rather than token buses.

802.5 Token-Ring LAN

This category defines the standard at both the Data Link Layer's MAC sublayer and Physical Layer of the OSI model. IBM developed the standard for token-ring networks.

802.6 Metropolitan Area Network (MAN)

This standard defines the Distributed Queue Dual Bus (DQDB) which is a network with two physical channels. MANs are usually characterized by high-speed connections using fiber-optic cable or other digital media.

802.7 Broadband Technical Advisory Group

Defines the technical advisory group concerned with broadband issues.

802.8 Fiber-Optic Technical Advisory Group

This specification describes the groups that advise on fiber-optic technology.

802.9 Integrated Voice and Data Networks

This standard addresses networks that integrate data and voice traffic.

801.10 Network Security

This standard focuses on network security issues.

802.11 Wireless Networks

Wireless networks are starting to become more common. This IEEE group creates standards for this emerging technology. The draft standard specifies a single Medium Access Control (MAC) sublayer and three Physical Layer specifications.

802.12 100VG-AnyLAN

Hewlett-Packard developed this network standard. The technology supports 100-Mb transmission speeds.

Protocols and Protocol Suites

A protocol is a set of rules that apply to a particular process. A collection of protocols that describe a multi-step process is called a protocol suite. In networking architecture, a protocol suite is a collection of rules that define a network system. The remainder of this chapter will focus on the protocols and protocol suites that make up the most common computer network systems. Figure 2.3 represents a protocol suite and how it corresponds to the OSI model.

Figure 2.3 Protocol Suites and OSI Model

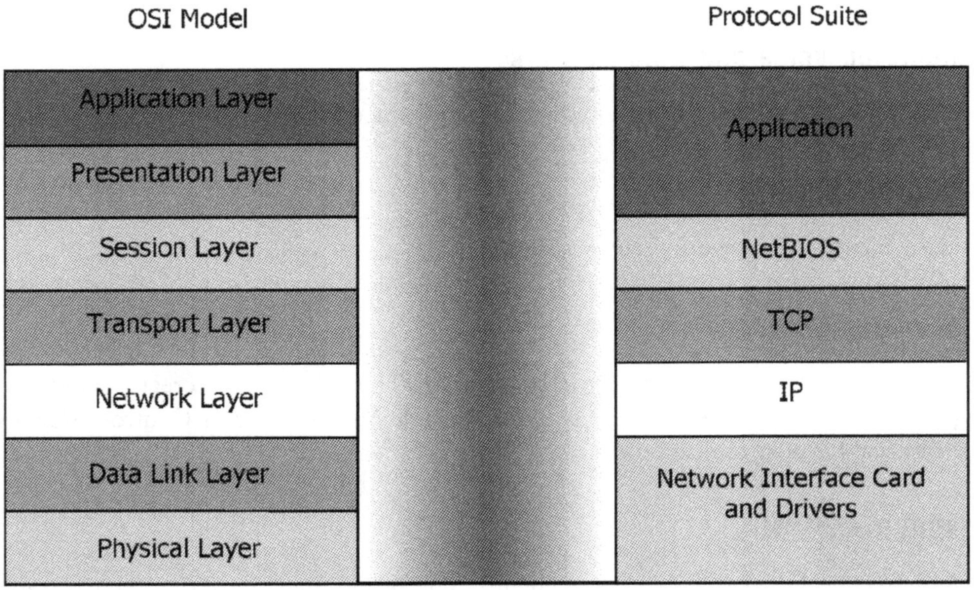

OSI Model	Protocol Suite
Application Layer	Application
Presentation Layer	Application
Session Layer	NetBIOS
Transport Layer	TCP
Network Layer	IP
Data Link Layer	Network Interface Card and Drivers
Physical Layer	Network Interface Card and Drivers

NetBIOS Extended User Interface (NetBEUI)

NetBEUI is a fast, easy-to-use protocol for establishing small Microsoft Windows LANs. NetBEUI (pronounced net-buoy) was one of the first network protocols to become widely adopted. Because of its ease of use and relative speed, NetBEUI is the default network protocol for Microsoft Windows, except Windows 2000. The NetBEUI protocol uses computer names for network identity. Because no logical addressing is required, setting up this kind of network is very easy.

NetBEUI has a significant limitation that restricts its use to small networks. NetBEUI is not routable. The ease of setup made possible by eliminating logical addressing becomes a limiting factor on everything except simple networks. Complex networks invariably use routers that rely on logical addressing to direct, or route, network traffic.

 Tip: NetBEUI is not routable; as a result, its practical use is limited to small networks.

Network Basic Input/Output System (NetBIOS)

Sytek originally developed NetBIOS for IBM in 1983. NetBEUI and NetBIOS are linked in the minds of many computer industry veterans because NetBIOS and NetBEUI were originally considered one protocol. NetBIOS and NetBEUI functions are distinct, however, and today NetBIOS has evolved into a standard (or optional) component of nearly every network system. In contrast, NetBEUI is a protocol limited to small Windows networks.

Major NetBIOS Services

NetBIOS provides services that applications use to communicate over a network. NetBIOS provides the following two major services:

A standard Application Programming Interface (API)—Computer programs use API to communicate with underlying network protocols.

Regulation and resolution of computer names on a network—NetBIOS regulates and resolves network computer names.

Internet Packet Exchange/Sequenced Packet Exchange (IPX/SPX)

Although several companies are prominent in computer networking, Novell's NetWare is a force to be reckoned within the LAN industry. NetWare networks use different protocols than Microsoft Windows networks. Microsoft and Novell acknowledge the need to provide connectivity tools that allow their respective products to coexist. NWLink is Microsoft's product that bridges the two protocols.

IPX

IPX is the Novell solution for the Network Layer of the OSI model. Successful transmission acknowledgment is not required in this implementation. IPX can be thought of as a send-and-forget protocol. IPX delegates message acknowledgement and related issues to the upper layers of the OSI.

SPX

SPX is Novell's implementation of the Transport Layer. Reliable packet delivery, recovery of missing data, and recovery from errors are handled by SPX. IPX works in coordination with SPX as data moves through the OSI model.

NWLink

NWLink is a Microsoft implementation of Novell's IPX/SPX protocol for Windows NT, Windows 95/98/2000 and Microsoft DOS. NWLink also supports NetBIOS. Using NWLink, Windows clients can access NetWare client/server applications. NetWare clients can also access client/server applications running on Windows servers by using NWLink. Windows clients can use NWLink and other software to access some NetWare network devices, such as printers and file servers.

Tip: In some situations, for instance if a Windows client accesses a client/server application on a NetWare server, NWLink is the complete connectivity solution. In other situations, for instance if a Windows client accesses print resources on a NetWare server, additional software is required.

IPX/SPX and its Windows implementation, NWLink, is a mature networking technology capable of solving complex networking challenges. The fact that IPX/SPX is a Novell proprietary standard has probably kept it from becoming the current networking standard. That honor goes to the open standard Transmission Control Protocol/Internet Protocol (TCP/IP). Nevertheless, NetWare remains a major presence in networking technology. Its routability, scalability, reliability, and advanced features keep Novell administrators loyal to NetWare.

TCP/IP

TCP/IP is a suite of open standard protocols. Originally designed for the UNIX platform, TCP/IP started as a Department of Defense-sponsored (DOD) program to develop a large network system that could remain functional under wartime conditions. During the last thirty years, TCP/IP has evolved into a sophisticated protocol suite that can meet virtually any network requirement. The original program was conducted by a DOD branch called the Advanced Research Projects Agency (ARPA). The network created at ARPA (originally call ARPAnet) is what we now refer to as the Internet. In addition to being the Internet standard, TCP/IP is the most common protocol suite for all networks.

Note: One significant difference in functionality between TCP/IP and IPX/SPX is the client-to-client capabilities built into TCP/IP. NetWare was conceived as a client/server system, and client-to-client connectivity was not built into its network architecture.

Internet Protocol (IP)

IP is a connectionless protocol that performs the Network Layer functions of the OSI model. The send-and-forget aspect of IP means that it is not dependant on acknowledgement from the remote device to perform its functions. IP also attaches header information to data packets that facilitates the partitioning and assembly of information in the data stream.

Transmission Control Protocol (TCP)

TCP is a connection-based protocol that performs the Transport Layer duties of the OSI model. TCP maintains the connection between a host, a central or control computer on a network, and a remote access computer. TCP assigns a unique port number, a form of computer address, to a communication session that directs the data packets to the correct host and remote machine. By assigning unique port numbers, TCP ensures the data is sent only to the correct host and remote computer.

 Note: Although a correlation exists between the OSI model Transport Layer (for TCP) and Network Layer (for IP), TCP/IP is actually a collection of many protocols that add functionality to networks.

TCP/IP was designed to be reliable under adverse conditions, to scale to very large networks, to work in complex routed systems and to have an open standard. All of these features have contributed to the popularity of TCP/IP. Figure 2.4 compares the OSI model to TCP/IP and IPX/SPX.

Figure 2.4 OSI Model, TCP/IP and IPX/SPX

IPX/SPX	OSI Model	TCP/IP
	Application Layer	Application Layer
	Presentation Layer	
	Session Layer	
SPX	Transport Layer	TCP
IPX	Network Layer	IP
	Data Link Layer	Network Interface Layer
	Physical Layer	

Vocabulary

Review the following terms in preparation for the certification exam.

Term	Description
algorithm	A set of rules for specific calculations.
Application Layer	The seventh or top layer of the OSI model that establishes a common interface between a computer program, such as an e-mail application, and the lower layers of the OSI model.
bridge	A network hardware device used to connect network segments into one logical network. Bridges also have functions that control broadcast traffic on a network.
broadcast storm	A self-perpetuating broadcast cycle on a network. Broadcast storms completely dominate network traffic and shut down a network. A bridge using the Spanning Tree Algorithm can prevent a broadcast storm.
checksum	A calculation result that is compared to an expected result. Computers use checksums for error control.
Data Link Layer	Second layer in the OSI model that facilitates reliable communication between two points on a network. This layer is divided into the LLC and MAC sublayers.
encryption	Transforms data into a form unreadable to everyone except those that have the correct algorithm or key to unlock the data.

Term	Description
IEEE 802	A set of twelve industry standards developed to define how devices function when moving data across a network.
IPX/SPX	A robust proprietary protocol suite developed by Novell. NetWare networks operate using IPX/SPX.
LAN	A Local Area Network is a computer network where all devices are located in the same site.
logical address	A network device address that is assigned in software. This address contains information about the location of the device on a network.
LLC	Logical Link Control is a sublayer of the Data Link Layer. The MAC sublayer senses network traffic to avoid data collisions and identifies the physical address of the computer.
MAC	Media Access Control is a sublayer of the Data Link Layer. The MAC sublayer senses network traffic to avoid data collisions and identifies the physical address of the computer.
NetBEUI	NetBIOS Enhanced User Interface is a fast and easy-to-use protocol in Microsoft Windows. NetBEUI is not routable.
NetBIOS	Network Basic Input/Output System. NetBIOS provides a standard API for computer programs to communicate with other network protocols.
NIC	A Network Interface Card is a device that allows computers to connect to a network. A unique MAC number is hard-coded into each device.

Term	Description
Network Layer	The third layer of the OSI model, the Network Layer performs routing functions that determine the path the data follows on a network.
NWLink	A Microsoft implementation of the IPX/SPX protocols used in NetWare.
open standard	Computer programming that is freely available to the public and industry.
OSI model	The Open System Interconnection is a conceptual model that establishes protocols for seven independent and sequential processes, or layers, for network data transmission.
packets	Large blocks of data are broken into smaller packets in the Transport Layer to conform to network requirements for efficiency and reliability. Packets have header and trailer information about them that is used to assemble the data at the remote destination.
Physical Layer	The first or bottom layer of the OSI model. The physical connection to the network.
protocol	A set of rules or standards that enable computers to connect with each other and exchange information with as few errors as possible.
protocol suite	A collection of protocols that define a multi-step process on a network. TCP/IP is a protocol suite that establishes how the Internet works.
Session Layer	Layer six in the OSI model. The Session Layer is responsible for beginning, maintaining, and ending a communication between two points on a network.

Term	Description
Spanning Tree Algorithm	Defined in IEEE 802.1, this standard establishes protocols for network bridges and is responsible for controlling broadcast storms.
TCP/IP	Transport Control Protocol/Internet Protocol. The most commonly used protocol suite, TCP/IP was originally developed by the military on UNIX computers to create very large, durable networks. The Internet is based on TCP/IP.
Transport Layer	The fourth layer of the OSI model, the Transport Layer divides and assembles network data into efficient packets to facilitate reliable transmission.

In Brief

If you want to...	Then do this...
Connect network segments into one logical network and control broadcast traffic on the network	Use a bridge to connect network segments.
Create a small, fast, easy-to-set-up Windows network	Use the Windows default NetBEUI protocol to set up a small Windows network.
Communicate between a Windows network and a Novell NetWare network	Use NWLink and other software if needed to allow the different protocol suites to communicate.
Establish a connection with the Internet	Use the TCP/IP protocol to establish a connection with the Internet.
Connect a local computer to a network	Install a NIC to enable network communication.
Divide a network into connected segments and control the path a signal takes en route to its final destination	Use a router to control signal destination paths.

Lesson 2 Activities

Complete the following activities to test your knowledge and then refer to the answers.

1. Diagram the OSI model and show how the TCP/IP and IPX/SPX protocol suites map to it.

2. Describe IEEE 802.

3. Explain the significance of IEEE 802.3.

4. Explain when NetBEUI would be an appropriate network protocol choice.

5. Name the two sublayers of the Data Link Layer.

6. Explain the term MAC address and describe where is it located.

7. Describe the origins of the Internet.

8. Explain the function of NWLink and when you would need it.

9. Explain the meaning of the word protocol and describe what constitutes a protocol suite. Give an example of a protocol suite.

10. Explain what is meant by the term connectionless protocol.

Answers to Lesson 2 Activities

1.

IPX/SPX	OSI Model	TCP/IP
	Application Layer	
	Presentation Layer	Application Layer
	Session Layer	
SPX	Transport Layer	TCP
IPX	Network Layer	IP
	Data Link Layer	Network Interface Layer
	Physical Layer	

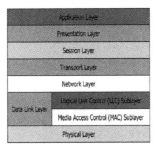

2. The IEEE 802 project began in February 1980. A group of engineers and computer scientists began a project with the goal of creating open standards that defined the functionality of network devices and how data is transmitted on a network.

3. IEEE 802.3 is the original standard for Ethernet.

4. When setting up a simple Windows network that does not need to communicate with other networks or the Internet, NetBEUI is a good choice because it is fast and easy to use.

5. Logical Link Control (LLC) and the Media Access Control (MAC).

6. The MAC address is the hard-coded identification number burned into the NIC. This address cannot be changed.

7. The DOD originally assigned the task of developing a large robust network system to the ARPA in 1969. ARPA developed a packet-switching, fault-tolerant, network system originally called ARPAnet. Today ARPAnet has evolved into the Internet.

8. NWLink is a Microsoft implementation of Novell's IPX/SPX protocol suite. NWLink allows Windows clients to communicate with NetWare servers and NetWare clients to communicate with Windows servers.

9. A protocol is a set of rules that define a specific process. A protocol suite is a collection of protocols that define a system. TCP/IP is a protocol suite that establishes the networking standards for the Internet.

10. A connectionless protocol does not require acknowledgement to perform its function. It is a send-and-forget protocol. Connectionless protocols usually work in tandem with other protocols that provide transmission receipt acknowledgement, error control, and other session related functions. Internet Protocol (IP) is a connectionless protocol.

Lesson 2 Quiz

These questions test your knowledge of features, vocabulary, procedures, and syntax.

1. What protocol is necessary for a Windows client to communicate with a NetWare server?

    A. NetBIOS

    B. NWLink

    C. NetBEUI

    D. IPX/SPX

2. What sublayers comprise the Data Link Layer?

    A. NetBEUI and NetBIOS

    B. Session layer and Network layer

    C. LLC and MAC

    D. LLC and NetBIOS

3. Which two of the following are not OSI model layers?

    A. Transition layer

    B. Session layer

    C. Physical layer

    D. Internet layer

4. Which of the following are true about NetBEUI?

    A. Routable

    B. Runs on Windows computers

    C. Fast

    D. Uses computer names

5. To which layers in the OSI model do TCP/IP and IPX/SPX correspond?

    A. Session

    B. Data Link

    C. Transport

    D. Network

6. Which statement is not true about TCP/IP?

    A. It is a single protocol

    B. It was originally designed for UNIX operating systems

    C. It is used on the Internet

    D. It is an open standard

7. Which IEEE 802 standard defines Ethernet?

    A. 802.1

    B. 802.2

    C. 802.3

    D. 802.11

8. Which two statements are true about the difference between a bridge and a router?

    A. A router is a physical device, while a bridge is performed in software

    B. Bridges connect network segments and routers do not

    C. Routers maintain logical address tables and redirect network traffic, while bridges only control broadcast traffic

    D. Routers operate at the third layer of the OSI model, and bridges are layer two devices

9. Which statements are true of both MAC addresses and logical addresses?

    A. They both contain information about where a device resides on a network

    B. They both contain information used to identify computers on a network

C. Both addresses are hard coded into NIC

D. Both addresses are set in software

10. Which statements accurately describe the OSI model?

A. The first layer is the top layer

B. The OSI is a conceptual model

C. There is only one protocol per layer

D. The OSI is an open standard

Answers to Lesson 2 Quiz

1. Answer B is correct. NWLink is the Windows implementation of IPX/SPX.

   Answer A is incorrect because NetBIOS is an upper layer API used in many protocol suites.

   Answer C is incorrect because NetBEUI is a simple Windows only protocol.

   Answer D is incorrect because IPX/SPX is the Novell protocol suite and is incompatible with TCP/IP, which is used on most Windows networks. NWLink is needed for Windows and NetWare networks to communicate.

2. Answer C is correct. The MAC and the LLC are sublayers.

   Answer A is incorrect because NetBEUI and NetBIOS are not OSI model sublayers.

   Answer B is incorrect because the Session layer and the Network layer are primary layers of the OSI model, not sublayers.

   Answer D is not correct because NetBIOS is not an OSI model sublayer.

3. Answers B and C are correct.

   Answers A and D are incorrect because the transition layer and the Internet layer are not part of the OSI model.

4. Answers B, C and D are correct. NetBEUI is a fast, Windows networking system that uses computer names for network identity.

   Answer A is incorrect because a major limitation of NetBEUI is that it is not routable.

5. Answers C and D are correct. TCP and SPX map to the Transport layer of the OSI model. IP and IPX map to the Network layer.

   Answers A and B are incorrect because neither map to TCP/IP or IPX/SPX.

6. Answer A is not true about TCP/IP.

   Answer B is a true statement because the military originally developed TCP/IP on the UNIX platform.

   Answer C is true. TCP/IP is the Internet protocol.

   Answer D is true.

7. Answer C is correct. Ethernet was originally defined under IEEE 802.3.

    Answer A is incorrect. 802.1 set the standards for the Spanning Tree Algorithm.

    Answer B is incorrect. 802.2 is the standard for the LLC sublayer of the Data Link layer of the OSI.

    Answer D is incorrect. 802.11 establishes standards for wireless networks.

8. Answers C and D are correct. Routers can redirect traffic according to logical address stored on an internal table. Bridges can connect network segments and limit broadcast traffic to the appropriate segment, but bridges cannot redirect general traffic.

    Answer A is incorrect. Bridges are physical devices. Routing can actually be accomplished in software by a computer that has two NICs installed.

    Answer B is incorrect. A bridge connects two network segments into one logical segment, while a router connects two network segments into two logical networks. In both cases, properly configured devices can communicate across all connected segments.

9. Answer B is correct. Both MAC addresses and logical addresses are used to establish network identity.

    Answer A is incorrect because a MAC address contains only computer identity information. It contains no location information.

    Answers C and D are incorrect because logical addresses are set in software. Only MAC address are hard coded into the NIC card.

10. Answers B and D are correct. The OSI was developed as an open standard conceptual model with the goal to promote connectivity in emerging network technologies.

    Answer A is incorrect because the first layer of the OSI model is the bottom layer or the Physical layer.

    Answer C is incorrect because developers often create multiple protocols to accomplish the functionality described in a singe OSI model layer. The OSI model itself expresses this refinement of layer function by dividing the Data Link Layer into the LLC and MAC sublayers.

Lesson 3: TCP/IP

Transmission Control Protocol/Internet Protocol (TCP/IP) is used more than any other network protocol. TCP/IP initially connected military bases, universities, and research facilities. That project has evolved into a large, robust global network—the Internet. This chapter takes a more in-depth look at TCP/IP.

After completing this lesson, you should have a better understanding of the following topics:

■ Network Layer Internet Protocol (IP)

■ Internet Protocol (IP) Addressing

■ Routing Architecture

■ Domain Name System (DNS)

■ Windows Internet Naming Service (WINS)

■ Troubleshooting

Network Layer Internet Protocol (IP)

IP is the Network Layer in the TCP/IP protocol suite. Sometimes called the Internet Layer, this layer primarily performs these three addressing services:

- Message addressing

- IP address to physical address translation

- Computer name to physical address translation

IP also controls how the subnet mask (a 32-bit number that determines how an IP address is interpreted) routes messages from the host computer to the destination computer. Although IP is the primary protocol used at the Network Layer, other protocols in the suite also add functionality. These protocols are discussed in the following paragraphs.

Address Resolution Protocol (ARP)

This protocol matches a physical address (MAC address) to an IP address. This process is called address resolution.

Internet Control Message Protocol (ICMP)

This is an error-reporting protocol that monitors packet delivery.

Internet Group Management Protocol (IGMP)

This protocol supports certain kinds of router transmissions.

 Tip: Protocol suites are also called protocol stacks. The term stack is descriptive, suggesting the sequential layering of a system. The TCP/IP stack has four layers.

Figure 3.1 TCP/IP Stack and OSI Model

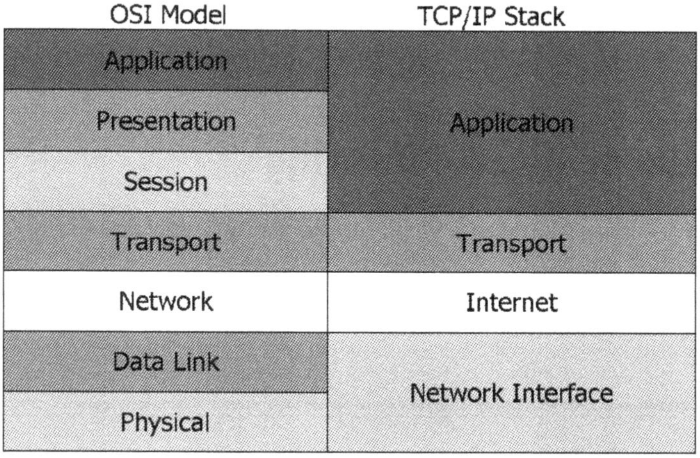

OSI Model	TCP/IP Stack
Application	Application
Presentation	Application
Session	Application
Transport	Transport
Network	Internet
Data Link	Network Interface
Physical	Network Interface

Transport Layer Functionality

The Transport Layer, as the name implies, provides services to move data across a network. The TCP/IP protocol stack has two protocols available to handle Transport Layer services.

Transmission Control Protocol (TCP)

This protocol is a reliable connection-oriented service that requires a channel to be established between the sender and receiver before any messages are transmitted. TCP handles message segmentation, error detection, and datagrams. A datagram is a packet of information and its delivery information. TCP is an appropriate protocol for sending large amounts of data or any data that cannot contain errors. Slower transmission speeds can be a consequence of using TCP.

User Datagram Protocol (UDP)

This send-and-forget protocol is also called a best-effort delivery protocol. Because UDP does not perform error control or check for reliable delivery, transmission is typically faster than with TCP. Error control and datagram recovery become the responsibility of applications that use UDP.

Internet Protocol (IP) Addressing

IP addresses are 32-bit binary numbers. The 32 bits are divided into four groups of 8 bits. Each 8-bit group, or octet, describes a part of the address. Because working with binary numbers is impractical, the dotted decimal system is used to represent each binary octet as a decimal number from 1 to 255. Each decimal number is separated by a period.

 Note: The enormous complexity of today's computers and layers of programming language obscure the fact that computer processing depends on an open or closed circuit dependant upon two-digit binary numbers, 0 or 1, that match the on/off computer circuit.

The following is an example of a typical IP address in binary:

10000100 00100001 00010111 00001011

Applying the decimal system yields the following:

132.33.23.11

Upgrading IP Version 4 to Version 6

IP Version 4 is a 32-bit architecture. IP Version 6.0 will be 128-bit architecture. Version 4 is the current version of the IP addressing system that has not changed in design since the 1970s. Although the original design for IP addressing is extremely clever and functional, it is not able to keep up with the enormous demand for new addresses created by the Internet. In the last few years, IP addresses have become a scarce commodity.

A new version of IP, called IPv6, creates more IP addresses and improves functionality. While the theoretical number of available addresses in the 32-bit architecture of IP Version 4 is a very large number, due to a variety of limiting factors and the enormous demand created by the Internet, the actual number of available addresses has shrunk dramatically in recent years.

Since IPv6 uses a 128-bit number architecture, the number of addresses (billions and billions) created by this system will meet addressing needs for a long time.

IPv6 is meeting some resistance in the developer community because of the large base of users running software developed around IP Version 4. Even with the reluctance to adapt a new standard, the need for IPv6 is undeniable.

Address Classes

IP addresses are divided into the following four classes:

- Class A addresses are assigned to very large networks

- Class B addresses are assigned to large networks

- Class C addresses are normally assigned to small networks

- Class D addresses are reserved for multicasting

 Note: A Class E address is reserved for experimental purposes and possible future use.

The design of the IP address system is such that relatively few Class A addresses were created. In theory, each Class A address can accommodate up to 16 million unique number schemes to identify networked computers, called host IDs. Class B addresses are more common, but also more limited in the number of available host IDs. The most plentiful address type is the Class C. A class C address is limited to 254 host IDs per network.

As a practical matter, all Class A addresses are taken and Class B addresses are very difficult to obtain. Large companies are often unable to get an IP address that can accommodate all of the host computers on their network. It is common for large companies to acquire multiple Class C addresses to meet their addressing needs. Small organizations may only get a portion of a Class C network address. IPv6 will relieve the shortage of network addresses, once it is adopted.

Public and Private Addresses

The organization responsible for managing the registration of IP addresses is Internet Network Information Center (InterNIC). To avoid IP address duplication, every address used on a public network, such as the Internet, must be unique. InterNIC maintains a large database of all registered and available IP addresses.

It is possible to design a private network using any IP address system that suits your network requirements. The limitation to this strategy is that your network can never connect to a public network like the Internet (or another private network for that matter) without potential IP address conflict. In an age where Internet access is considered a necessity for most organizations, it rarely makes sense to build networks with unregistered addresses.

There are situations where a company has practical reasons to create a private network. Technical schools may have student computer labs on isolated networks. Private industry and governmental organizations may have departments that are not connected to public networks for security reasons. Although these network environments could theoretically use any addressing system, a better solution is built into the IP addressing system. Within each of the three major address classes, there are reserved address blocks for private networks. These addresses will never be registered for public use.

 Note: Although private IP addresses are sometimes referred to as non-routable IP, this name is misleading. While it is true that an Internet Service Provider (ISP) will never route these addresses to the Internet, they can be routed by standard routing equipment within private networks and intranets.

The reserved private network IP address blocks for each class are as follows:

■   Class A: 10.0.0.0 to 10.255.255.255

■   Class B: 172.16.0.0 to 172.31.255.255

■   Class C: 192.168.0.0 to 192.168.255.255

Tip: One other IP address is reserved for network testing. This address is 127.0.0.1, and it is called the loop-back address. This address is used to troubleshoot networks.

Subnet Masking

An IP address actually contains two types of address information. The subnet mask is another 32-bit number that defines which part of the IP address is used for network address information and host address information.

Figure 3.2 shows a typical class B IP address and how a subnet mask is used to allocate network ID and host ID information.

Figure 3.2 IP Address and Subnet Mask

Network ID		Host ID	
IP Address			
165	26	135	19
Subnet mask			
255	255	0	0

The portion of the 32-bit IP number allocated for the network address and the host address varies with each class of IP address. Only the first octet of a Class A network refers to the network portion of the address, leaving the three remaining octets available for host addressing. This explains why there are so few Class A networks in existence (8 bits, or a byte, of binary information has a maximum value of 255) and the large number of host IDs that a single Class A address can support.

A Class C address has the reverse allocation. The first three octets are available for network addressing (approximately 16 million possible network IDs) with only one octet assigned for host IDs. Class B addressing has two octets each for network IDs and host IDs.

 Note: Subnet masking is complex. The introduction to the topic on these pages is only a starting point. Individuals planning a future in network administration should do additional reading on the subject.

The first number in an IP address has a range assigned by class as follows:

■   1 to 126 for Class A

■   128 to 191 for Class B

■   192 to 223 for Class C

A computation is done between the binary numbers of the IP address and subnet mask to determine the network portion and the host portion of the IP address. This is called a logical bitwise AND calculation. Using this method, any subnet mask octet with a decimal value of 255 means the corresponding octet in the IP address is network ID information. From that point on, it logically follows that the subnet number 255 is used in place of the actual number in a portion of the address to mask it's identity for each network class.

The subnet number masks the original identification numbers in the network classes as follows:

■   Class A networks have 255 in the first octet

■   Class B addresses have 255 in the first two octets

■   Class C addresses have 255 in the first three octets

Note: A zero in the subnet designates the host portion of the IP address. This puts all host addresses in a single network. While that organizational system may be practical for a Class C network, it is unworkable for larger networks.

Table 3.1 Subnets for Class A, B, and C

Class A IP address	32.120.65.12
Subnet mask	255.0.0.0
Class B IP address	131.28.69.121
Subnet mask	255.255.0.0
Class C IP address	211.23.115.69
Subnet Mask	255.255.255.0

Subnet masks do more than separate network and host information in an IP address. Subnets also allocate host address resources to create network addresses called subnets. For example, a large company may have a Class B IP address that provides for approximately 65,000 host addresses in a single network. The network designer may decide that the organization is best served by dividing the network into subnets.

A simple solution is to designate the third octet entirely to network ID information. This effectively creates 255 Class C networks. In practice, some other division of resources is likely to best suit an organization. It is also possible to allocate portions of an octet to network IDs and host IDs. Table 3.2 shows possible subnets in a Class B address.

Table 3.2 Class B IP Address Allocations

Subnets	Hosts	Borrowed Bits	Subnet Mask
0	65,534	0	255.255.0.0
2	16,382	2	255.255.192.0
6	8,190	3	255.255.224.0
14	4,094	4	255.255.240.0
30	2,046	5	255.255.248.0
62	1,022	6	255.255.252.0
126	510	7	255.255.254.0
254	254	8	255.255.255.0

The subdivision of resources follows binary rules. Rather than use all 8 bits to define host addresses, some bits are borrowed to create subnets. Borrowing 2 bits from the 16 bits available for host addresses in a Class B network allows for the creation of two subnets. Because only 14 bits are left for host IDs, each subnet may only have 16,382 hosts. As more bits are borrowed, the number of available host addresses diminishes. Finding the right combination of subnets and host IDs (with consideration for current and future needs) is a primary goal of network design.

Note: It is also possible to combine network IDs in a process called supernetting. Because of the scarcity of Class B addresses, large organizations may have to register several Class C networks to meet capacity. Rather than contend with the inconvenience of having multiple network IDs, they can supernet their Class C networks into one network address.

Routing Architecture

Routing is the process of directing information from one device to another on an internetwork. Two devices can only communicate without routing information when they are located on the same subnet (logical network). When one device needs to communicate with another device located on a remote network, a route or path must be determined for successful delivery. The system for routing network traffic from segment to segment is an important function of IP.

Network Segments

A network segment consists of all the connected network devices that are not separated by a router (also called a gateway in IP terminology).

A simple network may have only one segment. Every computer on the same network segment listens to all local traffic. Routers join network segments and remote traffic is introduced into the local subnet. Each segment could quickly be overwhelmed with network traffic if all of the signals on every other connected segment were simultaneously present. Routers prevent this from happening.

Routers

Routers connect network segments, direct network traffic, and maintain tables of host addresses for segments to which they are directly connected. In addition, routers forward network traffic to its destination or to other routers.

IP Traffic Routing Processes

The following processes occur in IP traffic routings:

1. The originating computer compares the destination IP address to its own IP address and subnet mask, and determines whether or not the destination address is on the same subnet. If the destination is local, the message is put onto the network where the destination computer picks up the message. If the destination address is not local, the originating computer directs the datagram to its default gateway (a pre-assigned router).

2. The default gateway compares the destination IP address to its internal table of IP addresses (the table has addresses for every host on every segment that connects to the router). If the host address is found, the message is deposited on the appropriate network where it is identified and picked up by the destination device. If the router does not find the host address on any internal table, the message forwards to another router.

3. This process repeats until the message forwards to a router connected to a network segment containing the destination IP address. From there the message is delivered.

Tip: Routers are special purpose computers. They perform Network Layer services (called the Internet Layer in the TCP/IP stack) and are sometimes called layer three devices. Routers have at least two IP addresses and one IP gateway for each connected segment. Any computer with the appropriate software and at least two Network Interface Cards (NICs) can be configured to serve as a router.

Routing Information Protocol (RIP) and Open Shortest Path First (OSPF)

Routers use protocols to make logical path choices, allowing datagrams to arrive at their intended destinations. The most common routing protocol is Routing Information Protocol (RIP). RIP functions by broadcast. A table of known routers, routes, networks and the hop count between each are shared between routers. This information makes logical routing choices when more than one path is available.

RIP protocol is relatively simple. A broadcast is made every 30 seconds to update router tables and to keep routers synchronized with each other. However, these RIP broadcasts create network traffic and can cause network congestion.

Open Shortest Path First (OSPF) protocol is a newer, more efficient routing protocol designed to perform optimum route analysis without generating as much broadcast traffic as RIP. OSPF also supports variable-length subnetting. This system allows organizations to use any IP address class for internal addressing while only registering a single subnet with InterNIC. OSPF is rapidly replacing RIP as the routing protocol of choice.

Default Gateways

With IP addressing, the host address and the destination address are compared and a determination is made if the destination device is on the local network segment. If not, the datagram is sent to the default gateway. A default router (also called a default gateway) address is part of the IP address. Once the originating computer determines the datagram is bound for a remote device, its only responsibility is to direct the datagram to the default gateway. From that point forward, routers are responsible for forwarding the datagram to its destination.

Note: Default gateways are not required in an IP address. However, if no default gateway is specified, only destinations on the local subnet are available.

IP addressing also facilitates assigning alternate gateways should the default gateway be unavailable. Routers use RIP or OSPF protocol to track which gateways are available.

Domain Name System (DNS)

In the early days of the Internet, the entire system was made up of relatively few computer servers. Servers were identified by their IP address or with a special text file that matched IP addresses to computer names. This was called a HOSTS file. To use the HOSTS file, each user installed a copy of it on their computer. As server names and IP addresses were added to the HOSTS file, early adapters regularly downloaded the updated file.

Internet Domain Names

As the Internet began to take off, it became apparent that a more sophisticated method for finding resources on the Internet by name was needed. The Domain Name System (DNS) was developed to meet that need.

DNS is a distributed database (the data is spread over multiple servers) organized in a hierarchical system. Hierarchical means that information is organized in a system of layers. Detailed information is grouped as subsets of more general categories. DNS is designed to be centrally administered and is fast, reliable, and available to anyone with Internet access.

Root Servers

At the heart of the DNS system are the root servers. The root servers are maintained predominantly by the U.S. Government and updated daily by a designated contractor. The servers are physically located in multiple locations to serve an international audience and to create redundancy in the system.

Top-Level Servers

Internet domain names are at the top level of the DNS hierarchy. This level contains the following familiar domain names:

- .com

- .edu

- .gov

- .org

Recent additions to the top-level domain names include:

- .net

- .mil

Countries request top-level designations such as the following:

- .ca for Canada

- .au for Australia

Top-level names are under constant review and more are added all the time.

The next level in the DNS hierarchy is the second-level domain that names a company or organization.

Figure 3.3 DNS Database

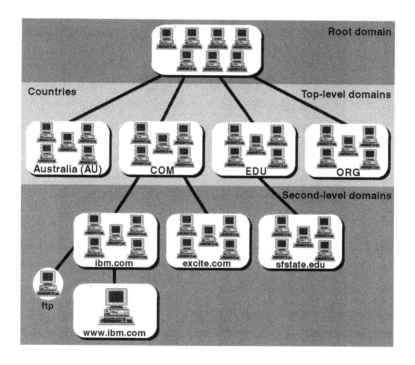

 Tip: A common point of confusion about DNS is that the hierarchical order is reversed in a URL address. Read a URL address right to left to understand the DNS hierarchy. For instance, www.ibm.com is an address in the .com domain on the IBM network for a computer named WWW.

Caching

Large organizations may have many DNS servers. These servers get requests from local computers for name-to-IP-address resolution. The DNS server has the responsibility to communicate with all the name servers necessary to discover the IP address associated with the name request. The DNS server could communicate with Internet Root servers of the DNS, and then drill down through many layers of the DNS hierarchy of servers, communicating with DNS servers on several continents, to find information or an answer to a request.

It is inefficient to repeat this process for every name-to-IP-address resolution request. Of the millions of IP addresses, only a few are the target of the majority of name resolution requests. Rather than doing a new search for every request, a DNS server maintains the current address request in the computer cache for instant retrieval. An amount of time, called Time To Live (TTL), is set for each cached IP address. If a new request for the address does not arrive before the TTL expires, the address is purged from the cache.

 Note: Systems that serve many DNS resolution requests, such as an Internet Service Provider (ISP), will typically designate a server as a DNS cache-only server. This server stores a large number of frequently requested IP addresses and can respond quickly to a high volume of DNS traffic. The primary DNS server is then free to devote its resources to resolving the IP addresses of infrequently requested names.

Static and Dynamic Systems

The current DNS system is static. The database updates when an administrator performs manual edits to the database to add, modify, or delete IP addresses and names. Because of the large size and rapid changes in the Internet, static database maintenance is a huge task.

A new system called Dynamic Domain Name System (DDNS) is under review, and is implemented in the Windows 2000 technologies. The goal of DDNS is to dynamically (automatically and in real time) update DNS databases to reflect changes. This service should eventually improve the accuracy of the system and virtually eliminate manual editing of the very large DNS distributed database.

HOSTS Files

Before there was DNS, there were HOSTS files. As mentioned in the introduction to this section, a HOSTS file is a text file list of IP addresses and corresponding computer names. Not every network is connected to a DNS server. For that and other reasons, HOSTS files continue to be a viable method of name-to-IP-address resolution. HOSTS files are easy to create and administer for any network with a small number of names and addresses. Another advantage of HOSTS is that name- resolution information resides on every user's computer which makes the resolution process virtually instantaneous.

Windows Internet Naming Service (WINS)

As the names suggests, WINS is a Microsoft solution for IP name resolution. Windows networks use NetBIOS naming services for TCP/IP clients. WINS resolves NetBIOS names to IP addresses.

Dynamic Configuration

WINS provides name-resolution services for Windows networks similar to the Dynamic DNS service. WINS has a client side and a server side.

A WINS client sends a registration message to the specified address of the WINS server during the TCP/IP start-up process. This information is then dynamically stored on the WINS server for use in name-resolution requests from other computers on the network.

The WINS server stores NetBIOS/IP information for every client computer that registers with it. It also stores NetBIOS/IP information for all other WINS servers on the internetwork via a broadcast synchronization process. If a WINS server does not have the information it requires, the request will be given to another WINS server until the address is resolved or returned when the request is determined to be irresolvable.

WINS provides the following advantages:

- Current and accurate NetBIOS/IP name resolution

- Dynamic database updating

- Reduced name-resolution broadcast traffic

LMHOSTS

Just as HOSTS files provide name/IP address information for the Internet, LMHOSTS files provide NetBIOS/IP address resolution for Windows networks.

An LMHOSTS file is a text list of NetBIOS names and their corresponding IP addresses. A copy of this file resides on every computer on a Windows network. If no WINS server is available, this resident list is available for name resolution. LMHOSTS files are static, which means that all changes must be made manually on every computer in the network.

WINS and DNS

WINS and DNS are not exclusive of each other. As a practical matter, they work together on virtually all large-size Windows networks connected to the Internet.

Resolving Names

The following is the name-resolution process for many Windows networks:

1. WINS client requests an IP address from a WINS server based on a NetBIOS name.

2. WINS server checks its database and, if necessary, forwards the request to other WINS servers on the internetwork.

3. If the address cannot be resolved by any connected WINS server, the request is forwarded to a DNS server.

4. The DNS server processes the request according to the DNS protocols.

Ports and Sockets

TCP/IP uses a port system to channel information in and out of a computer. A number from 0 to 65,536 is assigned to each application using TCP/IP services on a host computer. To standardize port number assignments, certain numbers are commonly used for popular TCP/IP applications. These are well-known port numbers. Ports keep information from different applications separate. Some services also use a sophisticated system of port assignment for security purposes.

Note: Multitasking computers are capable of running multiple sessions of the same application. In this case, each active session of a program is assigned a unique port number.

When a port number is paired with the IP address of a host number, the combination is called a socket. Sockets provide the following information:

- Identify an IP address

- Identify a port number

- Identify an application or process (associated with a well-known port number)

Warning: A port in IP terminology is a special number assigned to an application, not the physical connection on the back of a computer for printers, a mouse, or modems. While a socket is the combination of a port number and an IP address, Windows Sockets is an Application Programming Interface (API) that provides a standard interface for TCP/IP and applications written for the Windows OS.

Troubleshooting

Networks are complex systems. The interaction among computer hardware, communication applications, and network hardware make it difficult to isolate problems. Tools and procedures are available to help resolve network problems.

IPCONFIG and WINIPCFG

IPCONFIG is a TCP/IP command line utility that runs in an MS-DOS window on a Windows computer. IPCONFIG is a useful utility for computer IP settings checks and for IP settings updates when linked to a DHCP server.

 Note: A Dynamic Host Configuration Protocol (DHCP) server provides IP addresses to clients dynamically. Rather than having a client computer permanently assigned an address, this service provides IP addresses on an as-needed basis.

IPCONFIG is easy to use. In a DOS window simply type **ipconfig** with the **/all** switch to display current IP settings as shown in Figure 3.4.

To release current settings, use the command line **ipconfig /release all**. The command **ipconfig /renew all** will retrieve fresh IP settings from a DHCP server.

 Warning: IPCONFIG will release your current IP settings whether or not you are able to access a DHCP server. It is a good idea to confirm the availability of a DHCP server before you release an IP address.

Figure 3.4 IPCONFIG Utility

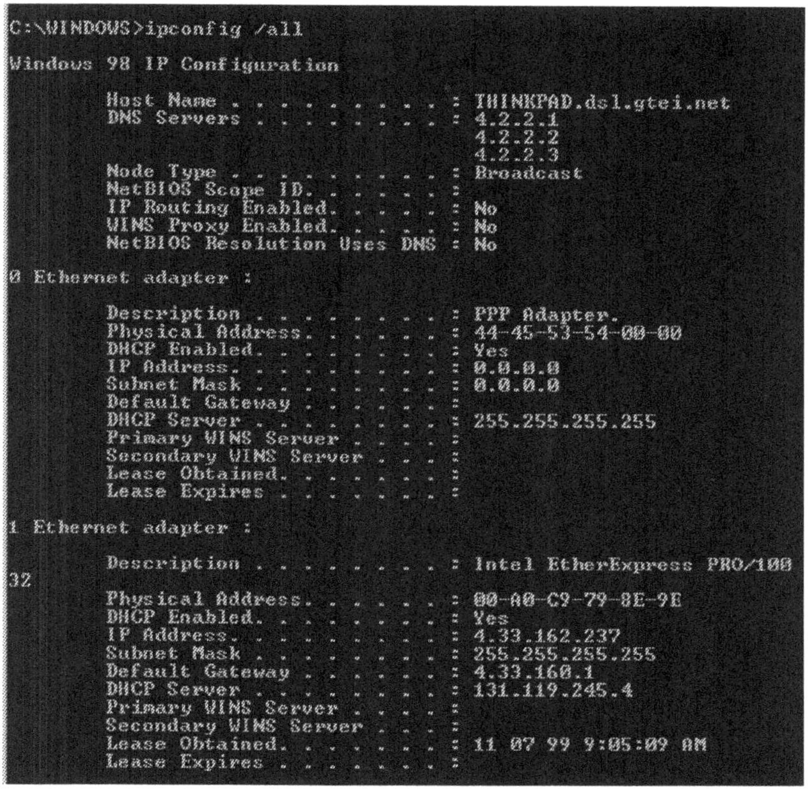

```
C:\WINDOWS>ipconfig /all

Windows 98 IP Configuration

        Host Name . . . . . . . . . . : THINKPAD.dsl.gtei.net
        DNS Servers . . . . . . . . . : 4.2.2.1
                                        4.2.2.2
                                        4.2.2.3
        Node Type . . . . . . . . . . : Broadcast
        NetBIOS Scope ID. . . . . . . :
        IP Routing Enabled. . . . . . : No
        WINS Proxy Enabled. . . . . . : No
        NetBIOS Resolution Uses DNS   : No

0 Ethernet adapter :

        Description . . . . . . . . . : PPP Adapter.
        Physical Address. . . . . . . : 44-45-53-54-00-00
        DHCP Enabled. . . . . . . . . : Yes
        IP Address. . . . . . . . . . : 0.0.0.0
        Subnet Mask . . . . . . . . . : 0.0.0.0
        Default Gateway . . . . . . . :
        DHCP Server . . . . . . . . . : 255.255.255.255
        Primary WINS Server . . . . . :
        Secondary WINS Server . . . . :
        Lease Obtained. . . . . . . . :
        Lease Expires . . . . . . . . :

1 Ethernet adapter :

        Description . . . . . . . . . : Intel EtherExpress PRO/100
32
        Physical Address. . . . . . . : 00-A0-C9-79-8E-9E
        DHCP Enabled. . . . . . . . . : Yes
        IP Address. . . . . . . . . . : 4.33.162.237
        Subnet Mask . . . . . . . . . : 255.255.255.255
        Default Gateway . . . . . . . : 4.33.160.1
        DHCP Server . . . . . . . . . : 131.119.245.4
        Primary WINS Server . . . . . :
        Secondary WINS Server . . . . :
        Lease Obtained. . . . . . . . : 11 07 99 9:05:09 AM
        Lease Expires . . . . . . . . :
```

WINIPCFG is essentially the IPCONFIG command utility wrapped in a graphical interface for Microsoft Windows 95 and Microsoft Windows 98. WINIPCFG can be launched from the Start menu Run command. Figure 3.5 shows WINIPCFG in the IP configuration screen.

Figure 3.5 WINIPCFG Utility

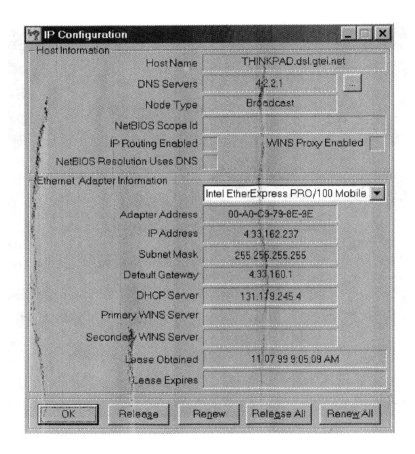

PING

The PING command line utility is a very simple and indispensable network analysis tool. PING generates echo requests and records echo replies using the Internet Control Message Protocol (ICMP). Use PING to verify a physical connection on a TCP/IP network.

Checking a System

The recommended order for checking a system with PING is:

1. PING the 127.0.0.1 loopback address to verify that your computer communicates with its own network card.
2. PING the IP address of your default gateway to verify that the connection works. (You can get the IP address of the default gateway using the IPCONFIG).
3. PING the IP address of a remote device.

To use PING, type **ping** and a Fully Qualified Domain Name, FQDN, or IP address in a command-line window. The Fully Qualified Domain Name consists of a computer's hostname and full domain name, such as www.lightpointlearning.net). Figure 3.6 shows the PING utility.

Figure 3.6 PING Utility

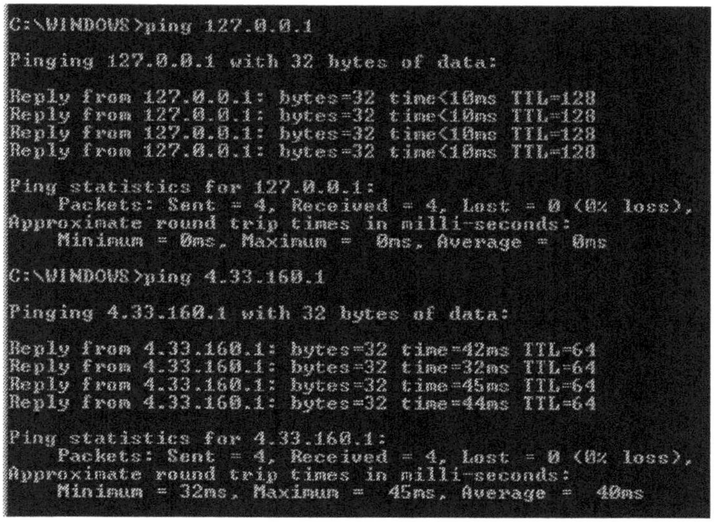

```
C:\WINDOWS>ping 127.0.0.1

Pinging 127.0.0.1 with 32 bytes of data:

Reply from 127.0.0.1: bytes=32 time<10ms TTL=128
Reply from 127.0.0.1: bytes=32 time<10ms TTL=128
Reply from 127.0.0.1: bytes=32 time<10ms TTL=128
Reply from 127.0.0.1: bytes=32 time<10ms TTL=128

Ping statistics for 127.0.0.1:
    Packets: Sent = 4, Received = 4, Lost = 0 (0% loss),
Approximate round trip times in milli-seconds:
    Minimum = 0ms, Maximum =  0ms, Average =  0ms

C:\WINDOWS>ping 4.33.160.1

Pinging 4.33.160.1 with 32 bytes of data:

Reply from 4.33.160.1: bytes=32 time=42ms TTL=64
Reply from 4.33.160.1: bytes=32 time=32ms TTL=64
Reply from 4.33.160.1: bytes=32 time=45ms TTL=64
Reply from 4.33.160.1: bytes=32 time=44ms TTL=64

Ping statistics for 4.33.160.1:
    Packets: Sent = 4, Received = 4, Lost = 0 (0% loss),
Approximate round trip times in milli-seconds:
    Minimum = 32ms, Maximum =  45ms, Average =  40ms
```

Tip: A common use for PING is to test name resolution. If you cannot connect to a remote address by name, but you can successfully PING its IP address, you have isolated your problem to a name-resolution issue.

TRACERT

TRACERT (Trace Route) is a command utility which tracks a connection route from a local host to the remote destination. Like PING, TRACERT uses ICMP to identify the path a signal takes. Each hop (the path from router to router) is listed by IP address and by signal travel time. TRACERT will log up to 30 hops. TRACERT can help identify where (which router) on a path a problem exists. Type **tracert** and a destination IP address to start the utility.

NETSTAT

NETSTAT, as the name implies, is a utility that generates statistics about TCP/IP connections and protocols. Netstat provides protocol statistics for:

- IP
- ICMP
- TCP
- UDP

A report displays the volume of network traffic by protocol. Network analysts can use this information to help determine if they are dealing with a protocol configuration problem or a network hardware problem. To view statistics type **netstat** with one of the following switches:

- **-a**   shows all connections
- **-e**   shows Ethernet statistics

- **-n**   shows addresses and ports as numbers (no name lookup)

- **-s**   displays statistics for default protocols

Address Resolution Protocol (ARP)

ARP is the protocol in TCP/IP that handles IP to physical address resolution. The physical network address is the hard-coded hexadecimal number written on every NIC. Ordinarily a physical address/IP address map will be stored in temporary memory space (cache) for a specific time period. It is possible to designate an address map as static. In this case, the map will only be purged if the machine is restarted or a broadcast is received updating the current static ARP map. A static map can speed the processes of hardware/IP address resolution of a frequently requested address.

From a troubleshooting point of view, bad information in a static ARP address is a potential problem. The ARP utility is a command line tool used to view and edit the ARP cache. The ARP utility can also add, delete and modify static address maps.

Type **arp** in a command window followed by one of the following switches:

- **-a**   displays current ARP cache entries

- **-d**   deletes a cache entry

- **-s**   designates a map address as static

Note: Command utilities usually have several switches (function controllers) associated with them. Only the basic switches are listed for the utilities discussed in this section.

Vocabulary

Review the following terms in preparation for the certification exam.

Term	Description
ARP	Address Resolution Protocol is a TCP/IP protocol that provides IP to physical address resolution services.
binary	A mathematical system that has only 2 values (1 or 0) for each number. In computer terminology, each binary number is called a bit.
cache	A special memory space used to store frequently accessed information.
computer name	The descriptive name assigned to a host computer. Examples of computer names are Library and Jonscomp.
datagram	IP terminology for a basic unit of transmission data.
default gateway	A dedicated network device with at least two IP addresses that routes packets to other networks.
DHCP	Dynamic Host Configuration Protocol is a service that provides IP addresses on an as-needed basis to host computers.
DNS	Domain Name System is a hierarchically organized distributed database that stores host name/IP address resolution information for the Internet and any connected TCP/IP host.

Term	Description
IP address	A 32-bit number represented as four decimal numbers separated by periods. Each IP address contains network and host ID information.
loop-back	This special IP address (127.0.0.1) will cause the PING utility to detect a host computer's own NIC.
NETSTAT	A command line utility that generates datagram statistics sorted by protocols used.
octet	A group of eight. In binary language an octet is 8 bits of information. Another term for 8 bits is a byte. In decimal format, a byte has a value range of 0 to 255.
OSPF	Open Shortest Path First is a routing protocol that minimizes broadcast transmissions between routers supports variable-length subnetting.
packet	A unit of transmission data with fixed size and header information about source, destination, and data assembly.
physical address	The hexadecimal number associated with a Network Interface Card (NIC).
PING	A command line utility used to check network connections.
port	IP terminology for a number assigned to an application to differentiate it from any other application using TCP/IP.
RIP	Routing Information Protocol is a common service provided by routers that use broadcasts to communicate with other routers, gathering path and host ID information.

Term	Description
root servers	Primary servers at the foundation of DNS.
socket	A port number paired with an IP address.
subnet	A subnet is a portion of a network on which computers share a common subnet mask and host ID. All devices on a subnet can communicate without routing datagrams.
subnet mask	A 32-bit number, represented in dotted decimal form, that defines information contained in an IP address. The subnet mask determines which part of an IP address is network information and which part is IP information.
supernet	A process where bits are borrowed from network ID bits and used to combine networks. This process is used to combine multiple Class C networks into virtual class B networks.
switch	Function controller for a command line utility.
top-level servers	The second tier of DNS, these computers store registration data about domain names.
TRACERT	A command line utility that generates datagram path information on an internetwork.
UDP	User Datagram Protocol is available as an alternative protocol to TCP. UDP is fast but contains no error checking or delivery confirmation services.
URL	Uniform Resource Locator is a standardized addressing system for locating Internet resources.
variable-length subnetting	A system for creating internal IP addressing that allows use of any class address while registering a single subnet with InterNIC.
WINS	Windows Internet Naming Service is a Microsoft solution for NetBIOS/IP address name resolution.

In Brief

If you want to...	Then do this...
Connect to the Internet	Use TCP/IP protocol.
Create a private network	Use the private network IP addresses set aside in the IP class numbering system.
Identify which part of an IP address is Network ID and which part is Host ID	Look at the subnet mask number 255 on the left to see the Network ID. Look for the Host ID on the right portion of the IP address.
Create additional network subnets	Borrow bits from that host address space.
Combine networks	Borrow bits from network address space to create network addresses.
Route data across subnets	Use a default gateway address and a router.
Reduce router broadcast traffic and use variable-length subnetting	Use OSPF protocol.
Assign IP addresses among hosts on an as-needed basis	Use a DHCP server.
Identify the hierarchy of a URL address	Read the address from right to left.
Create a dynamically updated system for NetBIOS/IP address resolution on a Windows network	Use a WINS client/server service for dynamic NetBIOS-name-to-IP address resolution.

If you want to...	Then do this...
Create a static resident list of computer names and IP address for each computer on a network	Use a LMHOSTS file for Windows environments and a HOSTS file for a non-Windows TCP-IP network.
Verify that your computer communicates with your NIC	PING the loop-back address (127.0.0.1) in a command window.
Verify a network connection	Use the PING utility.
Discover a datagram network path	Use TRACERT command line utility.
Display your IP configuration	Use IPCONFIG command line utility and/or WINIPCFG on a Windows 95/98 computer.
Check network traffic sorted by TCP/IP protocol	Use NETSTAT command line utility.
Check and/or modify ARP cache	Use ARP command line utility.

Lesson 3 Activities

Complete the following activities to better prepare you for the certification exam.

1. Review the TCP/IP stack and map it to the OSI model.

2. Explain the difference between TCP and UDP.

3. Explain how a 32-bit IP address is divided.

4. Explain the significance of IPv6.

5. Describe the four classes of networks and how they are used.

6. Explain the difference between a public and private network.

7. Explain the purpose of a subnet mask.

8. Describe the function of DNS and WINS and when you use each protocol.

9. Explain the advantage of using OSPF over RIP.

10. Name five command utilities that help troubleshoot networks.

Answers to Lesson 3 Activities

1. The Application Layer of the TCP/IP stack maps to the Application, Presentation, and Session Layer of the OSI model. The Transport Layers of each model maps directly, while the Internet Layer of the OSI model maps to the Network Layer of the OSI model. The Network Interface Layer of the TCP/IP stack maps to the Data Link and Physical Layer of the OSI model.

2. TCP is a reliable-link connection protocol with error detection and datagram recovery capabilities. UDP is a send and forget protocol that delegates error control and other connection duties to the Application Layer. UDP is faster than TCP.

3. An IP address is a 32-bit number divided into 4 groups of 8 bits. Each group, or octet, can represent a decimal number from 0 to 255. Some of the octets are network ID information and some of the octets represent host ID information. It is possible to delegate a portion of an octet for network ID and a portion for host ID information.

4. IPv6 is a successor protocol to IP Version 4, which is the current version. IPv6 is based on a 128-bit architecture and will solve the current scarcity of IP addresses. Ipv6 also has improved functionality for some IP services.

5. The four classes of networks in use are A,B,C, and D. A is for very large networks, B is for large networks and C is for small networks. D is used for multicasting.

6. A public network uses registered IP address. DNS uses registration information for name/IP resolution. InterNIC regulates the regulation process and is responsible for preventing duplicate registered IP addresses. A private network uses a special block of IP addresses reserved for that purpose. These IDs cannot be registered with InterNIC.

7. A subnet mask is a 32-bit number that is part of every IP address. The subnet mask defines which part of the IP address is network ID and which part is host ID.

8. DNS and WINS are both name/IP resolution services. They can work together. WINS is a dynamic service created for Windows networks while DNS is a static service available to Internet users.

9. OSPF is a newer routing protocol that performs routing services with less broadcast traffic. OSPF supports variable-length subnetting.

10. PING, IPCONFIG, NETSTAT, TRACERT, and ARP are command line utilities useful in troubleshooting networks.

Lesson 3 Quiz

These questions test your knowledge of features, vocabulary, procedures, and syntax.

1. Which layer of the OSI model maps to IP?

    A. Session Layer

    B. Application, Presentation, and Session Layers

    C. Network Layer

    D. Data Link Layer

2. Which statements are true about IP addresses?

    A. Every valid IP configuration has three components; the IP address, the subnet mask, and a default gateway.

    B. An IP address is a 32-bit number and a subnet mask is an 8-bit number.

    C. IP addresses must be registered to use them on the Internet.

    D. Private IP addresses are available to large companies which can afford them.

3. What is a subnet?

    A. A subnet is a private network not registered with InterNIC.

    B. Subnets are divisions within a network separated by routers.

    C. A subnet is the host portion of the IP address.

    D. A subnet is two or more segments connected by routers.

4. What are true statements about default gateways?

    A. Every valid IP configuration must have a default gateway.

    B. Default gateways are the dotted decimal address for a router.

    C. Both hosts and routers use default gateways.

    D. Default gateway services can be provided by another router if specified.

5. Which are true statements about DNS and WINS?

    A. Anybody with Internet access can use both WINS and DNS services.

    B. WINS is a dynamic system and DNS is a static system.

    C. DNS is a Microsoft solution while WINS is an open standard.

    D. DNS and WINS provide IP/name resolution services.

6. When would you use a HOSTS file?

    A. When no WINS server is available

    B. On a small Windows network

    C. When no DNS server is available

    D. On any small non-windows network

7. What is the difference between IPCONFIG and WINIPCFG?

    A. IPCONFIG has a graphical interface and WINIPCFG does not

    B. WINIPCFG works on Windows 95/98 machines and IPCONFIG does not

    C. IPCONFIG is a command line utility and WINIPCFG has a graphical interface

    D. WINIPCFG has substantially different functionality than IPCONFIG

8. In which of the following troubleshooting situations would the PING utility be useful in problem diagnosis?

    A. Proper function of local NIC

    B. Name resolution problems

    C. Connectivity problems

    D. Datagram route information

9. Which two numbers make up a socket?

    A. IP address and MAC number

    B. Port number and subnet mask

C. IP address and subnet mask

D. Port number and IP address

10. Which of the following is not a top-level domain name (choose all that apply)?

A. . com

B. . microsoft

C. . edu

D. . ibm

Answers to Lesson 3 Quiz

1. Answer C is correct. IP maps to the Network Layer of the OSI model.

    Answer C is incorrect. The Network Layer of the OSI model maps to the Internet Layer of the TCP/IP stack.

    Answer A is incorrect. The Session Layer maps to the Application Layer of the TCP/IP model.

    Answer D is incorrect because the Data Link Layer and the Physical Layer of the OSI model map to the Network Interface Layer of the TCP/IP stack.

2. Answer C is correct. Only registered IP addresses are allowed on a public network like the Internet.

    Answer A is incorrect. A valid IP configuration does not require a default gateway. A default gateway is only required to contact devices on remote subnets.

    Answer B is incorrect. A subnet mask is also a 32-bit number.

    Answer D is incorrect. Private IP addresses are built into IP and are freely available to anyone to use.

3. Answer B is correct. Subnets are divisions within a network separated by routers.

    Answer A is incorrect. Subnets can exist on public networks. IP addresses, not subnets, are registered with InterNIC.

    Answer C is incorrect. A subnet mask, not a subnet, defines the host potion of an IP address.

    Answer D is incorrect. Subnets are a single logical segment.

4. Answers B and D are correct. A default gateway in an IP address is another 32-bit number represented in dotted decimal form. This gateway is on the same subnet as the host, which allows the host to communicate with it. IP allows for the designation of additional routers if the default gateway is unavailable.

    Answer A is incorrect. Valid IP addresses do not require default gateways if communicating to other devices on the same subnet.

Answer C is incorrect. Routers do not use default gateways. Routers use RIP or OSPF to locate other routers and direct traffic.   5. Answer B is correct. WINS is a dynamic system and DNS is a static system.

Answer D is correct. DNS and WINS provide IP/name resolution services.

Answer A is incorrect. Only Windows computers can make use of WINS.

Answer C is incorrect. WINS is a Microsoft solution and DNS is an open standard.

6.   Answer C is correct. When no WINS server is available you can use a HOSTS file because HOSTS files are the original IP/name resolution solution for IP and can still be useful when a DNS server is not available.

Answer D is correct. Any IP network using a non-Windows operating system can use HOSTS files.

Answer A is incorrect. WINS is a Windows solution and HOSTS files are not.

Answer B is incorrect. WINS is a Windows solution and HOSTS files are not.

7.   Answer C is correct. IPCONFIG is a command line utility and WINIPCFG has a graphical interface.

Answer A is incorrect. WINIPCFG has a graphical interface, not IPCONFIG.

Answer B is incorrect. IPCONFIG will work on a Windows 95/98 computer in an MS-DOS window.

Answer E is incorrect. The two utilities offer the same functionality.

8.   Answer A is correct. The PING utility would be useful in diagnosing proper functionality of a local NIC.

Answer B is correct. The PING utility would be useful in diagnosing name resolution problems.

Answer C is correct. The PING utility would be useful in diagnosing connectivity problems.

Answer D is incorrect. Use the TRACERT utility to display route information.

9.   Answer D is correct. The port number and the IP address numbers make up a socket.

Answer A is incorrect. The IP address and MAC numbers do not make up a socket.

Answer B is incorrect. The port number and the subnet mask numbers do not make up a socket.

Answer C is incorrect. IP addresses and subnet mask numbers do not make up a socket.

10. Answer A is correct. The domain name .com is a top-level domain name.

    Answer C is correct. The domain name .edu is a top-level domain name.

    Answer B is incorrect. The domain name .microsoft is a second-level domain name.

    Answer D is incorrect. The domain name .ibm is a second-level domain name.

Lesson 4: Internet Services and Connectivity

The protocols in the Application Layer level of the TCP/IP stack govern how applications interact with the rest of the networking protocols. E-mail programs use the upper level protocols to send and retrieve messages, client/server applications understand Application Program Interfaces (APIs) and Web browsers communicate with HyperText Transfer Protocol (HTTP).

This lesson covers the protocols and utilities that occupy the Application Layer in the TCP/IP stack. A good understanding of upper-layer services is a practical necessity for every internetwork professional.

After completing this lesson, you should have a better understanding of the following topics:

- HyperText Transfer Protocol (HTTP)

- E-mail Access Protocols

- Net News Transfer Protocol Services (NNTP)

- Internet Message Access Protocol (IMAP)

- File Transfer Protocol (FTP)

- Telnet

- Simple Mail Transport Protocol (SMTP)

- Transmission Control Protocol/Internet Protocol TCP/IP

- Dynamic Host Configuration Protocol (DHCP)

- Line Printer (LPR)

- Troubleshooting

HyperText Transfer Protocol (HTTP)

HTTP is perhaps the best-known protocol in the Transmission Control Protocol/Internet Protocol (TCP/IP) Application Layer. HTTP is the language of the Internet. The World Wide Web is actually a huge collection of computers acting as clients and servers communicating with HTTP.

HTTP transfers numerous types of data, including the following:

- Text
- Graphics
- Audio
- Video

All Internet users can communicate with each other regardless of the computer operating system, the Internet browser, or the connection method because they have HTTP in common.

Using HTTP Commands

HTTP provides a standard data type (computer code organized in a way that an application understands). HTTP also standardizes the basic commands for opening a connection, requesting a service, responding to a request and closing a connection. The process follows these steps:

1. The client requests a TCP connection to a specified Uniform Resource Locator (URL) address.

2. Information establishing parameters for the session is exchanged between client and server.

3. Data and header information about the data type and transaction status is sent to the client.

4. The connection closes after transmission of data to the client. A new connection is initiated every time the user activates a HyperText Markup Language (HTML) link.

Accessing HTML Information

HTML documents are sets of instructions that Web browsers understand. The Web page you view is the result of those instructions. A single page may represent a collection of text and files scattered across many different computer hard drives.

HTTP is sometimes confused with HTML. HTML is the language that defines the way text and graphics display on a Web page. HTTP is the protocol that controls how HTML information is accessed. HTML is a subset of a vastly more complicated markup language called Standard Generalized Markup Language (SGML).

In the early days of the Internet, HTML was introduced because it was easy to use and had the basic functionality to display text and graphics transferred across the Internet. The sophisticated Web page designs of today stretch HTML to its functional limits. Because of this, a new language, XML (also a subset of SGML), is being developed to replace HTML.

Accessing Internet Text

A Web browser is an application that uses HTTP to access HTML documents. HTML documents can be on a local hard drive or a hard drive connected to the Internet on the other side of the world. The browser displays the HTML document according to instructions, called tags, associated with each HTML object. These tags, or markups, are where the markup language name comes from. They can be viewed with most browsers by using the **view source** command.

A selection of text is treated as an object in HTML. The tags associated with text may include size, color, font, style, and justification. The actual text used to create text information is irrelevant. Your browser has the task of assigning the tag attributes to the text information displayed in your browser window. Figure 4.1 shows HTML code with tags.

 Tip: HTTP has been around longer than the Internet. Early use of HTTP was restricted to linking text to other information on the same computer. Using this feature, HyperText authors could embed footnotes and other reference material in a document. Enhancing this linking technology so that it worked across TCP/IP networks has made the World Wide Web possible.

Figure 4.1 HTML Code and Tags

```
<P><FONT face=Arial size=1><STRONG>Operating
System: </STRONG></FONT></P>
</td>
      <TD colSpan="2" style="line-height: 1.5; padding-left: 4; padding-right: 4;">
         <P><FONT face=Arial size=1><STRONG>
         Required Windows 2000 Upgrade Flyer for Dell Latitude Notebooks,Tied
(460-7801)</STRONG></FONT></P></TD></TR>
      <td colspan="2" style="line-height: 1.5; padding-left: 4; padding-right: 4;">
<P><FONT face=Arial
size=1><STRONG>Modem: </STRONG></FONT></P>
</td>
      <TD colSpan="2" style="line-height: 1.5; padding-left: 4; padding-right: 4;">
         <P><FONT face=Arial size=1><STRONG>
         3COM,56K-10/100,LAN/Modem Combo,For Dell Latitude C-Series
Notebooks,Factory Install (313-0279)</STRONG></FONT></P></TD></TR>
      <td colspan="2" style="line-height: 1.5; padding-left: 4; padding-right: 4;">
```

Using Internet Graphics

A Web page graphic is also an HTML object controlled by tags. The graphic file is not really part of the page. HTML tags define the page display attributes such as size and position. Tags also define the object as a graphic. The graphic object is really a name and location of a particular graphic file. There is no requirement that the graphic file be located on the same computer as the HTML document.

Accessing Audio Files

Audio files, like graphic files, are not really a part of the HTML document. HTML assigns attributes to the audio object, such as when to execute, while the name and location of the audio file is merely referenced.

Streaming Audio and Video Files

Streaming is a data transfer technique that allows audio and visual information to be processed as a steady and continuous stream. Streaming technologies allow access to large audio and video files from the Internet and enable the client browser or plug-in to start playing or displaying the data before the entire file has been transmitted.

Streaming audio and video files are referenced in an HTML document like any other type of graphic or audio file. The HTML document points to the actual file. The browser retrieves and displays the file according to the markup instructions.

For streaming to work, the client side receiving the data must be able to collect and send the data as a steady stream to the application that processes and converts it to sound or pictures. If the streaming client receives the data faster than required, the excess data need to be saved in a buffer or cache. If the data do not come fast enough, however, the presentation of the data will not be smooth.

Video and audio formats, other than streaming audio and visual, cannot be smoothly presented before the entire file has been delivered. Streaming technology answers the need for faster and continuous download of multimedia files. It allows data to be displayed before the entire audio and video file has been sent.

There are a number of competing streaming technologies, although current transmission limitations keep the Internet from eclipsing traditional radio and television. A current industry accepted application for downloading streaming audio and video media is the G2 Player by RealNetworks, Inc.

Moving Picture Experts Group (MPEG), an International Standardization Organization (ISO) group, develops audio and visual streaming technology standards. The MPEG streaming video format achieves high compression rates by storing only the changes from one frame to another instead of each entire frame. The audio format MPEG, Audio Layer 3, uses the file extension MP3.

Two major MPEG standards are MPEG-1 and MPEG-2. The most common implementations of the MPEG-1 standard provides a video resolution of 352-by-240 at 30 frames per second (fps). This produces video quality slightly below the quality of conventional VCR video. MPEG-2 can compress a 2-hour video into a few gigabytes.

Streaming Audio/Video Transmission

Although a discriminating audiophile or videophile may argue the point, data integrity is not critical in streaming audio or video. A blip on a video signal or click on the sound track, which represent a missing bit of data here and there, are not nearly as important as replenishing the data buffer before it is depleted.

Transmission Control Protocol (TCP) error control and packet delivery confirmation services create datagram overhead that may slow transmission speeds to unacceptable levels for streaming media.

The low packet overhead associated with the User Datagram Protocol (UDP) send-and-forget (also called best effort) design generates the fastest possible datagram delivery across a TCP/IP network. UDP is ideally suited for streaming audio/video.

Enhancing Text with Videos

As the Web matures, new forms of media are placed online. Far from its humble beginnings as a text and e-mail delivery system, the Web now accommodates diverse requirements from disseminating breaking news with audio and visual media to taking grocery orders.

New technologies are constantly being developed to enhance the Internet experience. News Web sites like MSNBC and CNN regularly include video clips on their Web pages to capture the attention of a demanding Web audience.

 Warning: Web sites that offer audio and video content usually allow the Web user to control whether or not to play the clip. Audio and video files are much larger than other file types used in HTML. Slow connections are unable to play streaming media smoothly.

E-Mail Access Protocols

It is important to understand that Post Office Protocol, Version 3 (POP3) is not a complete e-mail solution. Other protocols, such as the Lightweight Directory Access Protocol (LDAP), Simple Mail Transport Protocol (SMTP), for example, are used to send e-mail or facilitate the e-mail process. POP3 is the protocol used by e-mail applications to retrieve e-mail from a user account.

Using POP3

Local delivery requests for e-mail messages on a mail server are accomplished with POP3. The mail server also uses POP3 to send the e-mail to the client computer.

E-mail service was integral to the development of the TCP/IP and remains one of the Internet's most used services.

Retrieving E-mail with POP3

The following steps allow you to retrieve e-mail from a user account on an e-mail server:

1. Connect to an e-mail server (typically provided by your Internet Service Provider (ISP)) with the e-mail application of your choice and log on to your account with your password.

2. Request the server to send the accumulated messages to your local computer.

3. Disconnect from the e-mail server.

4. Open your e-mail at any time.

Tip: Today's e-mail programs automate steps 1 through 3, which gives the impression that the messages are on the mail server. In reality, the messages are retrieved before they appear in the your e-mail inbox. Most mail servers erase the messages after delivery to a local device.

Accessing E-mail Directories with Lightweight Directory Access Protocol (LDAP)

In the late 1980s, the X.500 standard for implementing device-and-network-independent directory services was introduced. Directory Access Protocol (DAP) is a TCP/IP compliant portion of the X.500 protocol. DAP, although very powerful, is difficult to implement and contains advanced features that are seldom used.

LDAP is a subset of DAP with a reduced feature set and an easy-to-use structure. LDAP provides services for text-based queries from a LDAP client to a LDAP server. LDAP has become an Internet standard because it simplifies the task of creating queries for searchable directories.

Creating LDAP Searches

LDAP uses ordinary text entries to search directories. Name searches, e-mail address queries, telephone numbers and other list-type information are excellent candidates for LDAP client/server configuration.

 Note: LDAP was created in the early 1990s when desktop computers were far less powerful and could not supply the processing power that DAP required. That limitation has essentially disappeared and a debate has rekindled about the need to continue with the more limited LDAP.

Network News Transfer Protocol (NNTP)

NNTP is a TCP/IP protocol based upon text strings. It allows users to transfer articles between servers and then reads and posts articles. Members of special interest groups, called newsgroups, conduct extended conversations in the form of text postings and responses on just about every subject imaginable. Due to the vast amount of information in the system, a process for retrieving postings of particular interest is required.

Accessing News Services

Like many TCP/IP services, using NNTP started out as a protocol based command-line utility. Third-party developers soon introduced applications that provided graphical interfaces called news readers. Today, a newsreader interface is bundled with other TCP/IP software such as Microsoft's e-mail program Outlook and also the Netscape Communicator suite.

Subscribing to Newsgroups

Because there are thousands of newsgroups, the first step is to sort through all of the offerings for topics of particular interest. The directory for newsgroup topics is hierarchical. After locating the topics of interest, the next step is to subscribe to selected newsgroups. The newsreader software will retrieve headings (the user specifies how many) from the newsgroup. Many newsgroups accumulate hundreds of postings every day.

Retrieving Newsgroup Postings

You can load posted headings onto a local computer and then view headings for postings of interest. Headings can be sorted into subtopics called threads. From that point, you can initiate the process of retrieving a particular posting.

Creating a Newsgroup Posting

Postings are created in the following two ways:

Reply to an existing post—Your post becomes part of a hierarchical goup of the existing thread.

Start a new thread—Your post is not associated with any existing threads.

Internet Message Access Protocol (IMAP)

IMAP is a newer protocol, similar to POP e-mail, offering additional capabilities with expanded interactive client/server features. IMAP is more flexible and complex than the more popular POP3 but is more difficult to implement and manage. Although POP3 is used more often, IMAP could become the preferred protocol because it can provide the following capabilities:

- Retrieves and manipulates e-mail messages while they are on the server

- Searches for and saves e-mail messages according to given criteria

- Accesses and manages multiple e-mail accounts

Manipulating and Retrieving Messages

With IMAP, you stay connected to a mail server after logon. Where POP3 merely alerts an e-mail server to send all accumulated messages, IMAP allows you to review message headers on the server. As a result, individual messages or groups of messages can be selected for retrieval. IMAP can instruct the mail server to leave a message on the server after a copy of it has been retrieved.

Searching Message Headers

Another advanced feature of IMAP is the ability to search e-mail header information on the server prior to retrieving messages. Some e-mail accounts receive hundreds of messages daily. The search and sort capabilities of IMAP are powerful tools when looking for mail from a particular sender or about a particular subject.

Accessing and Managing Multiple E-Mail Accounts

IMAP also has the capability to handle multiple e-mail accounts. This feature is welcome now that having more than one e-mail account is becoming as common as having more than one telephone line. The complexity of IMAP is already being minimized with intuitive application user interfaces.

The popularity of IMAP is growing steadily as users need more powerful tools to deal with their ever-increasing volume of e-mail.

File Transfer Protocol (FTP)

The FTP utility transfers files between a client computer and a server running the FTP service. FTP offers platform independence because it is available to any system running TCP/IP. UNIX or Windows NT servers are routinely used to provide FTP services. FTP is an essential Internet service. Anyone who has purchased software electronically or downloaded a program update or an MP3 audio file onto a local hard drive has used FTP. FTP is the way most programs and computer files are transferred across the Internet.

Using FTP Configurations

FTP servers can be configured to allow anonymous connections or require user accounts and passwords. The URL of an FTP site looks similar to a WWW address except for the first part of the address. Table 4.1 compares FTP addresses to other Web addresses.

Table 4.1 FTP and URL Address Comparisons

Protocol	URL
FTP	ftp://sample.inet.com
HTTP (Web page)	http://sample.inet.com
HTTP (Web page)	www.inet.com

Using FTP Line Commands

The FTP command line utility is available to all computers running TCP/IP. Because modern browsers allow for browsing an FTP site with a graphical interface (making downloading files on FTP servers a point-and-click action), most users only use this utility for uploading files to a FTP site. A variety of powerful FTP utilities with graphical interfaces are available for managing the contents of FTP servers. Table 4.2 lists the most common FTP commands and their functions.

Table 4.2 FTP Commands

FTP Command	Function
`binary`	Changes file type to binary
`get`	Copies a remote file to a local computer
`put`	Copies a local file to a remote server
`quit`	Exits FTP

Anonymous Access of FTP Sites

Many FTP sites are configured for anonymous access. With this configuration, anyone who has the correct URL can access the site and download available files. Anonymous access is a common system for delivering software updates, public files and shareware applications. With an anonymous configuration, the FTP administrator has no way to determine who actually logs on to the site.

Tip: As a form of security-by-ignorance, some companies create FTP sites with difficult-to-guess addresses and then e-mail the URL only to those individuals who have authorization to access the site. In most cases, administrators will not allow users to transfer or upload their files to an anonymous FTP site.

FTP File Transfer

You can transfer files from your local computer or from a server to an FTP site by using FTP file transfer programs.

While retrieving FTP files is common, writing to FTP directories is usually only performed by network administrators. Powerful FTP file transfer applications with convenient graphical interfaces are available through private companies such as GlobalScape, Inc. at www.cuteftp.com and through Internet shareware and commerce sites such as www.winfiles.com, sponsored by CNET, Inc. Virtually all network administrators use these programs to help manage FTP sites.

Telnet

Telnet is a command-line utility that starts terminal emulation on a local computer when connecting to a remote computer that supports DEC VT 100, DEC VT 52, or TTY terminals. In the days before personal computers, all remote access to mainframe computers was through terminals that duplicated the screen and keyboard configuration of the mainframe computer's local workstation. With this type of connection, all processing occurs on the mainframe computer.

Using Telnet

Telnet is not used nearly as much as it once was, however a surprising number of legacy mainframe computer systems still perform their functions reliably. Although third party developers have built additional functionality into terminal emulation programs, the Telnet utility provides basic connectivity and terminal emulation to anyone running TCP/IP.

Emulating Terminals with Telnet

Emulation is the process of creating a virtual environment. Terminal emulation is the process of programming one kind of computer monitor and keyboard to behave as if it were another. When mainframe computers were the computing standard, there were relatively few protocols developed to describe how a computer screen and keyboard should function. Because virtually all communication with the device was in the form of command-line instructions, support for the graphical interface fine points like font selection and color management were unnecessary.

Telnet has the ability to mimic the attributes of the common terminal models of mainframe computers. Terminal emulation makes it possible for modern monitors and keyboards to become virtual terminals when connected to mainframe computers.

Connecting Remote Computers with Telnet

During a Telnet session, some systems allow for changes in the emulation mode. Several parameters can be set to better match the terminal environment the host system expects. All computing occurs at the host computer. Even the keystrokes that appear on your emulation screen are remotely generated. Emulation involves more than the monitor. For example, the character map of your keyboard must match that of the host computer or the characters that display on your monitor will be different from yours.

Entering Telnet Commands

One of the parameters that can be set in most terminal emulation environments is local echo. With this setting, the terminal does not write characters returned to the screen from the mainframe. Instead a local echo of the keystroke is drawn. This is very handy for fast typists who can type faster than the character returns from a slow connection. However, local echo makes it difficult to identify an incorrect keyboard-mapping problem.

Most command line utilities have help built into them. Type **?** after the command prompt (the **>** character) for the utility. A return keyboard input will display a list of all switches (commands) available for that utility. To display the function of each switch, type the word **help** after the prompt followed by a space and the switch name. Table 4.3 lists the most common Telnet commands and their functions.

Table 4.3 Telnet Commands

Telnet Command	Function
open (remote system name)	Connect to remote system
close (remote system name)	Close connection
quit (remote system name)	End session

Searching with Gopher

Once the most common search utility on the Internet, Gopher has all but disappeared. Gopher servers were designed to be searchable by Gopher clients at a time before modern search engines such as Yahoo, Excite, and AltaVista made it possible to search virtually any WWW server for content. The need for a special class of searchable TCP/IP server has effectively disappeared.

Simple Mail Transport Protocol (SMTP)

SMTP handles mail delivery to mail servers and between servers. Both IMAP and POP rely on SMTP for e-mail or E-commerce services. Local e-mail is exchanged among computers on the same network and is not routed through a mail server. SMTP does not provide local mail services but does provide remote services. A primary advantage to using e-mail servers is the ability to deliver mail at any time. The recipient, as far as the SMTP is concerned, is the e-mail server.

Using SMTP on E-Mail Servers

SMTP (like POP and IMAP) can be controlled using command-line instructions, but now, virtually everyone in the PC environment uses mail programs that have user-friendly graphical interfaces. Protocol selection is not automatic however, and the appropriate protocols must be specified in the e-mail setup program.

Using SMTP E-Mail Configuration

SMTP has a client and server side. The client-side configuration includes e-mail server address and connection type (dial-up or network). The server-side has variables for dealing with undelivered mail. SMTP has the ability to re-send messages that are not successfully delivered on the first attempt. SMTP servers also track the time a message remains on the server before being retrieved by the addressee. SMTP servers can be set to stipulate the number and frequency of e-mail delivery attempts, and they can be configured to return e-mail if the addressee fails to retrieve the mail after a specified period of time.

Establishing an SMTP Session

E-mail delivery sessions begin when a connection is established between the SMTP client and the SMTP server across a TCP/IP network. The transfer of e-mail involves the exchange of text string commands. Although the command-line exchange is hidden from the user because e-mail applications automate the process, a typical client/server dialog is shown in Figure 4.2.

Figure 4.2 SMTP Session

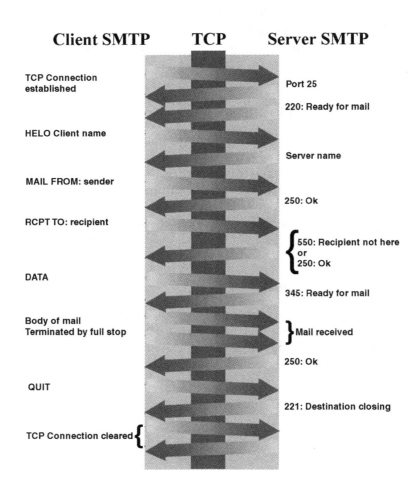

Resolving E-Mail Connectivity Problems

Whether trying to retrieve accumulated messages or send new ones, a connection must be established with an e-mail server. Although mail servers are considered mission-critical components of any network system, they occasionally go offline. Mail servers go offline for various reasons, including planned downtimes, maintenance routines, and unplanned system crashes.

You can determine if your e-mail problems are connection-related by using the diagnostic PING command to test the e-mail server's IP address. PING is a TCP/IP diagnostic utility that sends IP echo requests to a destination host on a local or remote network to determine if a destination TCP/IP host is available, functional, and has a valid IP address.

To confirm connectivity to your e-mail server, follow these steps:

1. From the **Start** menu, choose **Run**.

2. Type: **C:\windows\command** and then press **ENTER** to see the DOS shell command prompt.

3. From the **command prompt**, type: **ping** followed by the numeric IP address of your remote e-mail server.

4. Confirm the e-mail server connection. If you receive a response, then you have a remote connection.

5. Type: **EXIT**.

TCP/IP

TCP is responsible for the reliable delivery of data. Client/server applications can be designed to assume responsibility for data exchange integrity, but most programs rely on TCP for that service. TCP adds header information to datagrams to confirm the integrity of arriving data that may slow down transmission speed. However, this performance penalty is usually preferable to sending incomplete or corrupt data.

Establishing TCP/IP Parameters

Personal computers that use TCP/IP have tools for basic network configuration. The Windows Operating System (OS) uses the network control panel to access TCP/IP settings, while Macintosh computers employ a control panel cleverly named TCP/IP. The settable parameters in a TCP/IP configuration are the same parameters viewable with the IPCONFIG command-line utility. Some or all of the parameters can be set with a Dynamic Host Configuration Protocol (DHCP) server.

TCP/IP E-Mail Configurations

Certain information is typically required of a user when establishing an Internet e-mail account with an ISP. Configuration information can include the following:

- Incoming e-mail server type and address

- Outgoing e-mail server type and address

- Account name

- User name

- Password

- Connection type

DHCP

DHCP service is a significant advancement in TCP/IP network management. DHCP uses a centralized database to dynamically address and configure IP clients as TCP/IP services are requested. Additionally, DHCP provides for the recovery and redistribution of unused addresses. The following are two major DHCP services:

Dynamic assignment of IP addresses and other IP configuration settings—Eliminating manual IP addressing and host IP configuration greatly reduces the workload of network administration.

Distribution of IP addresses on an as-needed basis and recovery of unused IP addresses—IP addresses are distributed, recovered, and reused which increases the number of clients that an IP address pool can accommodate.

Assigning Dynamic IP Addresses

In a DHCP environment, a host broadcasts a request for an IP address and configuration settings at TCP/IP startup. The DHCP server retrieves an IP address from its database and transmits configuration information to the host. At a minimum, the DHCP server supplies the following information:

- IP address

- Subnet mask

Optionally, the server can be configured to supply the following:

- Default gateway

- DNS server

- WINS server

- Node type

- NetBIOS scope ID

Distributing IP Addresses

DHCP allocates IP addresses grouped according to host subnets. The available IP address pool for a subnet is called DHCP scope. Scopes must be defined on a DHCP server to regulate how addresses are divided on an internetwork. In this way, the address pool is divided so that the same IP address range is always associated with the same subnet.

Configuring IP Clients

Although DHCP servers have dramatically reduced the workload of network administrators by automating IP client configurations, there are times when the information must be entered manually. The client TCP/IP configuration includes the following:

- IP address

- Subnet mask

The following is additional information that may be required:

- DNS server address

- WINS server address

- Default gateway and alternate gateways

- NetBIOS scope ID

This information is entered into data fields in a system control panel or an IP configuration utility.

Retrieving and Transmitting Data

DHCP assigns IP information for a specified period called a lease in IP terminology. The negotiation and assignment for an IP address uses the following functions:

Discover—The discover function is a broadcast message from a client that requests an IP address. This message does not transmit across routers. If the DHCP server is not on the local subnet, a relay agent must be configured to forward the request to remote DHCP servers. To be serviced by a remote DHCP server, every subnet needs at least one host configured to listen for broadcast requests and forward them to DHCP servers. The DHCP relay agent also informs the DHCP server on which subnet the discover broadcast originates.

 Note: Some routers can transmit broadcast requests for DHCP services. These routers essentially have relay agent functionality programmed into them, and are designated RFC1542-compliant.

Offer—DHCP servers receiving the discover request determine if the request originated from a subnet for which they have a scope. If an address is available in the scope, the DHCP server sends an offer packet that contains an IP address, a subnet mask, and a lease duration.

Request—The client responds with a broadcast called a request, announcing the acceptance of the first address offer it receives. Clients may receive offers from multiple DHCP servers and the request broadcast informs all servers that either the offered IP address is accepted or that it is still available for other clients.

Acknowledgment—The DHCP server with the accepted offer responds to the client acknowledging acceptance. Included in the acknowledgment is the optional IP configuration information such as DNS and WINS server information.

Recovering Unused IP Addresses

A DHCP server can recover an unused IP address through the lease renewal process. Because the client computer initiates the renewal process, the DHCP server recovers the IP address if the client does not request a renewal.

The following is the process for IP address lease renewal:

After 50% of the lease expires, the client sends a request—The client computer tries to renew the lease with the same DHCP server that granted the original lease.

Renew request persists until 87.5% of lease expires—The client computer continues to try to renew its lease with the original server until 87.5% of the original lease is expired.

After 87.5% of lease expires, client broadcasts for a new lease—The client computer abandons attempts to communicate directly with the original DHCP server and starts broadcasting for a new lease.

A DHCP server acknowledges a renewal request and renews the lease—The responding server can renew the lease and the client retains the IP address.

A DHCP server cannot renew the lease—The server terminates the old lease and offers another lease with a different IP address if able.

No DHCP server acknowledges the request—The lease expires and the client must request a new IP address.

Excluding IP Addresses

The utility that reserves a specific IP address for a computer is called client reservation. Another option to consider when configuring DHCP is which addresses to exclude from the scope. The excluded scopes can be a range or a single address. Most often, excluded addresses are manually assigned and should not be included in the available address pool.

The following are examples of possible IP address classifications:

- WINS server

- DNS server

- Router addresses

- WWW server

Line Printer (LPR)

LPR defines a print server standard for sending documents across a TCP/IP internetwork. The process has a client-side and a server-side. While network printing is the standard for medium-to-large organizations, the benefits of sharing a printer across a network of any size should be considered.

 Tip: Although the printing service called FAX (facsimile) is not TCP/IP-based, today, it is a form of network printing used by nearly every business as well as individuals. FAX (facsimile) is a service for remote printing across a telephone network.

Establishing LPR Client/Server Connections

The LPR client sends a print document to a Line Printer Daemon (LPD) print server. Any networked computer running LPD with a printer physically attached to a serial or parallel port effectively becomes a LPD print server to other LPR clients.

Printers specifically designed for network service have their own Network Interface Card (NIC) installed. A NIC is an expansion board installed in computers and servers and controls the flow of information over the network. The printer manufacturer builds LPD services into the printer's firmware or software to allow LPR clients to directly connect to the network printer. LPR and LPD run on any TCP/IP device including Windows and UNIX-based computers.

Troubleshooting

If you experience problems, always verify that the configurations are correct. As more TCP/IP-related components such as DHCP are added to configuration options, problems can multiply. It is important to follow structured basic problem analysis and elimination steps to identify Internet service and connection issues such as the presence of a slow server and Web site communication problems.

Follow these basic troubleshooting steps to first eliminate and isolate service and connection problems:

1. Identify the symptoms of the problem, such as hanging connections or changes made since it last worked.

2. Determine current TCP/IP settings.

3. Determine which component is faulty.

4. Determine which utility can best diagnose the problem.

Identifying Slow Server Problems

A mail server can slow down for a variety of reasons, but the most common culprit is high e-mail volume. A network administrator experiencing slow e-mail response times can collect data on peak activity periods, available hard disk space and SMTP parameters to isolate the cause of the problem. Solutions can involve hardware upgrades, configuration changes, and screening for unsolicited e-mail (junk mail) and deliberate hacker attacks to increase capacity.

Identifying Web Site Communication Problems

The TRACERT utility identifies a router path, and then a datagram packet goes on its journey from destination to source. In a situation where connection performance varies over time, TRACERT can be helpful in identifying bottlenecks. The PING utility also determines connectivity to a Web server. A common linking problem is incorrect domain name information. You can ping an IP address or a URL to confirm connectivity. If that fails, the problem is probably an IP/name-resolution issue.

Vocabulary

Review the following terms in preparation for the certification exam.

Term	Description
API	Application Programming Interface provides application developers with consistent rules for designing programs to interact with the TCP/IP stack.
buffer	Temporary memory space used for constantly changing data.
client	The requestor of server services.
Gopher	Once the most popular client/server search engine on the Internet, Gopher has been almost completely replaced by modern search engines like Yahoo and AltaVista.
graphical interface	A computer interface designed with a visual metaphor to help users intuitively know how to perform operations.
LDAP	Lightweight Directory Access Protocol is a client server service for search databases using ordinary text queries.
local computer	The computer that can be accessed directly rather than by means of a communications line.
LPR	Line Printer is a client/server protocol for sending and receiving print documents across a TCP/IP network.

Term	Description
NNTP	Network News Transfer Protocol provides services for special interest group forums to organize posted discussions in hierarchical threads.
parameters	Properties represented by user-settable variables.
query	An inquiry for information from a database.
remote computer	The computer that an operator accesses by way of a modem.
server	A computer or program on the Internet or other network that responds to commands from a client.
SIG	Special Interest Group is any group of people that meet in person or via discussion groups over the Internet to exchange ideas and information about a single topic.
streaming media	A data transfer system that allows the media to be accessed while it is still being transferred.
Telnet	A command-line utility for remote connectivity across TCP/IP.
terminal emulation	Software designed to make a PC mimic the behavior of a particular monitor/keyboard model associated with mainframe computers.
XML	Extensible Markup Language is a new markup language similar to HTML but with a richer feature set.

In Brief

If you want to...	Then do this...
Access HTML documents	Use HTTP commands with your browser to access pages from the Web.
View an HTML document	Use a Web browser.
Create an HTML document	Learn the HTML tagging system or use an HTML editor.
Listen to or view streaming media over the Internet	Start the streaming media using a fast connection with a browser enabled with the necessary software helpers (plug-ins).
Create leading-edge Web pages	Include multimedia functionality in your page.
Retrieve your e-mail	Use POP3.
See e-mail headers and selectively retrieve copies of your e-mail	Enable and use IMAP e-mail applications.
Create searchable databases that allow users to easily create text queries	Build your database with LDAP client/server services.
Follow and contribute to an Internet discussion about a particular topic	Enable and use an NNTP news reader to join a news group.
Download a file or application from an Internet server	Use the FTP functionality built into your browser.
Upload a file to an Internet server	Use an FTP utility or the FTP command-line utility.
Connect to a mainframe computer	Use Telnet utility to start terminal emulation.
Search Gopher Server	Use a Gopher client utility.
Automate the TCP/IP address and configuration process	Use a DHCP server service.
Send print documents to a remote printer across a TCP/IP network	Use LPR to connect to a print server running LPD.

Lesson 4 Activities

Complete the following activities to better prepare you for the certification exam.

1. Describe the function of HTTP and HTML.

2. Explain the purpose of an HTML tag.

3. Explain the difference between streaming audio/video files and other forms of audio/video file formats and explain why UDP is a better choice than TCP for streaming data transmission.

4. Discuss the function of SMTP, POP3, and IMAP.

5. Discuss a client server protocol suitable for creating searchable databases that clients can access over the Internet with simple text queries.

6. Explain the purpose of FTP and the two different user access configurations.

7. Explain terminal emulation, the Telnet utility, and what types of computers require this type of connection.

8. Discuss the services of a DHCP server and when you would not use them.

9. Explain what an IP address lease is and how it is renewed.

10. Explain LPR and LDP.

Answers to Lesson 4 Activities

1. HTTP defines connectivity to HTML documents on the World Wide Web. HTTP initiates, nego-tiates, and ends a connection to a URL address across a TCP/IP network.

2. HTML is a markup language. Text and file references are treated as objects subject to the instruc-tions contained in tags. For instance, a text object may have attributes of font, size, color, and jus-tification assigned by tags.

3. Streaming audio and/or video information can be accessed while the data are being transferred. Other forms of audio and video files can only be played after the entire file is received. Because the efficiency of the data stream across a network is more important than data integrity (TCP ensures data integrity at a cost of high overhead and slower speeds), the low overhead and high speed of UDP is the best choice for transferring streaming media.

4. E-mail is conducted by using two types of protocols. The sending protocol is SMTP and handles mail transfers to and between mail servers. Retrieving e-mail from servers is handled by either POP3 or IMAP. IMAP has a richer feature set and can manipulate e-mail while it is still on the mail server.

5. LDAP is an Internet standard for creating client/server databases on the Internet. An LDAP server allows for easy-to-construct text queries from an LDAP client.

6. FTP is a file transfer protocol. Many FTP sites are designed so that anyone can access files, such as application updates, using anonymous logons. FTP sites can also be configured to require user accounts and passwords to gain access.

7. Mainframe computer terminals (monitors and keyboards) are used to access the computer hard-ware. PCs must emulate a terminal to interface with a mainframe computer. Telnet is a terminal emulation protocol that can mimic the most common mainframe computer terminals. Telnet also has the ability to start and end a PC-to-mainframe session.

8. DHCP servers provide automated IP address and configuration to TCP/IP clients. This process increases the efficiency of an IP address pool and reduces network administrator workload. DHCP should not be used for locations requiring static IP address like servers and routers.

9. DHCP servers issue temporary IP addresses. Each address is leased to a host computer for a specified time. Halfway through the lease the host computer automatically tries to renew the lease. This process continues until the client is successful and receives a new lease for the address. If

the host does not communicate with the DHCP server, the IP address will be recovered by the DHCP server at the end of the lease and made available to other host computers.

10. LPR is the TCP/IP protocol for sending documents to a printer on a network. LPD is the protocol that accepts print jobs sent using LPR. LPD forwards the document to a local printer for production.

Lesson 4 Quiz

These questions test your knowledge of features, vocabulary, procedures, and syntax.

1. What language determines how a Web page is displayed in a browser?

    A. HTTP

    B. TTPT

    C. C++

    D. HTML

2. Which of the following does not describe the function of a HTML tag?

    A. Sets text attributes

    B.   file names

    C. Assigns object positions

    D. Describes information types

3. What is not true about streaming media?

    A. The best protocol to use when sending is UDP

    B. Streaming media works well on relatively slow connections

    C. Streaming media files can be accessed while the data are being transferred

    D. Streaming media works best on relatively fast connections

4. Which of the following protocols is used with e-mail?

    A. LDAP

    B. IMAP

    C. UDP

    D. PING

5. Which protocol is used to access Special Interest Groups (SIGs) and view and contribute to text-based postings?

    A. IMAP

    B. ASIG

    C. CNNP

    D. NNTP

6. What statement is never true about FTP?

    A. FTP requires logon authentication

    B. FTP allows anonymous logon

    C. Administrators record user information from anonymous logons

    D. FTP clients upload files to FTP servers

7. Which of the following is a Telnet service?

    A. Monitor bit-depth

    B. Connection speed

    C. Font selection

    D. Session control

8. Which protocol is not associated with e-mail?

    A. IMAP

    B. LDAP

    C. SMTP

    D. POP3

9. Which service is not associated with DHCP assignment?

    A. WINS server address

    B. Subnet Mask

C. Default gateway

D. POP3 account

10. What protocol works with LPR?

A. LDAP

B. UDP

C. LPD

D. Postscript

Answers to Lesson 4 Quiz

1. Answer D is correct. HTML is the markup language that determines how a Web browser displays an HTML document.

    Answer A is incorrect because HTTP is the protocol that determines how Web sessions progress.

    Answer B is incorrect because TTPT is not a protocol.

    Answer C is incorrect because C++ is an application development language and has nothing to do with Web page display.

2. Answer B is correct. Tags do not name files; they assign attributes to objects (which can be files).

    Answers A, C, and D are incorrect because they are functions of HTML tags.

3. Answer B is correct. Streaming media does not work well across slow connections.

    Answers A, C, and D are incorrect because they are true statements about streaming media.

4. Answer B is correct. IMAP is a feature-rich mail retrieval service.

    Answer A is incorrect because LDAP is a client/server service for searchable databases.

    Answer C is incorrect because UDP is a connection-less protocol for sending fault-tolerant data across a TCP/IP network.

    Answer D is incorrect because PING is a connection diagnostic utility.

5. Answer D is correct. NNTP is the protocol used by news reader applications to read and post hierarchical threads on a topic of interest to a SIG.

    Answers B and C are incorrect because they are not protocols.

    Answer A is incorrect because IMAP is an e-mail protocol.

6. The correct answer is C. FTP site administrators cannot determine any user information from an anonymous visitor.

    Answers A, B, and D are incorrect because they are conditionally true statements about FTP.

7. Answer D is correct. Telnet, among other services, initiates and terminates a session with a remote computer.

Answer A is incorrect because Telnet does not control that monitor parameter.

Answer B is incorrect because Telnet does not control connection speed.

Answer C is incorrect because Telnet does not offer font control services.

8. Answer B is correct because LDAP is not associated with e-mail.

    Answers A, C, and D are incorrect because they are protocols associated with e-mail.

9. Answer D is correct. POP3 configurations are not DHCP server services.

    Answers A, B and C are incorrect because they are all basic or optional configuration settings included in DHCP service.

10. Answer C is correct. LPD is the server-side protocol to the client side LPR service.

    Answer A and B are incorrect because LDAP and UDP are not printing protocols.

    Answer D is incorrect because Postscript is a page description language, not a printing protocol.

Lesson 5: Internet Infrastructure

The data on the Internet consists of millions of devices connecting and communicating across Transmission Control Protocol/Internet Protocol (TCP/IP) networks. The connections are transmitting across copper wires, through fiber-optic cables, and over the airwaves through microwave energy. Hardware devices detect, sort, repeat, and redirect signals and send them to network cards attached to computers. This lesson covers hardware and transmission conduits, network concepts, and the systems that make up the global network infrastructure called the Internet.

After completing this lesson, you should have a better understanding of the following topics:

- Internet Bandwidth and Transmission

- Data Transmission Media

- Hardware and Software Connections

- Bandwidth Link Technologies

- Network Operating Systems

Internet Bandwidth and Transmission

The Internet is often compared to the freeway and road transportation infrastructure. Just as highways, roads, and streets connect to the freeways, the fiber-optic Internet connects T1 connections, twisted-pair wire, coaxial cable, and fiber-optic media.

The data on the Internet finds its way to computers over various paths and media. Most home computers connect to the Internet with dial-up access, a connection to a data communications network through a Public Switched Telephone Network (PSTN), and modems. Data transmissions traveling over the Internet have speed requirements in terms of throughput and bandwidth much like a car goes at 55 miles per hour on a four-lane freeway.

Line Throughput

Modems are communication devices that transmit information over standard telephone lines. A modem sends information over a telephone line by converting or modulating binary (digital) data into analog (radio frequency) data for transmission on telephone lines. Binary computer data, the 1s and 0s, are the numerical representation of signals.

To receive information, a modem converts or demodulates the analog signals from the telephone line back to digital information. The term modem is the short form of MODulation/DEModulation. While the word modem originally referred to the device that modulated and demodulated digital information across telephone lines, it now describes a wide variety of data interfaces for computers.

Throughput is the rate at which data are transferred on the network, and it is measured at Bits Per Second (bps) or by Kilobits Per Second (Kbps).

Wire cable connections are capable of much higher throughput speeds. Wire offers some resistance to electrical energy, a process called attenuation, which causes a loss of signal over distance and limits throughput.

Broadband and Baseband Bandwidth Limitations

Bandwidth is the amount of data that can be transmitted over a given communications channel (such as a computer network) in a given unit of time (usually one second). Internet connections are limited to a certain amount of data transfers at any given time. For example, if too many files download at once, the Internet connection lags.

The speed of the dial-up modem connection, for example, cannot transmit large amounts of data at one time. A higher bandwidth connection, such as a cable modem, can download more files before the connection lags.

All connections to the Internet are limited in the same way. Dial-up connections are measured by Kbps, such as 14.4K, 28.8K, 33.6K, and 56K. Other types of transmission connections are measured in Megabits Per Second (Mbps). A megabit is a measurement of storage capacity equal to about 1 million bits (1,048,576 (2^{20})). In general, baseband technologies are faster than broadband methods. Most Local Area Network (LAN) connections are made using baseband transmissions, while many Wide Area Network (WAN) connections use slower broadband connections.

Broadband and Baseband Bandwidth Transmissions

Broadband transmissions are encoded, single data signals carried over a data transmission medium, such as wire, with several channels being carried at once. Cable TV, for example, uses broadband transmission. In contrast, baseband transmission transmits only one signal at a time. Most communication on Local Area Networks (LAN) is baseband communication.

A system that uses cable medium such as fiber optic to transmit encoded digital signals is a baseband system. Digital signals comprised of either light or electricity pulse through the cable in discrete increments. Baseband transmissions use the complete communication channel to transmit just one data signal.

Broadband networks are LANs connected with coaxial or fiber-optic cable medium, so that both inbound and outbound analog channels transmit signals as electromagnetic or optical waves. A large portion of the electromagnetic spectrum, ranging from frequencies of 50 Mbps to 600 Mbps, is used by broadband systems. The networks accommodate voice, data, television, and many other services over multiple transmission channels.

Data Transmission Media

The primary conduit for transmitting Internet information is high-capacity fiber-optic cable that connects large cities, governmental organizations, and universities. Fiber-optic cable transmits signals with light rather than with electricity, as do other types of cable. All other portals to the Internet eventually connect into this fiber-optic conduit.

LANs use the following three major cabling types to connect to the Internet backbone:

- Twisted-pair cable
- Coaxial cable
- Fiber-optic media

Twisted-Pair Cabling

Twisted-pair cabling consists of two independently insulated wires twisted around one another. One wire carries the signal while the other wire is grounded and absorbs signal interference. Twisted-pair cable is used by older telephone networks and is the least expensive type of LAN cable.

Two types of twisted pair cable are Unshielded Twisted-Pair (UTP) and Shielded Twisted-Pair cable (STP).

UTP consists of at least two (and typically eight) insulated copper wires. UTP is the most popular type of twisted-pair cable for LAN cabling. Most telephone systems use a type of UTP that is often installed to meet future cabling requirements for a computer network.

 Warning: Common telephone wire may not have the twisting and other electrical characteristics essential for a clean, secure computer data transmission, which Internet access requires.

Five categories specified by the Electronic Industries Association and the Telecommunications Industries Association (EIA/TIA) 568 Commercial Building Wiring standard are shown in Table 5.1.

Table 5.1 UTP Wiring Standard Categories

Standard Category	Description	Certified Data Transmission
Category 1	Traditional UTP telephone cable carries voice and no data	—
Category 2	UTP cable, four twisted-pairs	4 Mbps
Category 3	UTP cable, four twisted-pairs with three twists per foot	10 Mbps
Category 4	UTP cable, four twisted-pairs	16 Mbps
Category 5	UTP cable, four twisted-pairs of copper wire	100 Mbps

UTP is susceptible to cross-talk, which is a problem with all types of cabling. Twisting and shielding can help prevent cross-talk, the signal overflow from another line. The more twists per foot in cable, the greater the protection against cross-talk.

STP consists of two pairs of copper wires surrounded by a metal shield to prevent cross-talk. STP is made with a woven copper braid jacket, which is more protective than that of UTP. STP is less susceptible to electrical interference and supports higher transmission rates over longer distances than UTP. Both STP and UTP cable connections, however, cannot be longer than 100 meters.

STP or UTP cable connects computers on IBM token-ring networks. IBM has its own system of cable type classification. For example, Category 3 cable (voice grade UTP) is known as Type 3 in the IBM system.

Coaxial Cabling

Signal deterioration is a key factor that determines how far a cable can extend. Coaxial, or coax, cable can extend farther than twisted-pair cable. The coax design is different from STP in that the coax consists of a copper core that is surrounded by insulation, a braided metal shielding, and a jacket. The inner insulation assures that no signals can pass from the copper core, and no signals from outside the insulation pass into the copper core. The following are two types of coaxial cable:

Thicknet cable—Somewhat rigid with a 0.5-inch (1.25 cm) diameter and a thick copper core.

Thinnet cable—Flexible with a 0.25-inch (0.6 cm) thick diameter.

Thicknet cable is more expensive than thinnet cable, but it carries a signal farther. Larger networks combine thicknet and thinnet cable.

Manufacturers agree on designations for types of cable, and have assigned the following four types of coaxial cable designations for use with different types of LANs, as shown in Table 5.2.

Table 5.2 Coaxial Cable Types

Coaxial Cable Type Designation	Network Use	Standard Name	Also Known As
RG-58 /U, solid copper core or RG-58 A/U stranded copper core	Ethernet coax networks (10 Mbps, baseband, 185 meters)	10Base2	Thinnet
RG-8 or RG-11, copper core	Backbone to connect small, thinnet network types, (10 Mbps, baseband, 500 meters)	10Base5	Thicknet, Standard Ethernet
RG-59	Cable TV (CATV)		Broadband
RG-62	ARCnet and IBM terminals		Broadband

Fiber-Optic Cable Internet Access

Fiber-optic conduit is the Internet backbone's primary transmission media. The Internet backbone (also called a trunk) is fiber-optic cable. Fiber-optic cable transmits data at speeds of 2 Gigabits Per Second (Gbps). Gbps is the data transfer speed on a network in multiples of 1,073,741,824 (2^{30}) bits. The IEEE committee published a specification for running Ethernet over fiber-optic cable. The primary reason for using 10BaseFL is for long cable runs between buildings. The maximum distance for a segment is 2000 meters.

Fiber-optic cable is made from extremely precise round cores of glass or plastic strands, encased in a reflective material. Laser light is pulsed into the end of a fiber-optic strand, and the light and dark translates into binary information. As the light travels down the glass core, the cladding, a reflective coating, keeps the light from escaping. The light transmissions are immune to electronic eavesdropping, which makes fiber-optic cable a more secure data transmission medium. Figure 5.1 shows light traveling down a fiber-optic cable.

Figure 5.1 Fiber-Optic Cable

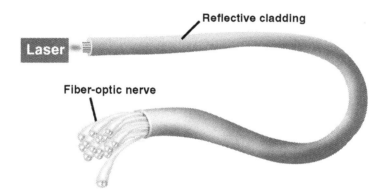

Fiber-optic cable produces no Electromagnetic Interference (EMI) because it uses light to transmit data. The glass fiber-optic core is encased in reflective cladding; signals from bundled cables do not interfere with each other. An unlimited number of fiber-optic cables can be bundled when burying cable for Internet backbones.

Fiber-optic cable is only used for one-way transmission of data. Fiber-optic cabling is usually laid in pairs, one strand dedicated for transmission and one strand dedicated for reception of data. This system is very efficient with attenuation only becoming a significant problem after cable runs of 10 miles.

Note: Fiber-optic cable does not leak EMI, but all other forms electric-wire cabling cause EMI. If leakage is too great, it can interfere with radio transmissions. The Federal Aviation Administration (FAA) takes EMI leakage seriously and will shut down any system that interferes with the Air Traffic Control System.

With all of the advantages of fiber-optic cable, you may ask why it is not always used. The answer is because of expense and difficult installation. When fiber-optic technology was first introduced, it was very expensive to manufacture. Costs should decrease as manufacturing processes advance and the market for the technology expands. In addition, it is difficult to work with it and to connect it to networks. Nevertheless, the advantages of fiber-optic cable are compelling. Aggressive programs by private industry are underway to crisscross the country with more fiber-optic cable. Experts predict that fiber-optic cable will connect businesses and residences in the not-too-distant future.

The advantages of using fiber-optic cable are as follows:

- It provides a fast connection

- EMI reduction

- Minimal attenuation problems

The disadvantages of using fiber-optic cable are as follows:

- It is difficult to install

- It is expensive

Other media such as terrestrial and satellite microwave transmission technologies will augment fiber-optic transmission to increase bandwidth and transmission capability far beyond current rates.

Terrestrial Microwave Internet Access

The primary advantage of terrestrial microwave connections is that they offer high-speed access to the Internet without the need to be directly connected to the fiber-optic backbone.

Microwave transmitters and receivers are capable of high-capacity data transmissions. Current service providers claim transmission speeds up to 100 Mbps, but these systems have limitations. Because focused high-energy microwave energy constitutes a health hazard, this type of Internet conduit is limited to the tops of tall buildings that have an unobstructed line-of-sight between transmitters and receivers (Figure 5.2).

Figure 5.2 Microwave Transmissions on Tall Building Rooftops

Transmission dishes focus microwave energy into tight beams so that only the receiving dishes are targeted, not the CEO in the top-floor office. Microwave energy is also subject to atmospheric attenuation. For example, a heavy rain shower can absorb a lot of microwave energy that limits transmission range to about a mile.

Warning: A brief exposure to the energy produced by terrestrial microwave connections is not harmful. Nor is there evidence that microwave transmissions are harmful to birds in flight. However, prolonged exposure to the relatively high levels produced by rooftop transmitters can be dangerous. Care must be taken during installation to prohibit access to any area located directly between the transmitter and receiver.

The advantages of terrestrial microwave connections to the Internet are as follows:

■ Very fast data transmission speeds

■ High-speed direct access to Internet for buildings not physically connected to fiber-optic backbone

The disadvantages of terrestrial microwave connections to the Internet are as follows:

■ Requires access to tall building rooftops

■ Weather may cause attenuation

■ Potentially dangerous

■ Expensive to install

Satellite Microwave Internet Access

From a data transmission perspective, the quality of residential telephone lines is relatively low in many parts of the country. People with 56 Kbps modems may only achieve reliable connection speeds of 20 Kbps or slower. Your Internet experience suffers when Web pages, documents with Hypertext Markup Language (HTML), other files for graphics, and scripts take minutes instead of seconds to load, or when a file transfer takes hours.

The good news is that relatively fast Internet access is currently available to those people without high-speed telephone line access. Residential customers can now surf the Internet with satellite dishes in the same way similar dishes pipe digital television to people without cable TV. In fact, some venders sell one satellite dish capable of receiving both TV and Internet information.

Note: The privately held Teledesic LLC company is undertaking a project it calls Teledesic Internet-in-the-Sky, or a constellation of 288 Low-Earth-Orbit (LEO) satellites, to create the world's first network to provide fiber-like access to telecommunications services. These access services include linking enterprise computing networks, broadband Internet access video-conferencing, and other digital solutions. This technology differs from existing satellite services because access speed will be much faster (64 Mbps on downlink and 2 Mbps on uplink). Users will both uplink and downlink data without modems.

Current satellite microwave systems claim access speeds of up to 400 Kbps but the following are some limitations of the service:

■ Installation requires an unobstructed line-of-sight between satellite and receiving dish

■ Signal attenuation can result from atmospheric conditions such as clouds and rain

■ The system is fairly expensive to install

■ Reception-only transmission is by traditional modem dial-up account

Current Internet Satellite technology allows small businesses or home users to receive data. However, available systems are expensive to install and still require a dial-up Internet account. Sending requests over telephone lines and receiving responses over a satellite dish is undesirable from a performance perspective.

Almost all significant blocks of data, such as Web pages, streaming data, and file transfers, require download processes. Even a very slow connection can transmit data on an Internet link with minimal delay. However, sending a file to a File Transfer Protocol (FTP) site will still take a relatively long time with this kind of arrangement.

Tip: A network connection that has different capabilities for sending and receiving data is called asymmetric. Because current satellite connection services have much faster downlink speeds than uplink speeds, they are asymmetric systems.

Hardware and Software Connections

If freeways, highways, city arterials, and neighborhood streets are a metaphor for the Internet, then freeway junctions, on-ramps, exits, street intersections, and traffic signals represent Internet connections. Examining how information is routed and processed from sender to recipient is fundamental to understanding the Internet.

From the initial concept of TCP/IP to the current state of internetwork technology, the driving requirement is reliable datagram delivery. In Internet Protocol (IP) networks, a packet containing both destination address and data is called a datagram. The marvelous flexibility of TCP/IP allows information to automatically re-route itself until it finds a way to get to the final destination.

Hubs

A hub is a connection device that splits one signal into many and is a central point on networks for signal and data distribution. Passive, active, intelligent, and switching hubs all provide a central point on networks for signal and data distribution. However, each type of hub provides distinctive features.

A passive hub functions by physically connecting multiple ports. A port is an interface through which data are transferred between computers and other devices or computers and a network. The number of cables attached to the port multiplies signal loss from attenuation. Figure 5.3 illustrates a passive hub.

Figure 5.3 Passive Hub

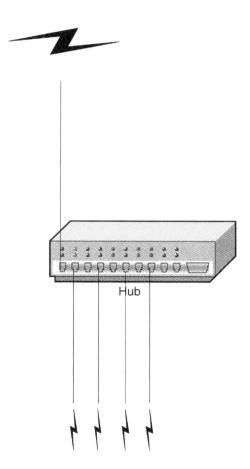

A passive hub serves as a conduit for the data, enabling it to go from one device (or segment) to another.

An active hub operates like a passive hub, but regenerates signals to reduce attenuation. Active hubs extend distances from one network node to another.

Intelligent hubs, or active hubs, include additional features that enable an administrator to monitor the traffic passing through the hub and to configure each port in the hub. Intelligent hubs are also called manageable hubs.

A fourth type of hub, called a switching hub, actually reads the destination address of each datagram and then forwards the datagram to the correct port.

Passive hubs are rarely used because signal loss limits cable lengths. Active hubs are no more difficult to use than passive hubs and have the repeater functionality built into them. This eliminates the signal attenuation problem posed by passive hubs.

 Note: Repeaters are simple devices that receive digital information, regenerate the signal, and pass it along. They are not signal amplifiers for digital signals. Repeaters, placed at appropriate intervals on network cables, indefinitely extend the distance data signals can travel.

Active hubs are basic building blocks of networks. They connect host computers to each other as well as to shared network resources such as servers. Hubs also connect to other hubs, allowing network segments to share information. Figure 5.4 illustrates network hub connections.

Figure 5.4 Network Hub Connections

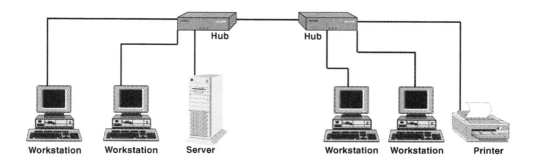

Bridges

Bridges, like hubs, are devices that connect network segments. Bridges, unlike hubs, provide datagram-filtering services. When a bridge is turned on, it has no network information and acts essentially as a repeater, passing along all network traffic. The bridge logs the Media Access Control (MAC) address of every datagram that comes along and very quickly builds a table of datagrams associated with each segment. Once the table is complete, the bridge only allows segment-to-segment network traffic to pass.

Local traffic on each segment remains available to all local nodes, such as client computers, servers, or shared printers, while cross-segment traffic passes through the bridge. This process of separating local traffic from segment-to-segment traffic greatly reduces unnecessary datagram traffic from slowing down a network.

The most common type of bridge is a transparent bridge. Two other types of bridges are a source-route bridge and a translational bridge. Source route bridges connect token-ring networks (a network technology developed by IBM) and translational bridges connect different types of networks, such as TCP/IP and token ring.

Although bridges provide datagram-filtering services, bridges do not filter broadcast traffic. When multiple bridges connect segments, a potential for a self-perpetuating broadcast loop exists, which is known as a broadcast storm. The Spanning Tree Algorithm, the standard that establishes protocols for network bridges, is responsible for controlling broadcast storms. The algorithm built into modern bridges detects and eliminates broadcast storms. Figure 5.5 shows the filtering function of bridge connections.

Figure 5.5 Bridge Network Connections

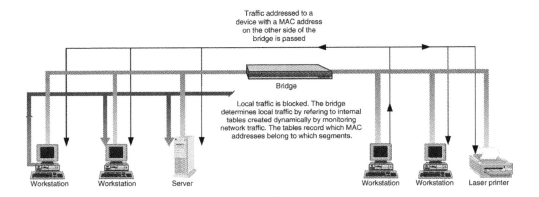

Routers

A router is a special-purpose device that processes network traffic. By definition, a router must have two or more Network Interface Cards (NICs). A NIC is an expansion card or other device that provides network access to a computer or other device, such as a printer.

NICs mediate between the computer and the physical media, such as cabling, over which transmissions travel. Any computer with two NICs can perform router functions, although routing on medium and large networks is usually performed by dedicated router hardware.

While repeaters, bridges, and hubs connect network segments into single logical segments, routers transfer data among networks and divide LANs into separate network segments called subnets. A router, like a bridge, maintains address tables. However, instead of MAC information, router tables contain network addresses.

Network addresses, or IP addresses, are unique 32-bit numbers that identify computers connected to the Internet to other Internet hosts. This enables communication through the transfer of datagrams, or packets. A packet in a packet-switching network is a transmission unit of fixed or maximum size that consists of binary digits, representing data, a header containing an identification number, source and destination addresses, and sometimes error-control data.

IP addresses contain two types of information: the network ID and the host ID. An IP address is expressed in dotted quad format, consisting of the decimal values of its 4 bytes, separated with periods. The first 1, 2, or 3 bytes of the IP address identify the network the host is connected to, and the remaining bits identify the host itself. The subnet mask determines which part of the 32-bit binary IP address is the network ID information and which part is the host ID information.

Routers direct traffic between networks and subnets using network ID information. Router protocols use network tables to make decisions about forwarding network traffic. When a router receives a network packet, it looks at the packet header information for sender/receiver network information.

Note: Since routers block broadcast messages, network protocols that rely exclusively on broadcast information for communication are not suitable for routed systems. NetBIOS Enhanced User Interface (NetBEUI) is a fast and easy-to-administer protocol that was once very popular, but because NetBEUI is inherently non-routable, its use has fallen off dramatically.

If the packet header indicates that both the sender and recipient exist on the same network segment, the router will not forward the message because it recognizes the data as local traffic. On the other hand, if the sender network ID is different than the recipient network ID, the router accepts the data and forwards the message according to routing protocols.

Routers contain tables of network address. Routers that are designed to service a single organization may contain the IP address of every subnet in the organization. In that situation, the routing protocol calculates a data path and forwards the data to another router. This step is called a hop. A hop is the path that data travel from one router to the next. For data to reach the backbone, several hops may be necessary, since each router repeats the process until the message is delivered to its intended subnet.

Note: Hops require processing time. When the message must be read and passed on by several routers before it reaches its destination, it can result in jitter. Jitter is an annoying and perceptible variation in the time it takes various workstations to respond to messages. Some respond quickly, while some respond slowly.

Huge networks, like the Internet, have multitudes of networks. Every router cannot have every network address stored on its internal tables. If the router does not have the network address on its table when it receives a data packet, the router still forwards the data.

The challenge is for the router to send the data along an efficient path that will eventually lead to a router that does contain the recipient's network ID on its internal table. Routers apply algorithms using the message destination and its internal tables to make routing decisions. The routing decision is conducted in the following sequence:

1. The host route sends the message to a specific IP address.

2. The subnet route directs the message to a router connected to a specific subnet.

3. The network route directs the message to a gateway router of an entire network. A gateway is a conversion service for data. It both transfers information and converts it to a form compatible with the protocols of the receiving network.

4. The default router directs the message to a default gateway router when there are no table matches.

Tip: The definition of the term router is constantly evolving. Companies at the forefront of router technology, like Cisco Systems, are building high-level services into their router products that greatly exceed traditional ideas of router functionality.

Switches

Switches are multi-port bridges. A switch is comparable to a hub with transparent bridge functionality built into each port. Bridges dynamically build MAC address tables when monitoring network traffic. Once a bridge associates MAC addresses with a physical port, only those addresses (and broadcast traffic) are passed through.

By extending this functionality to a multi-port hub, network traffic is efficiently directed between sender and recipient, bypassing other devices on the subnet. Switches can substantially reduce traffic and increase performance on all but the smallest networks.

 Note: Hubs with bridge functionality built into each port are also called switched hubs. Most manufactures are moving away from this terminology and are simply calling these devices switches.

Figure 5.6 compares data paths on a network using a switch and a hub.

Figure 5.6 Switches and Hubs

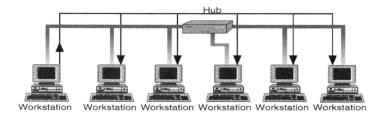

Gateways

Gateways are hardware or software setups that translate between two dissimilar protocols and perform conversion services. Although there are a few standardized gateway services, most gateways are customized to fulfill a special purpose.

You can use gateways for the following purposes:

■ To connect dissimilar networks like TCP/IP and token ring

■ To translate network protocols like TCP/IP and Internetwork Packet Exchange/Sequence Packet Exchange (IPX/SPX)

■ To convert file formats like Lotus cc:Mail and Microsoft Exchange

When data exchange is limited by compatibility constraints, a gateway is the likely solution. Creating a gateway may be as difficult as developing a custom application or as simple as attaching off-the-shelf hardware or software.

Backbones

A network backbone is the primary conduit of information for a system. The term backbone refers to a part of the network structure and not any particular physical specification. The Internet backbone is the fiber-optic cabling that connects major cities, government facilities, and universities. The backbone of a small business could be a relatively slow conduit that uses twisted pair cable. A metaphor for a network backbone is that of a tree trunk. The backbone is the tree trunk, and all smaller branches and limbs connect to the main trunk. Figure 5.7 shows a network design based on backbone topography.

Figure 5.7 Network Backbones

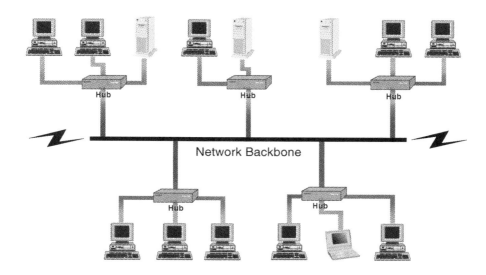

Adapters

Adapters are the computer hardware interface to a network. Adapters are commonly referred to as one of the following:

- NICs

- Network adapters

- Network cards

Adapters convert media signals into binary information that a computer recognizes. A NIC for a typical office computer detects and creates line voltage variances on a network that represent the 1s and 0s of binary computer code. A NIC connected to fiber-optic media translates bursts of laser light into computer data. Whatever the media, the adapter's job is to detect and generate network signals.

The computer and the NIC must be configured properly for usable data to flow across a network. Plug-And-Play (PnP) features on Macintosh and Microsoft Windows 98 and Windows 2000 operating systems may set some or all adapter configurations automatically. On Microsoft Windows 95 and Windows NT computers, it may be necessary to configure the following:

- Interrupt Request Lines (IRQs)
- Input/Output (I/0) addresses
- Shared memory addresses
- Direct Memory Addresses (DMAs)

Figure 5.8 illustrates a typical network adapter or NIC.

Figure 5.8 Network Adapter

Internet in a Box

For the average user, gaining Internet access several years ago was an intimidating process. The prospect of configuring a modem, connecting to an Internet Service Provider (ISP) and working with a Web browser was enough to discourage all but the most tenacious early users. Internet In A Box was an attempt to help the average user get online.

Internet In A Box is a software package that included Mosaic, the original Web browser, and other Internet utilities. Also included in the package were configuration and connection utilities. Although the product simplified the process of accessing the Internet in its day, current browsers, available free to everyone, are more integrated, more powerful, and far easier to use.

Modems

The term modem refers to devices that convert analog telephone signals into digital information used by computers. However, the meaning of the word modem has expanded to include just about any data interface for data lines and computers.

 Tip: The word modem comes from the words MOdulation and DEModulation. Analog modems send digital information across wires by voltage modulation and receive similar information by demodulating carrier voltages.

The following are five elements that link two computers communicating with modems:

1. First computer

2. Modem attached to first computer

3. Connecting wire (usually telephone twisted pair)

4. Modem attached to second computer

5. Second computer

The modems on either end of the connection must be able to understand each other. For this to occur, the modems must share common configurations and common protocols. ISPs provide modem configuration information to their subscribers to ensure that end-user configurations are compatible with the ISP modems.

Analog Modems

Analog modems are slow by network standards, but they are considerably faster than previous models. Until recently, most modems operated at 2400 bps or slower. Today's modems are 10 to 20 times faster.

Each possible modem speed is associated with a protocol. The current fastest modems use the V.90 protocol. Newer modems can also use older protocols so that they remain compatible with slower devices. When two modems connect, they negotiate a common protocol and the fastest connection speed the line signal quality permits.

Operators on either end may have to manually configure other modem parameters for the devices to communicate. These parameters include the following:

■ Data compression

■ Data flow (computer-to-modem speed)

■ Data flow (modem-to-modem speed)

■ Flow control

■ Error correction

■ Parity

■ Advanced Technology (AT) commands

Tip:AT commands are configuration and testing instructions between the modem and the computer. Some connections are only possible by running a string of AT commands when initializing the modem.

Integrated Services Digital Network (ISDN)

Virtually all of the main connections and switches within the telephone companies have been digital for years. The signal converts to analog from the last switch or transfer station to the end user. ISDN service requires digital service all the way to the end user.

ISDN interfaces are not really modems in the traditional sense. ISDN terminal adapters are devices that accept digital signals from a telephone line and translate them into digital data that are recognizable to a computer.

ISDN telephone lines deliver faster connections than analog connections. While anyone with a telephone has the connectivity needed for an analog modem, ISDN connections require digital telephone line hookups. ISDN is popular in some parts of the world but has never gained wide acceptance in the United States. Newer technologies like Digital Subscriber Lines (DSL) and cable modems offer faster, more convenient, and less expensive Internet access.

DSL

DSL is a telephone wire data delivery system that is rapidly growing in popularity. DSL technology sends digital data and analog data along the same telephone wire and does not require new telephone line connections. Digital information is separated from the analog signal at the point where the telephone wire connects to the house. From that point, the analog signal is passed into the network of telephone and other analog devices. The digital signal is routed to a DSL modem.

DSL modems (like ISDN modems) are not really modems in the sense of translating analog to digital information. DSL modems translate digital telephone signals into Ethernet packet information or frames as a single unit.

DSL modems connect to a computer NIC. DSL connection speeds vary according to the service level purchased, with top speeds of 9 Mbps for downstream traffic and from 32 Kbps to 1.5 Mbps for upstream traffic.

Cable Modem

The television cable industry has entered data delivery with cable modems. Similar to a telephone modem, which sends and receives signals over the telephone network to a PC, a cable modem sends and receives signals over a cable TV network. The important difference between telephone and cable TV networks is capacity.

Since telephone networks were built to carry only voice signals, the capacity or bandwidth is limited. Cable TV networks were designed to deliver full motion video and, as a result, have much greater bandwidth. This significantly greater bandwidth enables the cable TV network to deliver more information per second.

Because television cable is broadband transmission media, a cable modem has a tuner set to a specific frequency to which the digital data information is assigned. The modem translates the digital signal into Ethernet data for delivery to a NIC.

Tip: Cable modem service is typically less expensive than DSL service for the same level of connection speed. However, DSL bandwidth is dedicated and cable modem bandwidth is not. This means that the DSL customer is ensured throughput, while the cable modem subscriber will be sharing bandwidth. As subscriber traffic on cable modem services increases, the cable modem user will experience a decrease in throughput.

Network Firewalls

Any computer attached to a network is a potential target for hackers or crackers who attempt to access or vandalize other people's data. A hacker is an intrusive or unauthorized individual who is interested in gaining knowledge about a computer system and possibly using this knowledge for pranks. A cracker is an individual whose sole purpose is to sneak or break through security systems.

The first line of defense against these intruders is the installation of a firewall that represents the concept of a gatekeeper. A firewall detects and blocks uninvited access to a network or computer. Firewalls provide a variety of protection services that include the following:

- Allow only known trusted traffic onto a network

- Exclude the unknown and mistrusted from a network

- Detect certain types of suspicious activities and block access

A firewall may consist of inexpensive software solutions, similar to virus protection software, residing on host computers and operating unobtrusively in the background. At the other end of the spectrum, a firewall may also be very expensive hardware that guards an entire network.

Bandwidth Link Technologies

Organizations that need faster, more secure transmissions can use Digital Data Service (DDS) lines such as T1 and T3 connections, packet-switching technologies over wide areas networks such as X.25, and more advanced Wide Area Network (WAN) technologies with digital and fiber-optic media.

Networks can provide subscribers with the bandwidth they need with the following line connection technologies:

- T1 and E1 connections

- T3 and E3 connections

- X.25 protocols and packet-switching network

- Frame relay packet switching

- Asynchronous Transfer Mode (ATM) connections

- DSL

T1 and E1 Connections

T1 and E1 carriers are dedicated twisted-pair, coaxial cable, or fiber-optic media connections. They offer speed and flexibility at a price. The European equivalent of T1 is called E1 and is normally relegated to larger organizations because of its relatively high cost.

T1 connections are actually 24 64 Kbps channels delivered together for the combined connection speed of 1.5 Mbps. E1s are 32 channels for a combined connection speed of 2.048 Mbps. A device called a multiplexer can also divide the channels up for different purposes.

One common use of multiplexers is to divide a single T1 or E1 connection into data lines and voice lines. Because T1 and E1 connections support both data and voice, a medium-size business may lease a single connection and divide the bandwidth up among data and voice.

Reverse multiplexers aggregate channels. Using a reverse multiplexer, an organization with several individual 64 Kbps lines (typical of ISDN accounts) can combine them into a single higher speed connection. Multiplexers can also combine multiple T1s and E1s for very fast connections

Using T3 and E3 Connections

T3s and E3s are not merely the equivalent of three T1s or three E1s, as the name suggests. A T3 is the equivalent of 28 T1s with transmission speeds of 45 Mbps. A T3 connection is only delivered over fiber-optic cable. E3s are 16 E1s combined. E3s are usually delivered by fiber-optic cable, but they can use twisted pair. T3 or E3 connections are expensive, but they provide terrific throughput. Large companies, and businesses that generate a lot of network traffic such as Web hosting services, are candidates for T3s and E3s.

X.25 Technologies

X.25 is an older packet switching protocol dating back to 1974 that requires a dedicated X.25 line leased from a telephone company. A significant portion of the header information included in X.25 data packets were for error control because the telephone lines were not particularly reliable and generated a fair amount of corrupted datagrams. X.25 does a good job of detecting and correcting errors. However, the extra overhead needed to accomplish error detection and correction limits the maximum throughput to 64 Kbps.

Frame Relay

Frame relay is a packet-switching protocol based on X.25 but with less error control. As telephone lines improved, the need for extensive built-in error control has diminished. Frame relay takes advantage of low error rate telephone lines. Frame relay also introduced a technology called Permanent Virtual Circuit (PVC). PVCs allow a continuous open path between host and recipient. This speeds throughput by eliminating the need for switching calculations to accommodate each packet as it moves from destination to host. Frame relay can operate at speeds up to 1.5 Mbps.

ATM

ATM is a newer packet-switching technology that is capable of high-speed throughput. ATM can support bandwidth requirements of real-time audio and video over data lines. ATM achieves throughput speeds of up to 622 Mbps by including very little packet overhead. ATM sessions are created by sending one packet through the system to establish all of the routing information from host to recipient. That information is assigned a number, and subsequent packets only include the reference number. ATM has complicated implementation and is expensive to operate.

Network Operating Systems (NOS)

With the variety of business commerce available on the Internet today for both the business and home computer system, the NOS should best fit your business transmission needs and your cabling plan. Even with the growing popularity of peer-to-peer networks, client-server networks are more common. Network operations can run from a server, while other operations are stored on individual workstations.

The client-server model of the Web, however, takes advantage of the intelligence of the NOS on both sides of the network communication.

Network operating systems, such as UNIX and the Mac OS, include special functions to connect computers and devices to a LAN. The term NOS, however, generally means software which enhances a basic operating system and adds networking features.

In peer-to-peer networks, each computer has processing capabilities and can act as servers or workstations, using and providing resources as required. Some popular NOSs for include Novell Netware, Artisoft's LANtastic, Microsoft LAN Manager, and Windows NT 4.0 and Windows 2000. This is in contrast to server-based networks.

Server-based networks have one or more computers of special status as dedicated servers. Banyan VINES or Novell NetWare provide client-server or server-based operating systems. Application products to provide Internet functionality and address specific issues can enhance systems like Microsoft Windows NT.

Microsoft Internet Information Server (IIS), for example, allows Web site hosting. Any computer can be used as a Web server by installing server software and connecting the machine to the Internet. There are many Web server software applications, including public domain software from NCSA and Apache and more commercial packages from Microsoft, Netscape, and others.

Vocabulary

Review the following terms in preparation for the certification exam.

Term	Description
adapter	An adapter is the computer hardware interface to a network, also known as a network interface card (NIC), network adapter, or network card. It converts media signals into binary information that a computer recognizes.
address mask	Same as subnet mask; determines which part of the 32-bit binary IP address is the network ID information and which part is the host ID information.
analog	Signals with direct frequency and amplitude relationship with the source signal as in sound waves across telephone wires.
analog modem	Analog modems send information across wires by voltage modulation and receive similar information by demodulating carrier voltages.
asymmetrical	Sending and receiving data at different speeds.
AT	Advanced Technology commands are configuration and testing instructions between the modem and the computer.
ATM	Asynchronous Transfer Mode is a very fast packet-switching technology capable of quality real-time video transmission.
attenuation	A signal loss through media.

Term	Description
backbone	Primary conduit for an information system. Also called a trunk.
bandwidth	Amount of information a conduit can transmit over time.
baseband	Transmission that allows one signal at a time. Most communications among computers and local-area networks use baseband communications.
bridge	A hardware device that filters network traffic.
broadband	Type of data transmission in which a single medium (wire) can carry several channels at once.
broadcast storm	A self-perpetuating broadcast loop.
cable modem	Special tuner that detects digital information transmitted on a unique frequency on a TV coaxial broadband cable. It converts the information into Ethernet information and transmits it to a NIC attached to a computer.
cladding	Reflective covering that surrounds the glass core of a fiber-optic cable.
coax	Same as coaxial.
coaxial	Cabling (also called coax) that consists of one solid copper core which is surrounded by insulation, a braided metal shielding, and a jacket. The inner insulation ensures that no signals can pass from the copper core and no signals from outside the insulation can pass into the copper core. There are thick and thin types of coaxial cable.

Term	Description
conduit	A physical or virtual pipe through which information travels.
cracker	An individual whose sole purpose is to sneak or break through security systems.
cross-talk	Radio frequency signal overflow from one line to another.
datagram	In IP networks, a piece of a message that contains the destination address in addition to the data.
digital	Numerical representation of signals, such as the computer's binary-based digits or bits of 0 and 1.
down-link	Usually refers to receiving a satellite transmission.
DSL	Digital Subscriber Line is a system of high-speed data, which co-exists with analog signals on telephone lines, and delivers up to T1 speeds to home and business users.
EMI	Electromagnetic Interference is a byproduct of electricity moving through wire.
Ethernet	Ethernet is a Local Area Network (LAN) system developed by the Xerox Corporation in 1976. The IEEE Ethernet/ 802.3 standard for the 10- or 100-Mbps transmission for hardware and data packet construction specifications was derived from Ethernet.
fiber-optic cable	A cable that uses glass strands and light pulses instead of electrical signals to transmit data.
firewall	Security systems that protect computers and networks from outside hackers.

Term	Description
frame relay	Packet-switching technology based on X.25 with less error control and faster speeds.
gateway	Hardware or software setup that translates between two dissimilar protocols and performs conversion service for data.
Gbps	The abbreviation for Gigabits Per Second. Gbps is a measurement of data transfer speed on a network, in multiples of 1,073,741,824 (2^{30}) bits.
gigabyte	Written in powers of 2, a gigabyte is (2^{30}) or 1,073,741,824 bytes.
hacker	An intrusive individual who is interested in gaining knowledge about computer systems and possibly using this knowledge for pranks.
hop	The path that data travel from one router to the next.
HTML	HyperText Markup Language is the markup language used for documents on the World Wide Web.
hub	Hardware that splits a network signal and connects networks together.
IP address	An Internet Protocol (IP) address is a unique 32-bit number that identifies a computer connected to the Internet and other Internet hosts to enable communication through packet transfers.
ISDN	Integrated Services Digital Network is a high-speed digital communications network, which evolved from existing telephone services.

Term	Description
ISDN terminal adapter	Integrated Services Digital Network terminal adapters are devices that accept digital signals from a telephone line and translate them into digital data that is recognizable to a computer.
jitter	Jitter is an annoying and perceptible variation in the time it takes various workstations to respond to messages.
Kbps	Kilobits Per Second.
MAC	Media Access Control manages access to the physical network, delimits datagrams, and handles error control.
Mb	Abbreviation for Megabit (1,048,576 bits (2^{20})), sometimes referred to as 1 million bits.
Mbps	Abbreviation for Megabits Per Second.
Megabit	A Megabit is a measurement of storage capacity equal to about 1 million bits or 1,048,576 bits (2^{20}).
modem	Originally referred to a device that MOdulated and DEModulated digital information across telephone lines. Now used to describe a wide variety of data interfaces for computers.
multiplexer	A device that can divide a single T1 or E1 connection into data lines and voice lines.
NetBEUI	NetBIOS Enhanced User Interface is a simple fast network protocol that is not routable.
network adapter	Another name for Network Interface Card (NIC).

Term	Description
NIC	A Network Interface Card is an expansion card or other device that provides network access to a computer or other device, such as a printer. NICs mediate between the computer and the physical media.
node	A device, such as a client computer, server, or shared printer that connects to the network and communicates with other network devices.
packet	A unit of transmitted data that consists of binary digits represented by data and a header. A header contains an identification number, source and destination addresses, and sometimes error-control data.
port	A port on the Internet his a logical channel through which data flows for decoding and routing to destinations. Internet service applications for routing and decoding are assigned specific logical port numbers.
PSTN	Public Switched Telephone Network is the telephone system that carries analog voice data.
repeater	Repeaters are simple hardware devices that receive digital information, regenerate the signal, and pass it along.
router	Any device having multiple NICs that filter, forward, and redirect network traffic.
segment	Connected devices not separated by a bridge or a router.
source-route bridge	Connect token-ring networks, a network technology developed by IBM.

Term	Description
Spanning Tree Algorithm	A standard that establishes protocols for network bridges and is responsible for controlling broadcast storms.
STP	Shielded Twisted-Pair cable.
subnet	A local area network (LAN) that has been divided into separate network segments. Routers can divide LANs into subnets and transfer data among subnets.
subnet mask	The subnet mask, or address mask, determines which part of the 32-bit binary IP address is the network ID information and which part is the host ID information.
switch	A hub with bridge functionality for each port.
T1	High-speed carrier with 24 64-Kbps channels combined into one 1.5-Mbps connection.
T3	High-speed carrier that transmits at 45-Mbps connections.
thicknet	A thick type of coaxial cable that is somewhat rigid and measures about 0.5 inch in diameter with a thick copper core.
thinnet	A thin type of coaxial cable that is flexible and measures about 0.25 inch thick in diameter.
throughput	The rate at which data are transferred on a network and measured as the number of transmitted bits per second (bps).
translational bridge	Connect different types of networks, such as TCP/IP and token-ring networks.
up-link	Usually refers to sending data to a satellite receiver.
UTP	Unshielded Twisted-Pair cable.
Web page	A document on the World Wide Web that consists of a HTML file with files for graphics and scripts.
X.25	Packet-switching technology with robust error control and maximum connection speeds of 64 Kbps.

In Brief

If you want to...	Then do this...
Get near-Internet backbone speeds from buildings not directly connected to the fiber-optic trunk	Connect with a terrestrial microwave system.
Connect to the Internet at high speeds from residential or rural environments	Use satellite connections to the Internet.
Have the fastest possible Internet connection	Connect through fiber-optic cable to the Internet backbone using ATM.
Connect multiple devices on the same subnet with minimum configuration	Use a hub to connect the devices.
Connect network segments with filtering features to isolate network traffic	Use a bridge to connect the network segments with filters to isolate the traffic.
Connect subnets to other subnets and use redirecting services	Use a router to connect subnets and redirect connections.
Connect multiple devices on the same subnet and direct traffic only to the intended recipient	Use a switch to connect device and direct traffic to specific recipients.
Connect a computer to a network	Use an adapter.
Configure a modem with line commands	Use AT command instructions.

If you want to...	Then do this...
Connect over digital telephone lines for faster connections	Use an ISDN modem.
Connect at fast speeds over analog telephone lines with a digital sub-carrier	Use a DSL modem.
Connect at fast speeds over TV cable lines	Use a cable modem.
Protect your computer or network against hackers	Use a firewall with appropriate software or hardware protection.
Connect at the fastest possible speed over copper twisted-pair lines	Use a T1 or E1 carrier connections.
Connect over extremely fast lines	Use T3 or E3 carrier connections.
Connect at the fastest speeds possible	Use ATM technology and fiber-optic cable.

Lesson 5 Activities

Complete the following activities to prepare for the certification exam.

1. Name some advantages and disadvantages to Internet access using terrestrial microwave connections.

2. Describe the data path of uplink and downlink information using current consumer satellite connection technology to the Internet.

3. What are the advantages and disadvantages of using fiber-optic cable?

4. Describe the difference between an active and passive hub.

5. Describe how bridges differ from repeaters.

6. Explain the primary features and services of a router.

7. Explain the difference between a hub and a switch.

8. What is meant by the term network backbone?

9. Name and briefly describe four different types of modems.

10. Briefly explain the process of protecting a network with a firewall.

Answers to Lesson 5 Activities

1. A terrestrial microwave Internet connection is nearly as fast as a direct fiber-optic link to the Internet backbone. This type of link can work up to a mile away from a backbone portal. Terrestrial microwave connections are expensive, require rooftop access to tall buildings, are affected by weather, and are potentially dangerous.

2. With today's consumer-grade satellite Internet services, the uplink to the service is via a traditional dial-up account on telephone wires. The pointing and choosing information is sent to the ISP like any traditional dial-up service. The downlink results, the Web page loads, and file download are sent to a small TV satellite-type dish at the user's site. That signal is integrated with the user's Internet session at speeds of up to 400 Kbps.

3. Fiber-optic cable is the fastest technology available for transmitting TCP/IP traffic. It has very low attenuation over distance and creates no EMI. Fiber-optic cable is expensive and difficult to work with.

4. A passive hub is essentially a signal splitter. The signal strength is cut in half every time it is split. Passive hubs create highly attenuated systems. An active hub repeats the signal across every port, so that the split signal is procreated along wires as if it originated at the hub. Active hubs increase the line distance a signal can travel, as will any repeater.

5. A repeater is a purely hardware device with no higher layer functionality. A repeater senses all types of IP traffic and regenerates the signal and sends the traffic on its way. Repeaters correct the effects of attenuation so that line lengths can be extended indefinitely. A bridge has repeater functionality and some filtering capabilities. Bridges have internal tables of MAC address information for the network segments they span. Bridges will filter cross-segment traffic for all datagrams that are actually addressed to a local segment. This keeps local traffic local and reduces overall network traffic. Bridges will pass all broadcast traffic.

6. A router filters and redirects network traffic. Routers sense traffic on one NIC and determine whether to forward or not to forward the traffic to another NIC. Routers use tables of IP addresses to compute the best path to forward a datagram to a destination.

7. A hub is a purely physical device, while a switch provides higher layer services. A switch is a multi-port bridge. Switches are very efficient at reducing network congestion for a busy network segment.

8. A network backbone (or trunk) is the primary physical conduit of information for a system. The Internet backbone is made of very high-speed fiber-optic cable that connects large cities, government and research facilities, and major universities.

9. An analog modem is a device that senses the modulated waveforms of computer information which are sent on traditional telephone lines. This information is then translated into digital information understandable to a computer. An ISDN modem receives digital information directly from the telephone company on a dedicated phone line and translates the information into a dataform compatible with computers. DSL modems sense a digital subcarrier on traditional telephone lines and translate the information into Ethernet signals compatible with any Ethernet network. Cable modems tune to a specific frequency on a TV cable and sense a digital carrier. That signal is translated into Ethernet information and is sent to a computer NIC or any Ethernet network.

10. Firewalls protect computers or computer networks by a combination of services. Firewalls only permit known friendly IP traffic through; they specifically exclude known unfriendly IP traffic, and they monitor and block suspicious IP activity.

Lesson 5 Quiz

These questions test your knowledge of features, vocabulary, procedures, and syntax.

1. Which of the following are not advantages to terrestrial microwave Internet connections?

    A. High-speed Internet access

    B. Synchronous data flow

    C. Virtually unlimited range from transmitter to receiver

    D. Relatively low cost

2. Who are good candidates for Internet Satellite service?

    A. Anybody with cable modem or DSL access

    B. Companies in large cities

    C. Rural customers with low-quality telephone connections

    D. Government agencies

3. Which of the following are advantages to fiber-optic cable connections?

    A. Very high levels of EMI transmission

    B. Very low levels of attenuation

    C. Very high levels of attenuation

    D. Ease of installation

4. Which of the following are true statements about switches?

    A. Switches are low-cost alternatives to hubs

    B. Switches have bridge functionality

    C. Switches filter broadcast traffic

    D. Switches are multi-port routers

5. In which situation would a router be an appropriate solution?

   A. Reducing network congestion within a network segment

   B. Connecting two network segments into one logical segment

   C. Connecting two subnets and filtering traffic between the two

   D. Connecting two network segments and filtering traffic between the two

6. Which of the following is not a use for a gateway?

   A. Connecting dissimilar networks

   B. Translating network protocols

   C. Translating application file formats

   D. Bridging internetworks across InterNIC

7. What type of modem tunes to a specific frequency to detect a digital carrier signal?

   A. Analog

   B. Cable

   C. ISDN

   D. ADSL

8. Firewalls offer which of the following services?

   A. Network protection from computer viruses

   B. Network protection from hackers

   C. Detection and prevention of broadcast storms

   D. Virtual Private Networks (VPN)

9. Which is the fastest connection?

   A. T1

   B. E3

   C. X.25

   D. ATM

10. What is an advantage to X.25 connections?

   A. Extremely high speed

   B. Wide spread availability

   C. Robust error control

   D. Asynchronous connections

Answers to Lesson 5 Quiz

1. Answer C is correct. The range from transmitter to receiver is not virtually unlimited. In fact, limited distance is a disadvantage of terrestrial microwave connections.

   Answer D is correct. Relatively low cost is not an advantage of terrestrial microwave connections. High cost is a disadvantage of terrestrial microwave connections.

   Answers A and B are incorrect. High-speed Internet access and synchronous data flow are not disadvantages but advantages of terrestrial microwave connections.

2. Answer C is correct. Rural customers with low-quality telephone connections are good candidates for Internet Satellite service.

   Answer A is incorrect. Cable modems and DSL connections are better solutions in terms of cost and speed than satellite connections.

   Answers B and D are incorrect. Either companies in large cities or government agencies and organizations will have access to better Internet connection solutions than consumer satellite services.

3. Answer B is correct. Very low levels of attenuation occur in fiber-optic cable connections.

   Answers A, C and D are incorrect. Fiber-optic cable connections produce no EMI, do not have high levels of signal attenuation, and are not easy to install.

4. Answer B is correct. Switches have bridge functionality.

   Answers A, C, and D are incorrect. Switches are not low-cost alternatives to hubs. They are more expensive than hubs, do not filter broadcast traffic, and are multi-port bridges, not routers.

5. Answer C is correct. Routers connect subnets and filter traffic.

   A is incorrect. A router would not be the best solution for reducing network congestion within a network segment. The best way to reduce traffic congestion within a segment is to use a switch.

   Answers B and D are incorrect. Connecting two network segments into one logical segment and connecting two network segments and filtering traffic between them are services best provided by a bridge.

6. Answer D is correct. A gateway does not bridge traffic across InterNIC.

Answers A, B, and C are incorrect. Gateways connect dissimilar networks, translate network protocols, and translate application file formats.

7.   Answer B is correct. A cable modem tunes to a specific frequency to detect a digital carrier signal.

Answers A, C, and D are incorrect. Analog modems, ISDN modems, and ADSL connections do not tune to frequencies to detect a digital carrier signal.

8.   Answer B is correct. Firewalls offer network protection from hackers.

Answers A, C and D are incorrect because firewalls do not offer services to protect against computer viruses, nor do they detect or prevent broadcast storms or provide VPN.

9.   Answer D is correct. ATM is the fastest connection.

Answers A, B, and C are incorrect. T1, E3, and X.25 connections are not as fast as ATM.

10. Answer C is correct. Robust error control is an advantage of X.25 connections.

Answers A, B, and D are incorrect. The X.25 packet switching connection is relatively slow, only available through leased lines from telephone companies and asynchronous connections are not supported by X.25 (and they are not an advantage in any event).

Lesson 6: Client Setup

This lesson gives you the concepts necessary to connect a computer to remote networks, including the Internet. The material should enable you to explain remote control and remote access, how to configure a Web browser and set its cache, and understand software patches and updates. You will also see the differences in electronic mail systems, methods to connect to legacy mainframe systems, and learn to troubleshoot configuration problems.

After completing this lesson, you should have a better understanding of the following topics:

- Network Adapters
- Remote Access Service (RAS) and Dial-Up Networking (DUN)
- Transmission Control Protocol/Internet Protocol (TCP/IP) Configurations
- Browser Configuration
- Software Version Control
- E-mail Variations
- Legacy Clients Connections
- Troubleshooting Client Setup

Network Adapters

A network adapter must be installed in your computer before you can connect to a local or remote network. A modem (MOdulator-DEModulator) is a type of network adapter for connecting to remote networks by telephone line. A Network Interface Card (NIC) is another type of network adapter that makes direct network connections, such as to a Local Area Network (LAN). If your computer does not use a NIC to attach to a network, you must use a modem to make remote network connections.

Modem Data Transfer Rates

Modems are the most common devices to connect two computers by telephone line. The speed, or data transfer rate, of modems has increased over the years to the point that the common maximum data transfer rate today is 56,000 Bits Per Second (bps) or 56 Kilobits Per Second (Kbps).

 Tip: The Public Switched Telephone Network (PSTN) is also known as Plain Old Telephone System (POTS).

A new connection technology that also uses the POTS is called Asymmetric Dedicated Subscriber Line (ADSL). This high-speed modem is popular because it provides high quality connections at faster data transfer rates to homes and businesses at reasonable costs. Data transfer rates for ADSL modems range from 1.5 to 9 Megabits Per Second (Mbps) when receiving data (download stream rate) to as high as 16 to 640 Kbps when sending data (upstream rate).

ADSL is available in many areas of most major cities in the U.S. ADSL is requiring telephone companies to upgrade their local switching hubs with equipment that supports ADSL. As consumer demand for faster Internet connections increases, new equipment installations at local switching hubs will continue to support the adoption of ADSL.

Although it is possible to configure an ADSL modem for use through a dial-up connection, most people configure their ADSL modems to maintain a continuous connection to an Internet access server. Unlike regular dial-up connections, continuous ADSL connections do not interrupt the normal use of your telephone. This permits you to simultaneously browse the Web, upload or download files, send and receive e-mail, and talk on your telephone.

Installing a Modem

Modems are the most common network adapters and must be installed before you can establish remote network connections. This procedure assumes you are using a standard 56 Kbps modem. If you have not already installed the modem, you need to do so.

To manually install a modem in Windows 95 or 98, follow these steps:

1. Install the modem card in an empty slot inside your computer according to the manufacturer's directions and then re-boot your computer.

2. If Windows does not detect and configure the modem automatically during the boot-up process, then from the Task bar choose Start, Settings, Control Panel and then select Modems.

3. Follow the modem installation instructions displayed in the Wizard (Figure 6.1).

4. If your modem is not in the manufacturer's listing, use the software disk that came with the modem to install the necessary drivers.

5. After the drivers are installed, choose Finish.

Figure 6.1 Install New Modem Wizard

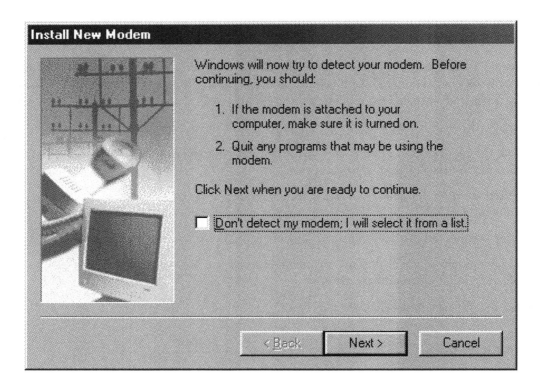

Remote Access Server (RAS) and Dial-Up Networking (DUN)

There are two different protocols you must use for communicating with remote networks when using modems. The first protocol is for establishing a connection from your modem to a remote modem using PSTN. Modems use these protocols to recognize each other (handshake) and establish a connection.

After the modems establish a connection, a different set of protocols allows your computer to access the remote network and become a client on that network. The following sections discuss the differences between the protocols for modem connections through telephone lines and protocols for network access.

Setting Up DUN Protocols

This section describes how to install, set up and configure RAS and DUN and to connect your system to remote network servers, including those of Internet Service Providers (ISPs).

Installing DUN

DUN is a feature built into Windows 9x and Windows NT 4.0 workstations. DUN is typically installed as part of the initial installation of Windows, but you can install it later from the Control Panel through the Add/Remove Programs option.

Dial-Up Networking uses all the major telephone line and network protocols to enable users to log onto various remote networks using a modem. If you do not see the Dial-Up Networking folder icon in My Computer, you need to install it. Refer to Figure 6.2, and then follow these steps to install DUN:

1. From **Control Panel**, choose **Add/Remove programs**.

2. Choose **Windows Setup** and then select **Communications** (not the check box).

3. Choose **Details** and then select **Dial-up Networking** (put a check in the box).

4. Click **OK** and then reboot the computer if prompted.

Figure 6.2 DUN Installation

Creating DUN Profiles

You can create and save separate dial-up configuration profiles, one for each ISP, such as America Online, Prodigy, or CompuServe.

Each ISP provides the following account information:

■ Your username

- Password

- Telephone numbers to their dial-in (RAS) server(s)

If not dynamically assigned, your ISP can assign the following:

- IP address of your computer

- Primary and secondary Domain Name Server (DNS) addresses

- A gateway address

- E-mail and News server addresses.

Creating a DUN Profile with a Wizard

Each DUN connection profile you create can have its own type of server connection. Use the Make a New Connection Wizard (Figure 6.3) and repeat the following steps to create a basic profile for each ISP or online service to which you subscribe to:

1. From My Computer, choose **Dial-Up Networking**.

2. Select **Make a New Connection** and then type a descriptive name for the connection such as: **My Primary ISP**

3. Choose **Configure** and then from the Port pull-down menu, select the Serial Communication Port (COM) port to which your modem is attached.

4. Choose **Maximum speed** and then select a modem speed.

5. Click **OK**, select **Next**, and then choose **Finish**.

Configuring DUN Profiles

You can configure each basic DUN profile you create to use a specific line connection and networking protocol. Follow the steps for configuring each protocol. Repeat the basic steps for each different profile but choose the applicable line and network protocols.

Figure 6.3 Make New Connection Wizard

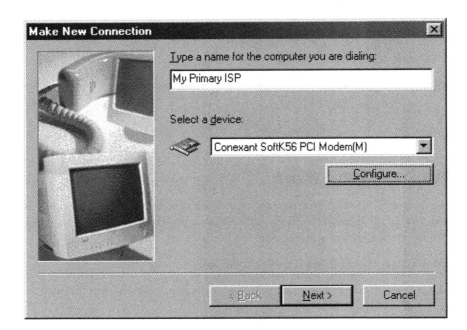

Configuring Point-to-Point Protocol (PPP)

This is the most common protocol for connecting to the Internet. To configure the profile to use the PPP line connection and the Transmission Control Protocol/Internet Protocol (TCP/IP) network protocol, follow these steps:

1. Choose **My Computer,** select **Dial-Up Networking** and then select the profile you created (such as My Primary ISP).

2. Right-click to display **Properties**, and then select **Server Types**.

3. Within **PPP: Internet, Windows NT Server, Windows 98** is displayed in the pull-down menu as the default (Figure 6.4).

4. Choose the logon options you want to use, such as data compression, password encryption, data encryption, and record a log file.

5. Under **Allowed**, choose the protocol options you want to enable (choosing all the options is typical.).

6. Choose **TCP/IP Settings** to configure the network access settings.

7. Unless your ISP tells you otherwise, choose **Server assigned IP address**, **Server assigned name server addresses** (often you will need to specify the Primary and Secondary DNS addresses), **Use IP header compression**, and **Use default gateway on remote network** options (Figure 6.5).

8. If your ISP assigns you a static IP address, select **Specify an IP address** and then enter the address in the spaces provided.

9. Click **OK**.

Figure 6.4 DUN Configurations

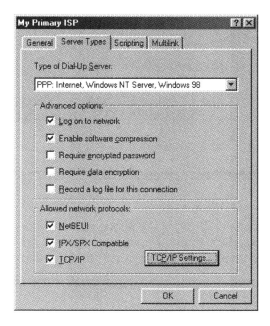

Figure 6.5 TCP/IP Settings

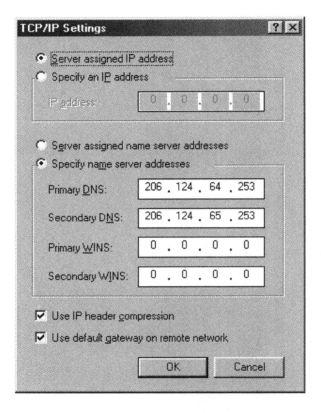

 Note: A Point Of Presence (POP) is the phone number your computer dials to access the modem on an ISP's Internet connection server. An ISP provides many POPs so that users can make a local call to gain Internet access.

Point-to-Point Tunneling Protocol (PPTP)

PPTP is a more secure version of PPP which is supported by Windows 98, Windows NT 4.0, and Windows 2000. This connection supports the encryption and compression of all transmitted data. PPTP requires use of a PPTP network adapter to connect to a remote tunnel server. Microsoft supplies a software-style network adapter for PPTP connections to Virtual Private Networks (VPN).

Tunneling uses one protocol inside another protocol to connect two networks through a third intermediate network. Once connected, PPTP supports all the same network protocols as PPP (TCP/IP, Internetwork Packet Exchange/Sequenced Packet Exchange (IPX/SPX), NetBEUI, etc.) to access the network.

Configuring PPTP

Follow these steps to configure your connection for a PPTP-supported remote server:

1. From **My Computer**, choose **Dial-Up Networking** and then select the profile that requires a PPTP server connection (Figure 6.6).

2. Right-click to display **Properties**, and then choose the **PPTP VPN** protocol.

3. Under **Allowed**, choose the network access protocol options you want to enable.

4. Choose **TCP/IP Settings**.

5. Set you options you want to use and then click **OK**.

Figure 6.6 Select Network Adapters for VPN

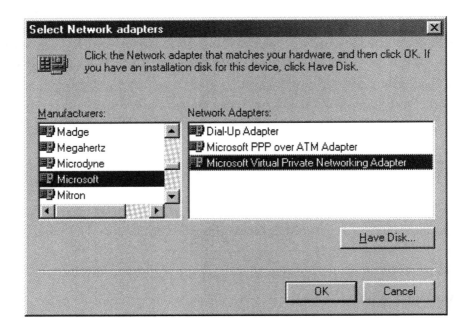

Configuring the Serial Line Interface Protocol (SLIP)

SLIP is the line connection to use with TCP/IP for remote access to UNIX Operating System (OS) networks. Follow these steps to configure the SLIP with TCP/IP connection:

1. From **My Computer, Dial-Up Networking**, select the profile to use for connection to a UNIX system.

2. Right-click to display **Properties**, and then choose **Server Types**.

3. Choose the **SLIP: UNIX Connection** listing so it appears in the pull-down menu window.

4. Choose the enabled logon check box options you want to use (ask your ISP for help).

5. Under **Allowed**, choose the available network protocols you want to enable.

6. Choose **TCP/IP Settings**, and then select your configuration options.

7. If a logon script is required, select **Script** and configure a logon script (ask your ISP for help).

8. Choose **Security**, and then select your security levels.

9. Click **OK**.

Configuring Compressed Serial Line Interface Protocol (CSLIP)

CSLIP is the same as SLIP, but it supports IP header compression. TCP/IP utilizes CSLIP for remote access to UNIX OS networks. Follow these steps to configure the CSLIP with TCP/IP connection:

1. Choose the DUN connection you created for a CSLIP-supported server and right-click to display the pop-up menu. Select **Properties**.

2. Choose **Server Types**, and from **Connection Settings**, select **CSLIP** from the drop-down menu.

3. Choose the enabled logon check box options you want to use.

4. Under **Allowed**, choose the available network protocol options you want to use. (SLIP and CSLIP line protocols require that the server and client both use TCP/IP. CSLIP also uses compressed IP header information).

5. Choose **TCP/IP Settings** and then specify an IP address.

6. Type your server address and DNS numbers if provided by your ISP.

7. Click **OK**.

Configuring Novell Interface Protocol (NRN)

1. Choose the DUN connection you created for a Novell-supported server and right-click to display **Properties**.

2. Choose **Server Types**.

3. From **Connection Settings**, choose **NRN NetWare Connect**, and then select the enabled logon check box options you want to use.

4. Under **Allowed**, choose the available network protocol options you want to use.

5. Choose **TCP/IP Settings** and then specify and IP address, server name and DNS specifications.

6. Click **OK**.

 Note: The SLIP protocol software for connecting a Windows 95 computer to a UNIX remote access server is only on the CD version of Windows 95, not the floppy disk version.

TCP/IP Network Protocol Configurations

If your computer connects to a LAN using a NIC, then you need to configure the NIC so it can communicate with the network. Although TCP/IP is the protocol for connection to the Internet and an Intranet Web server, you can use other protocols on networks to communicate in a heterogeneous computing environment.

A large company may use Novell, UNIX or other operating systems in addition to Windows NT and Windows 9x. To connect these networks together to share information requires the use of protocols those systems can understand. The following section briefly discusses how to configure TCP/IP and the other most widely used protocols for networking behind a proxy server firewall. Proxy servers' firewalls provide security to protect internal networks from attacks coming through external networks, such as the Internet.

Installing Network Adapters, Clients, Protocols, and Services on Windows 9x and Windows NT Workstations

You can install network protocol components to your computer, however, if this is the first install of any networking device, the Configuration list box will be empty. Figure 6.7 shows how to select the network component type.

Figure 6.7 Select Network Component Type

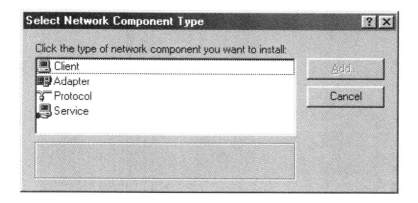

Installing Microsoft Network Adapter

To Install the Microsoft Dial-Up Adapter Network Component, follow these steps:

1. From **Control Panel**, choose **Network**.

2. Choose **Configuration**, and then select **Add**.

3. From **Select Network Components**, choose **Adapter**. Refer to Figure 6.8.

4. From the Manufacturer's list, choose **Microsoft**.

5. From **Network Adapters**, choose Dial-Up Adapter, and then click **OK**.

Figure 6.8 Microsoft Dial-Up Network Adapter

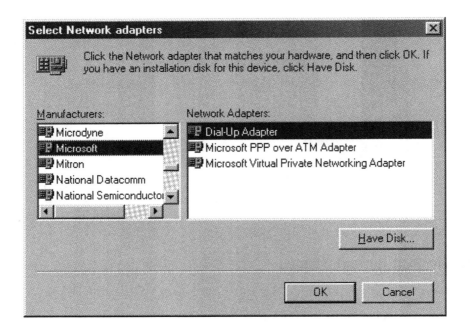

Installing Microsoft Network Client

Follow the steps below to install a Microsoft Network Client.

1. From **Control Panel**, choose **Network, Configuration,** and then select **Add**.

2. From **Select Network Components**, choose **Client** and then select **Add**.

3. From the Manufacturer's list, choose **Microsoft**, select **Client for Microsoft Networks** and then click **OK** (Figure 6.9).

Figure 6.9 Select Network Protocol

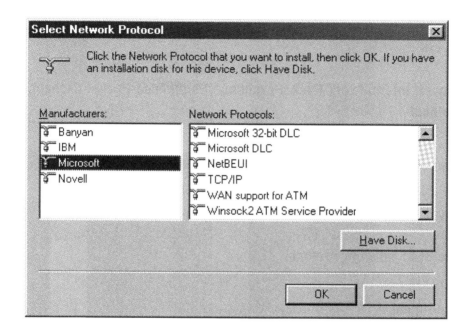

Installing Network Client for NetWare Networks

To install a network client for NetWare networks, follow these steps:

1. From **Control Panel**, choose **Network**, **Configuration**, and then select **Add**.

2. From **Select Network Components**, choose **Client** and then select **Add**.

3. From the Manufacturer's list, choose **Microsoft**, select **Client for NetWare Networks** and then click **OK**.

Installing TCP/IP Network Protocol

To install TCP/IP Network Protocol, follow these steps:

1. From **Control Panel**, choose **Network, Configuration**, and then select **Add**.

2. From **Select Network Components**, choose **Protocol**.

3. From the Manufacturers list choose **Microsoft**, select **TCP/IP** from **Network Protocols** and then click **OK**.

Installing Novell Internetwork Packet Exchange/Sequenced Packet Exchange (IPX/SPX) Network Protocol

To install IPX/SPX, follow these steps:

1. From **Control Panel**, choose **Network, Configuration**, and then select **Add**.

2. From **Select Network Components**, choose **Protocol**.

3. , choose **Microsoft**, select **IPX/SPX-compatible Protocol** and then click **OK**.

Installing NetBEUI Network Protocol

To install NetBEUI, follow these steps:

1. From **Control Panel**, choose **Network, Configuration**, and then select **Add**.

2. From **Select Network Components**, choose **Protocol**.

3. From the Manufacturer's list, choose **Microsoft**, select **NetBEUI** and then click **OK**.

Installing Network Service Components

To install network service components, follow these steps:

1. From **Select Network Components**, choose **Service** and then select **Add**.

2. Choose **File and printer sharing for Microsoft Networks** and then click **OK**.

3. Click **OK** again.

VPNs

VPNs can save companies the cost of long distance charges since these secure networks can be accessed by employees through the Internet rather than by using remote dial-up through telephone lines.

Installing Microsoft VPN Networking Dial-Up Adapter

This type of connection requires a connection to your ISP and a separate connection to the VPN tunnel server. However, if you are using PPTP to connect directly to a PPTP server through the Internet, only one connection is necessary.

To install a VPN networking dial-up adapter, follow these steps:

1. From the **Control Panel**, choose **Network**.

2. From **Select Network Adapters** (Figure 6.10) locate the **Dial-Up Adapter** in the installed components list and then select **Add**.

3. Choose **Adapter** and then select **Add**.

4. Choose **Microsoft** from the manufacturer's list.

5. Choose **Microsoft Virtual Private Networking Adapter** and then select **Add**.

6. Click **OK** and reboot the computer if prompted.

Figure 6.10 Microsoft VPN

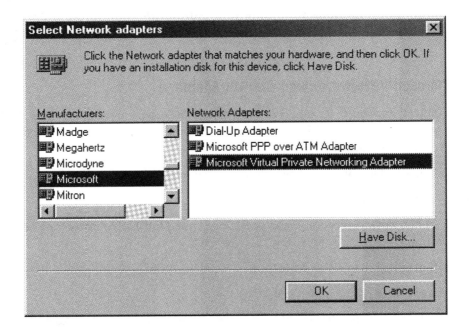

Dial-in Using PPTP and VPN

Although you make two connections with this arrangement, once both connections are established, it is like dialing directly into the PPTP server. You are using the Internet to access your company server with its file and printer resources.

To connect using your ISP and VPN DUN profiles, follow these steps:

1. From **My Computer, Dial-Up Networking**, choose the profile for your ISP connection.

2. Type your Internet account username and password.

3. Choose **Connect**.

4. Once connected to the ISP, choose **My Computer, Dial-Up Networking** and select the profile for the PPTP server connection.

5. Type the appropriate username and password.

6. Choose **Connect**.

Web Browser Configuration

The introduction of graphical Web browsers has sparked a tremendous public interest in the Internet. Many browsers are able to perform a number of tasks that once required separate tools. Today, you can browse Web pages, upload and download files from Web sites and send and receive e-mail all using your Web browser.

Customizing your Web browser allows you to:

■ Configure the proxy server settings in Internet Explorer and Netscape

■ Set and clear the cache in Internet Explorer and Netscape

■ Configure Multipurpose Internet Mail Extensions (MIME)

■ Enable and disable cookies

Proxy Servers and Web Browsers

Proxy servers allow multiple computers to share a single Internet connection. Most major corporations use one or more proxy servers to provide Internet access for their employees.

In addition to enabling access to the external Internet from a corporate intranet, most proxy servers also prevent unauthorized access of the intranet from the Internet. Most proxy servers are not full-featured firewalls, which are designed specifically to keep out unauthorized users. However, many of the higher-end (and more expensive) proxy server packages also include full firewall features and security.

When using proxy servers on an intranet, you must configure the intranet Web browsers to send all Internet requests through the proxy servers. Otherwise, no user will be able to access the Internet.

Configuring Internet Explorer's Proxy Server Settings

To configure the proxy server settings in Internet Explorer 5, which allows access to Internet sites outside a company firewall, follow these steps:

1. From the **Internet Explorer** menu bar, choose **Tools, Internet Options, Connections** and then select **LAN Settings**.

2. Choose the **Use a proxy server** option.

3. From **Automatic Proxy Settings**, type the URL or IP address as provided by your system administrator, such as: **www.proxy.yourbiz.com**.

4. Type a Port number, such as **31540**.

5. To manually set separate proxy addresses for HTTP, FTP, Gopher, WAIS, and Socks, choose **Advanced**, and then type the appropriate address and port number for each proxy server (Figure 6.11).

Figure 6.11 Manual Proxy Configuration

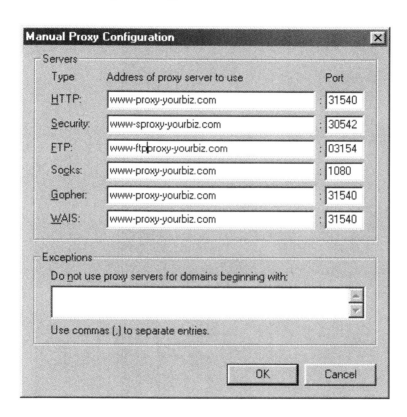

Configuring Netscape Communicator's Proxy Server Settings

To configure the proxy server settings in Netscape Communicator so you can access Internet sites outside your company firewall, you must provide the appropriate addresses and port numbers from your System Administrator.

Follow these steps to configure Netscape proxy server settings:

1. From the **Netscape Communicator** toolbar, choose **Edit**, **Preferences**, **Advanced**, and then select **Proxies**.

2. If you choose Automatic proxy configuration, type the appropriate http:// address and port number in the space provided like this: Address: www-proxy-yourcompany.com Port:31540

3. If you choose **Manual proxy configuration**, choose **View**.

4. Type an address and port number for each proxy server (Figure 6.12).

5. Click **OK**.

Figure 6.12 Netscape Communicator Proxy Settings

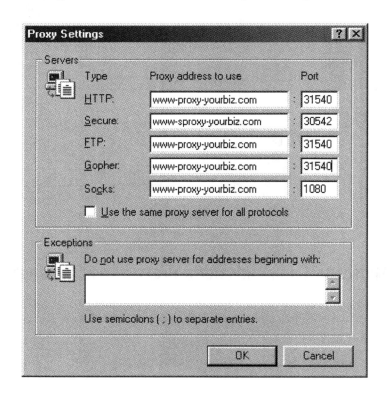

Web Browser Cache

Your browser stores recently viewed Web pages and files in storage areas called cache. The use of cache reduces the amount of Internet traffic by retrieving recently viewed material from these locations instead of repeatedly requesting and downloading Web pages from their original locations. Storage locations for cache are often configured to use portions of Random Access Memory (RAM), also called virtual memory.

Setting Cache Size in Internet Explorer

Internet Explorer makes its primary hard disk cache storage area in the Temporary Internet Files folder under the Windows folder. Follow these steps to set cache size:

1. From the **Internet Explorer** toolbar, choose **Tools, Internet Options** and then select **Settings**.

2. Choose how often you want the stored pages updated.

3. Select the slider and adjust the amount of hard disk space you want to reserve for cache (Figure 6.13).

4. Click **OK**.

Figure 6.13 Internet Explorer Cache Settings

Clearing All Files from Cache in Internet Explorer

To clear the entire hard disk cache from the Internet Explorer browser, follow these steps:

1. From the **Internet Explorer** toolbar, choose **Tools** and then select **Internet Options**.

2. Locate and choose **Delete Files** as shown in Figure 6.14.

3. Click **OK**.

Figure 6.14 Internet Explorer Cache Clearing

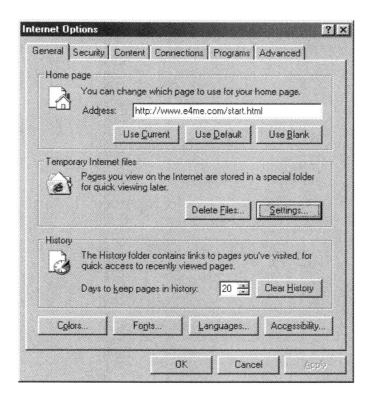

Clearing Individual Files from Internet Explorer Cache

If you would rather remove individual files from the hard disk cache in Internet Explorer, follow these steps:

1. From the **Internet Explorer** toolbar, choose **Tools, Internet Options** and then select **Settings**.

2. Choose **View** Files (Figure 6.15).

3. Hold down the **Control** (Ctrl) key on your keyboard, while using the left mouse button to select each file you want to remove from the list box.

4. After you select the files, simultaneously release the Ctrl key and the left mouse button.

5. Press the **Delete** key on your keyboard to delete the files.

Clearing History Files from Internet Explorer Cache

To clear all the History files from your browser's hard disk History cache, follow these steps:

1. From the **Internet Explorer** toolbar, choose **Tools, Internet Options**, and then select **Locate History**.

2. Choose **Clear History**, and then click **OK**.

Figure 6.15 Clear Individual Files from Internet Explorer Cache

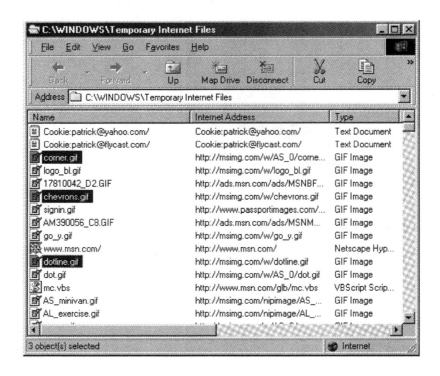

Setting and Clearing Netscape Communicator Cache

To clear the virtual and hard disk cache in Netscape Communicator, follow these steps:

1. From the **Netscape Communicator** toolbar, choose **Edit, Preferences, Advanced,** and then select **Cache**.

2. Choose **Clear Memory Cache** and then select **Clear Disk Cache** (Figure 6.16).

3. Click **OK**.

To set the amount of virtual memory or hard disk cache in Netscape Communicator, follow these steps:

1. From the **Netscape Communicator** toolbar, choose **Edit, Preferences, Advanced,** and then select **Cache**.

2. Type new numbers into the **Memory Cache** text box and the **Disk Cache** box (Figure 6.16).

3. Click **OK**.

Figure 6.16 Netscape Communicator Cache Settings

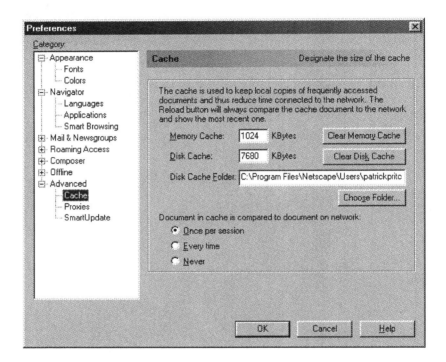

Cookies

Cookies are text files that a Web server sends to a user's Web browser and which are saved to the computer's hard disk. The main purpose of a cookie is to identify a visitor to a Web site. The information in cookies can change depending on the areas of a Web site entered by a user. Another name for these files is persistent cookies because they often remain on a user's hard disk for a long time. Cookies are not executable and do not pose a security threat to the operation of your computer.

Cookie text files are similar to: yourname@somewebsite.txt. This cookie message transmits back to the Web server that created it each time the browser requests a page from that server.

Cookies are often used to create customized Web pages for visitors that contain their name and particular items of interest. This customization is made possible when a person's browser enters a Web site that creates cookies. Visitors to a Web site often fill out forms to sign up as a free member of the site or to purchase items. This kind of personal information can be stored in a cookie and saved to the visitor's hard disk through the Web browser. The next time the visitor goes to the same Web site, the browser sends the cookie to the Web server, where a database updates the file then transmits the file back to the local hard disk. Web marketing and sales departments can use this information to help determine the focus and effectiveness of their Web site and to plan new features or services.

Enabling and Disabling Netscape Communicator Cookies

You can allow or deny the storage of cookies on your computer. Although cookies are not executable programs, they can prevent some features of a Web site from functioning when disabled. Some people, however, are willing to forego certain features if it requires them to give up some of their privacy. You can configure your browser to permit none, all, or only certain cookies to write to your hard disk.

To enable cookies in your Netscape Communicator, follow these steps:

1. From the **Netscape Communicator** toolbar, choose **Edit**, **Preferences**, and then select **Advanced** (Figure 6.17).

2. Choose the **Accept all cookies** option or choose **Accept only cookies that get back to the originating server**.

3. Click **OK**.

Follow these steps to disable cookies in Netscape Communicator:

1. From the **Netscape Communicator** toolbar, choose **Edit**, **Preferences**, and then select **Advanced**.

2. Choose **Disable cookies**, and then click **OK**.

Figure 6.17 Netscape Communicator Cookie Preferences

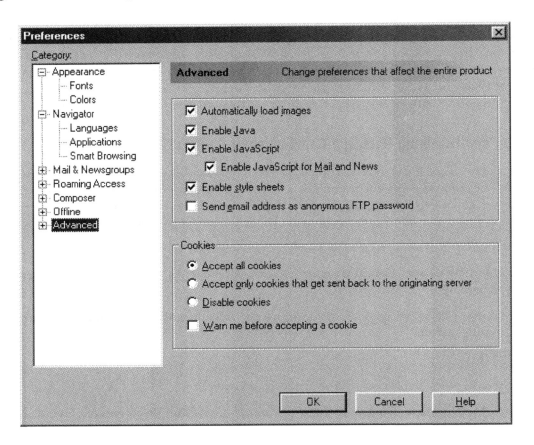

Enabling and Disabling Internet Explorer Cookies

To enable and disable cookies in Internet Explorer requires selecting options in the Security dialog at the Custom Level. There are two ways to enable cookies in Internet Explorer. You can enable or disable permanent storage of cookies on your hard disk.

To enable the cookie settings in Internet Explorer, follow these steps:

1. From the **Internet Explorer** toolbar, choose **Tools** and then select **Internet Options**.

2. Choose **Security** and then select **Custom Level**.

3. Scroll the **Settings** list box to display **Cookies** (Figure 6.18).

4. Choose the **Enable** option or the **Prompt** option under the label: **Allow cookies that are stored on your computer**. (The prompt option causes an Alert box to display.)

5. Choose the **Enable** or **Prompt** option under the **Allow per session** cookies (not stored) label or

6. Choose both **Enable** or **Prompt** options in both locations.

7. Click **OK**.

To disable Cookies in Internet Explorer, follow these steps:

1. From the **Internet Explorer** toolbar, choose **Tools** and then select **Internet Options**.

2. Choose **Security** and then select **Custom Level**.

3. Scroll the **Settings** list box to display **Cookies** (Figure 6.18).

4. Choose **Disable** under the **Allow cookies to be stored** or choose **Disable** under **Allow per-session cookies**, or choose **Disable** under both labels.

5. Click **OK**.

Figure 6.18 Internet Explorer Cookie Settings

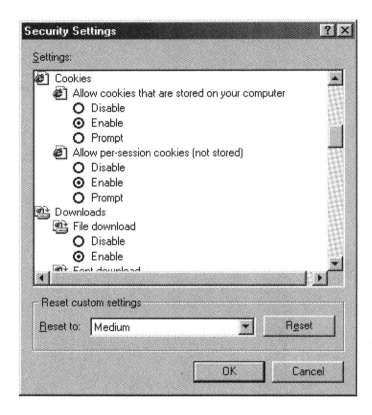

Disabling cookies prevents the writing of cookies to your hard disk. You can also set the browser to notify you when a server attempts to put a cookie on your computer. This notification dialog box allows you to accept or reject placement of a cookie on your hard disk.

Software Version Control

Software manufacturers release new versions of their products an average of every 18 months. This means you can expect to make a new purchase of an improved software product almost every two years. New software versions are often identified by the name of the software followed by a number, (Netscape Communicator 4.6 or Microsoft Internet Explorer 5.0).

Test Documentation

Test documentation contains patch release notes that provide detailed information about the purpose of a fix. Sometimes a software maker will notify you when a patch for your system is available and distribute test documentation to you from their Web site, on CD-ROM, DVD, or on a Bulletin Board System (BBS).

Applying Patches

Patches and updates distribute as executable files you can use to fix software problems (called bugs). These released patches often improve performance or fix problems in software that are discovered after the software is on the market. For example, if your browser software has a security problem, it makes your computer vulnerable to electronic attack, that takes advantage of the security hole. To close the security hole, the software manufacturer writes a fix for each problem, groups them together and creates an executable patch. It is common practice for software makers to place patches on their Web sites so you can download them and add them to your program.

 Tip: A hot patch is a bug fix to a software program that does not require you to reboot your system to activate it.

Applying a Software Patch

To keep your software secure from attack and at optimum performance, it is a good practice to check the software manufacturer's Web site for any new patches to download.

Follow these steps to apply a patch:

1. Download the patch from the software manufacturer's Web site to your hard disk.

2. Locate the executable file on your hard disk; execute it by double-clicking on its name or icon.

3. Wait while the patch installs itself into your software product.

4. Reboot your computer so the patch can take effect.

These software patches are temporary remedies for program and system software problems. Later, the fixes inside these patches will be incorporated into the next version of the software.

Applying Upgrades

Upgrades are new versions of a previous software release. Over the years, Microsoft and Netscape have released numerous patches and upgrades to their browser software.

Upgrades include all the previous patches released, plus other enhancements or functionality they have added to the software since its last major release. You may not want to upgrade to a new version with every release. Read about any enhancements that a new version offers and assess its value before you purchase it. You can often read about experiences with the new version by reading postings to Newsgroups on the Internet before you buy and install upgrades to your system. Read any test documentation, back up your system, then load and test the upgrade.

Consider installing a software upgrade if:

■   New functionality has been added

■   Improvements have been made to enhance the product

■   The manufacturer will not provide technical support for your current version of software

E-Mail Variations

Electronic mail, or E-mail, is the transmission of messages over communications networks. E-mail often consists of message files you can store on disk. Other electronic messages are just notes entered from the keyboard, often called messaging.

Most mainframes, minicomputers, and computer networks have an e-mail system in use, however the systems are often incompatible with one another. Some e-mail systems are limited to a single computer manufacturer's system or network. Use of gateways that recognize a standard protocol to pass mail along to other computer systems overcome the incompatibility.

ISPs and online services offer e-mail and support gateways that use the Messaging Application Programming Interface (MAPI) for exchanging mail with other systems. MAPI is a system built into Microsoft Windows that enables different e-mail applications to work together to distribute mail. Since almost all e-mail systems have a gateway to the Internet, it is the standard for exchanging e-mail among different systems. So long as both applications are MAPI enabled, they can share mail messages.

E-mail systems use a text editor so you can compose messages. You address it to a recipient's electronic mail box and send it. To facilitate the sending of messages to groups of people, e-mail systems allow the creation of electronic distribution lists. Distribution lists are used to send (broadcast) the same message to everyone on the list at the same time.

Messages are received on mail servers and stored in electronic mailboxes until the recipients retrieve them. Some e-mail systems display an alert when mail is received. With the increasing popularity of Web based e-mail, there are now tools that can also check Web mail accounts for new messages so you do not need to periodically log onto your account.

Some of the conveniences of electronic mail are that you can send it to one person or broadcast it to hundreds at the same time. You can read it, forward it to others, change it, print out paper copies, store it, or delete it. Electronic mail can often deliver a message to its destination mailbox in seconds.

Understanding E-Mail Protocols

E-mail has evolved from proprietary legacy systems that could not communicate outside their network environment to the vast intercommunications provided by today's Internet e-mail system. A number of e-mail protocols take advantage of the TCP/IP protocol and the Internet.

The following primary protocols make Internet e-mail possible:

1. Post Office Protocol (POP)

2. Internet Message Access Protocol (IMAP)

3. Simple Mail Transfer Protocol (SMTP)

4. MIME

5. UNIX-to-UNIX Encode (Uuencode)

6. BinHex

POP

POP retrieves e-mail from a mail server. Most e-mail client applications use the POP protocol. There are two versions of POP. The older version is called POP2. POP2 protocol became a standard in the mid-1980s and it requires use of the Simple Mail Transfer Protocol (SMTP) to send messages. The newer version, POP3, can use but does not require SMTP. Your ISP supplies you with the information you need to configure your Web browser, or other e-mail client, to access your POP e-mail account. POP e-mail account addresses often use this syntax: mail.ispname.com

IMAP

IMAP retrieves e-mail messages from an e-mail server. IMAP4 is the latest version. It is similar to POP3, but supports several enhancements. IMAP4 enables a person to do a keyword search of the messages on a mail server and allows you to download only the desired messages. Similar to POP, IMAP uses SMTP to communicate between the e-mail client and the mail server. Developers at Stanford University created the IMAP protocol in 1986.

SMTP

SMTP passes e-mail messages between Internet mail servers. Each message has a standard header that identifies the recipient's e-mail address, the sender's name and e-mail address, and the network nodes that the message passed through. SMTP is the standard methodology for e-mail transmission over the Internet.

MIME

MIME is built into Microsoft Windows allowing different e-mail applications to work together to distribute mail. Multipurpose Internet Mail Extensions (MIME) enables non-ASCII (American Standard Code for Information Interchange) applications and files to be transmitted and received on different e-mail systems. Messages that are MIME compliant can be read if the sending and receiving mail applications are both MAPI-enabled.

You can designate applications to recognize file formats received by a MIME compliant browser or e-mail client. When the browser or e-mail client receives a defined file type, the designated application launches and displays the contents of the file. For example, you can browse the Web and click on an Adobe Portable Document Format (PDF) file, and, if the PDF format is in the MIME list of formats and applications, the associated application such as Adobe Acrobat Viewer launches.

Uuencode

Uuencode started as a UNIX based code for the conversion of files into a series of 7-bit ASCII characters for transferring data over the Internet. It now also supports the transfer of files among different platforms such as Windows and Macintosh, as well as UNIX. Uuencode is popular, and many e-mail applications use it for sending and receiving e-mail attachments.

BinHex

This is a popular format for the transfer of data across the Internet. Its primary use is to transport Apple Macintosh graphics files, such as Tagged Image File Format (TIFF) and PICTs, across the Internet.

Using MIME in a Browser

MIME is a specification used to format non-ASCII messages like formatted documents, graphics, audio, and video files to enable them to transmit over the Internet. Web browsers use MIME to launch applications that can display or output files that are not in HyperText Markup Language (HTML) format. A new secure version, called S/MIME, supports encrypted messages.

Configuring MIME in Netscape Communicator

Enabling your browser to use MIME requires that you designate the format of a file that you want MIME to recognize. To configure MIME in a browser, follow these steps:

1. From the **Netscape Communicator** toolbar, choose **Edit**, **Preferences**, **Navigator**, and then select **Applications**.

2. Choose **New Type** and then type a description. This example uses WorldView, an Interleaf file-viewing product not widely recognized (Figure 6.19).

3. In the **File** extension field, type the extensions which the application recognizes, such as: **.pl, .wvw**

4. In the **MIME Type** field, type: **application/x-worldview**

5. In the **Application to use** field, type the full path to the executable file of the application you want to launch, such as:

C:\program files\iview2\ iview.exe%1

6. Choose **Option**, and then click **OK**.

Your browser will now recognize Interleaf formatted files and launch the WorldView application.

Figure 6.19 MIME Configuration for Netscape Communicator

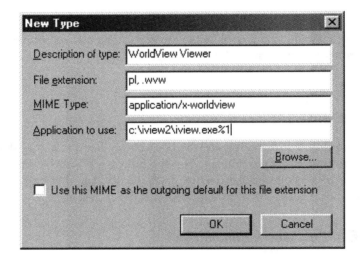

Configuring MIME in Internet Explorer

Internet Explorer 4.0, and later versions, use MIME Type Detection in the form of a data sniffer routine called FindMimeFromData. This routine runs a series of tests to identify and execute the correct server object or launch the correct application to read the associated file type so you can view it. This means you will never have to configure a MIME type in your Microsoft browser or e-mail client.

If the file type is unknown or not in your computer's registry, and it cannot be determined by the data sniffer routine, then it will either fail to launch the correct application or try to display it as a plain text or binary file.

Using HyperText Markup Language (HTML)

HTML is the code used to create and display Web pages. You can also elect to send and receive e-mail in HTML format, text format, or both when you configure your e-mail client (Figure 6.20). HTML documents can support interactivity using programming and scripting languages.

If you can create Web pages, you can e-mail them. Another way to let others view them is to post them to your own Web site and send a link in an e-mail message that, when selected, will launch a browser and display that Web page.

Figure 6.20 Netscape Preferences

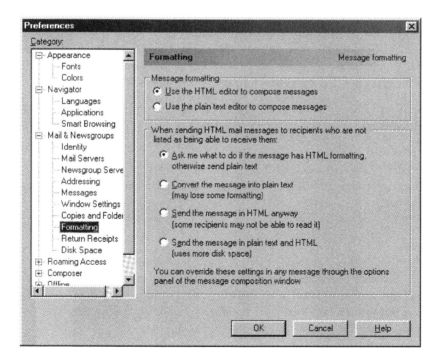

PC Client-to-Legacy System Connections

Legacy system refers to mainframe and mini-frame computing systems. Host connectivity to IBM mainframe computers, IBM AS/400 computers, UNIX systems, DEC VAX/VMS computers, HP 3000 systems, Wang systems, and others are possible using terminal emulation application programs that are Winsock-compliant.

Legacy systems are now increasing their support of Web browsers and protocols for Web-based computing. Browsers are not a burden on the computing resources of a legacy system in comparison to traditional remote computing solutions. Browser-based applications decrease the costs of clients that access legacy systems and increase the number of legacy systems they can connect to for use of the vast amounts of data they store.

The common network protocols that support legacy systems' host connectivity include:

TCP/IP—TCP/IP is the most common protocol used to permit connections among interconnected networks with many different OSs such as IBM, UNIX, and Microsoft. TCP/IP includes Telnet services such as TN3270 terminal emulators for connection to IBM mainframes, TN5250 emulators for AS/400s, and other gateways that support TCP/IP.

IPX/SPX—The IPX/SPX-compatible software from Microsoft is for connecting to Novell NetWare Connect networks and gateways. IPX/SPX are the acronyms for Internet Packet Exchange/Sequence Packet Exchange.

NetBEUI—NetBEUI supports a NetBIOS programming interface that supports the IBM NetBEUI protocol for connecting to legacy hosts using terminal emulation programs and gateways that support the NetBIOS interface

Sockets

A socket is a small piece of software that connects an application to a network protocol. In UNIX, a program can send and receive TCP/IP messages by writing and reading data to and from a socket. It makes the programmer's task easier by only having to deal with the socket. The programmer then trusts the OS to transport the messages across the network.

Winsock

A Windows Socket, or Winsock, is an Application Programming Interface (API) for creating Windows programs that enable them to communicate with other computers, including legacy systems, using the TCP/IP protocol. Windows 98 and Windows NT workstations come with the Dynamic Link Library (DLL) called WINSOCK.DLL that accomplishes these connections. This DLL file causes the API to tie Windows programs and TCP/IP connections together.

Using Sockets

Programmers created sockets to enable programs to connect using the TCP/IP protocol. When you connect to the Internet, the Winsock-compliant applications can find your Internet connection. If you close an application and start another, or the same application is running several instances at once, they all use the same Winsock connection to the Internet.

Considering Performance Issues

Accessing data stored on a legacy system through a terminal emulation program that does not support Winsock uses a large part of the resources on that legacy system. The legacy system needs to manage all of the connections to the system, including those that are idle. Traditionally, it has been up to the legacy computer to provide all of the support to an accessing client. This method results in slow and inefficient data processing and retrieval.

Applications that support the Winsock protocol have better performance than those that rely on older technologies, such as non-compliant terminal emulators.

If a remote network server does not support TCP/IP, you will need to install the protocols that allow direct connection to the remote network.

Compatibility Issues

Although Microsoft Winsock appears to be the most widely used version of sockets, there are other types of sockets available on the Internet at programming newsgroups as shareware and freeware. Shareware of freeware sockets not written by MicroSoft may differ slightly in their compatibility and how they perform.

Client Setup Troubleshooting

Systems administrators often need to deal with situations regarding customized client connectivity to the Internet or intranet. Company standard setup configurations do not always meet the needs of the person using the client computer. Troubleshooting a client computer often results in the determination that setting permissions and configurations for each individual's usage requirements solves the problem. The following scenario addresses a user's need to access the Internet from within an intranet.

Configuration Scenario

In this situation, a Web browser can connect to Web sites inside the company firewall but cannot communicate with Web sites outside the firewall. Determine what the most likely cause of this problem is and what you need to do to fix it. Look at the connections to the proxy server and determine if the client settings allow Internet Access. Then set the connections.

Repairing a Netscape Communicator Connection

To repair a connection to a proxy server, follow these steps:

1. From the browser, choose **Edit**, **Preferences**, **Advanced** and then select **Proxies**.

2. From **Proxy**, select the **Manual Proxy Configuration** option or the **Automatic Proxy Configuration** option.

3. Use the addresses and port numbers your Network Administrator provides.

Repairing an Internet Explorer Connection

To repair a connection to a proxy server, follow these steps:

1. Launch the browser and from the toolbar, choose **Tools** and then select **Internet Options**.

2. Choose **Connections** and then select **LAN Settings**.

3. Under **Proxy server**, select **Use a proxy server** option.

4. For **Automatic proxy configuration**, fill out the **Address** and **Port** text fields to make an automatic proxy connection and then click **OK**.

5. To configure the proxy settings manually, choose **Use a proxy server** and then choose **Advanced**.

6. Fill out the information for each proxy Address and Port number for each service you want the browser to use.

Vocabulary

Review the following terms in preparation for the certification exam.

Term	Description
browser	A software application that locates and displays Web pages by interpreting HTML codes to display graphics as well as text. They support programming languages like JavaScript to create interactive Web pages, and many browsers present full multimedia sound and video using small applications called plug-ins.
cookies	Cookies transmit to a user's Web browser by a Web server and save to the user's hard disk in a Cookie folder as text files. The main purpose of a cookie is to identify a visitor to a Web site. Sometimes cookies are called persistent cookies because they often stay on a user's hard disk for a long time.
CSLIP	Compressed Serial Line Interface Protocol is a UNIX telephone line protocol that allows compressed data transfers over the connection between remote hardware devices.
DUN	Dial-Up Networking allows you to gain access to shared information on a remote computer by dialing into a network server.

Term	Description
IMAP	Internet Message Access Protocol is designed to retrieve e-mail messages from an e-mail server. The latest version is IMAP4, which is similar to POP3, except that it supports several enhancements. With IMAP4 you can perform a keyword search for messages on a mail server and then download only the messages you want. IMAP uses SMTP to communicate between the e-mail client and the mail server.
line protocol	Enables a local computer to connect to a modem on a remote computer and connect the two devices.
MIME	Multipurpose Internet Mail Extensions is a specification for formatting non-ASCII messages for transmission over the Internet. Many e-mail client applications support MIME because it enables them to send and receive graphics, video, and audio files through the Internet mail system.
network protocol	TCP/IP, IPX/SPX, and NetBEUI, are the usual network communications protocols used to access remote Internet network servers.
POTS	Plain Old Telephone System refers to the public telephone system. Public phone lines are used to connect a local computer to a network computer using the DUN feature in Windows.
PPTP	Point-to-Point Tunneling Protocol is a more secure version of PPP. This connection supports the encryption and compression of all transmitted data. To use PPTP requires connection to a remote tunnel server. Once connected PPTP supports all the same network protocols as PPP (TCP/IP, IPX/SPX, NetBEUI, etc.) to access the network.

Term	Description
remote	Any files, devices, or other resources not connected directly to your workstation. Resources connected directly to a workstation are local.
Remote Access Server	A network server that enables you to log into a Windows NT-based LAN using a modem.
SLIP	Serial Line Internet Protocol is a UNIX protocol.
sockets	A software object that connects applications to a network protocol for sending and receiving TCP/IP messages.
Winsock	This API enables Windows programs to communicate with other computers by using the TCP/IP protocol. Winsock is designed upon the socket's API in UNIX. Windows 98 and Windows NT use the Dynamic Link Library (DLL) called WINSOCK.DLL to read and write data to and from TCP/IP-supported applications.

In Brief

If you want to...	Then do this...
Dial-up a new ISP's remote server to connect to the Internet	Create a new Dial-Up Networking connection profile and enter the necessary phone number, Server Type settings, IP address, DNS addresses, DHCP, and related items provided by that ISP.
Take control of a mainframe and run some of the programs on it using TCP/IP	Dial-up the remote computer and activate your Winsock-compliant terminal emulation program.
Print out a report on a remote network printer	Gain access to the remote network using your configured Dial-Up Networking profile, locate the printer and print the report to it.
Clear the cache in Netscape Communicator	Start the Web browser. From the main menu bar select Edit, Preferences, Advanced, Cache. Choose Clear Memory Cache and Clear Disk Cache.
Enable Cookies in Netscape Communicator	From the main menu bar select Edit, Preferences, Advanced and choose the Enable cookies option you want.
Change the amount of cache Netscape Communicator uses	Start the Web browser. From the main menu bar select Edit, Preferences, Advanced, Cache and type new numbers into the text boxes for Memory Cache and Disk Cache.

If you want to...	Then do this...
Create a new MIME type in Internet Explorer	Download the plug-in or add-on from the Web or install the software you will use to view or play the type of file you want. MIME types in Internet Explorer are automatically configured using a data sniffer and the Registry.
Clear the cache in Internet Explorer	Start the Web browser. From the main menu bar, select Tools, Internet Options. Choose Delete Files to empty the Temporary Internet Files folder. Choose Clear History to delete the files from the History folder.
Change the amount of cache Internet Explorer uses	Start the Web browser. From the main menu bar, select Tools, Internet Options. Choose Settings under Temporary Internet files. Move the slider bar to adjust the amount of cache you want or type the amount you want in the spinner text box to increase or decrease the amount of cache. Click OK to save the new settings.

Lesson 6 Activities

Complete the following activities to better prepare you for the certification exam.

1. Describe the function of cache.

2. Explain the advantage of IMAP over POP.

3. Define an e-mail broadcast.

4. Explain the purpose of MIME.

5. Describe the function that Winsock provides.

6. Describe the information a Network Administrator provides a user for connection of a Web browser to a proxy server.

7. Explain the purpose of SMTP.

8. Explain the significance of PPTP.

9. Describe the purpose of a modem and name the three most common line protocols for establishing connections between modems.

10. Name the two most commonly used network protocols for using remote access servers.

Answers to Lesson 6 Activities

1. The function of cache is to store recently viewed files and Web pages in volatile memory (RAM) or on a hard disk. Hard disk cache can be stored on either your local hard disk or on a cache server. Cache reduces traffic on the Internet by having a browser retrieve a recently viewed Web page or file from the cache rather than loading it into the browser from the actual Web site.

2. IMAP allows a person to do a keyword search on an e-mail server and select only the messages they want to download. POP also retrieves mail from an e-mail server, but it downloads all the messages at once. POP does not have an e-mail server search capability.

3. To broadcast an e-mail means you can send the same e-mail message to hundreds of people at the same time.

4. The purpose of MIME is to format non-ASCII messages, such as formatted documents, graphics, audio, and video files, to enable them to transmit over the Internet. Web browsers use MIME types to enable them to launch applications that can display or output files that are not in HTML format. A new, secure version called S/MIME supports encrypted messages.

5. A Windows Socket, or Winsock, is an API for creating Windows programs that enable them to communicate with other computers, including legacy systems, using the TCP/IP protocol.

6. A Network Administrator provides the addresses and port numbers to access proxy servers.

7. SMTP is designed to pass electronic mail messages between Internet mail servers. Each message has a standard header that identifies e-mail addresses of the recipients, the e-mail address and name of the sender, and the nodes on the network that the message passed through. SMTP is the standard methodology for electronic mail transmission over the Internet.

8. PPTP is a technology that allows you to create Virtual Private Networks (VPNs) that use the Internet to dial into a corporate network.

9. Modems are the most common hardware devices to connect two computers by telephone line. The most common line connection protocols are PPP, SLIP, and PPTP.

10. The two most common network protocols for remote network access are TCP/IP and IPX/SPX.

Lesson 6 Quiz

These questions test your knowledge of features, vocabulary, procedures, and syntax.

1. The public telephone system is also known by these acronyms. Select all that apply.

    A. X.400

    B. PSTN

    C. ADSL

    D. POTS

2. Select the answers that best define a patch. Select all that apply.

    A. A total upgrade to a new version of a software application.

    B. Another name for Winsock.

    C. A fix issued by a software manufacturer to repair a problem in a software application.

    D. The cord used to connect a modem to a telephone wall jack.

3. Which of the electronic mail protocols can perform a keyword search on an e-mail server?

    A. POP2

    B. SMTP

    C. POP3

    D. IMAP

4. Which of the following is not a line protocol?

    A. PPTP

    B. IPX/SPX

    C. SLIP

    D. PPP

5. Cache can be stored in which of the following locations

   A. A remote cache server

   B. Virtual memory

   C. Modem memory

   D. A local hard disk

6. What is the purpose of test documentation? Select all that apply.

   A. Notes from a software manufacturer that tell new users about the features in a new version of an application.

   B. These are notes about a patch release that provide detailed information about the purpose of each software fix in the patch.

   C. These are notes from software testers to the software manufacturer about bugs they have discovered while testing a new piece of software.

   D. This is a trial version of a user guide that is sent to software testers to help them do their software testing.

7. Choose the answer that best describes the role of a proxy server firewall.

   A. A type of protocol dedicated to passing electronic mail among Internet e-mail systems.

   B. A server configured to store temporary Web page information for quick retrieval.

   C. A program designed to keep unauthorized people from gaining access to a network.

   D. A program that dials-up a remote computer network.

8. In the Windows OS, remote access service is the server-side of which of the following?

   A. The Point-to-Point Protocol.

   B. Software used to connect to a local printer.

   C. The Dial-Up Networking feature on Windows clients.

   D. A modem.

9. Which of the following is not an electronic mail protocol specification? Select all that apply.

A. SMTP

B. Winsock

C. IMAP

D. POP3

10. Which of the following is true about cookies? Select all that apply.

A. A cookie is used to control a computer by remote control.

B. Cookies are used to collect information about visitors to a Web site.

C. Information placed in a cookie never changes.

D. Cookies are a network protocol for accessing remote servers.

Answers to Lesson 6 Quiz

1. Answer B is correct. PSTN is the acronym for Public Switching Telephone Network.

    Answer D is correct. The acronym POTS means Plain Old Telephone System.

    Answer A is incorrect. It is a specification for the X.400 Message Handling System. This electronic mail system is primarily used by government bodies and companies for its built-in security.

    Answer C is incorrect. ADSL is the acronym for Asymmetric Digital Subscriber Line, a type of high-speed modem technology that is becoming available in major metropolitan areas. It is popular for its high data transfer rates and reasonable cost for use in businesses and homes.

2. Answer C is correct. A patch is a fix issued by a software manufacturer to repair a problem in a software application.

    Answer A is incorrect. A total upgrade to a new version of software often contains fixes previously issued for a piece of software, but it is not a patch. New versions of software are released because they have new or improved functionality.

    Answer B is incorrect. A Winsock is a program that allows PCs to communicate with legacy systems.

    Answer D is incorrect. The cord that connects a modem to a telephone wall jack is telephone wire.

3. Answer D is correct. IMAP is the electronic mail protocol that can search an e-mail server by keyword. It also allows you to perform selective message downloads.

    Answer A is incorrect. POP2 is an old e-mail server protocol that was popular in the 1980s. POP also retrieves mail from an e-mail server, but downloads all the messages at once.

    Answer B is incorrect. SMTP is electronic mail protocol that is designed to pass electronic mail messages between Internet mail servers.

    Answer C is incorrect. POP3 is an electronic mail protocol, but it downloads all the messages from the e-mail server at once and does not support keyword searches.

4. Answer B is correct. IPX/SPX is Internet Packet Exchange/Sequenced Packet Exchange and is the network protocol for accessing Novell NetWare Connect servers.

    Answer A is incorrect. PPTP is a line protocol for connection to a tunnel server.

Answer C is incorrect. SLIP is the line protocol used to dial in to a remote Un server.

Answer D is incorrect. PPP is the line protocol used to dial in to most network servers, including Internet service provider networks.

5. Answer A is correct. A remote cache server is a location where temporary Web pages and files are stored for fast retrieval by Web browsers.

    Answer B is correct. Virtual memory is a location where temporary Web pages and files are stored for fast retrieval by Web browsers.

    Answer D is correct. The local hard disk can store temporary Web pages and files for fast retrieval by Web browsers.

    Answer C is incorrect. Modems do not have any kind of cache memory.

6. Answer B is correct. Test documentation describes patch release information about the purpose of each software fix in the patch.

    Answer A is incorrect. Notes from a software manufacturer that tell about the features in a new software version are promotional information.

    Answer C is incorrect. Notes to a software manufacturer from its software testers are designed to identify bugs and potential enhancements in a piece of software that is being prepared for release.

    Answer D is incorrect. Software testers receive basic notes from the software manufacturer to get them familiar with the purpose of the new software, some of the functions to test and how to report bugs and suggest enhancements, but this is not test documentation.

7. Answer C is correct. A proxy server firewall is a program designed to keep unauthorized people from gaining access to a network.

    Answer A is incorrect. The protocol dedicated to passing electronic mail among Internet mail servers is SMTP.

    Answer B is incorrect. A server configured to store temporary Web page information for quick retrieval is a cache server.

    Answer D is incorrect. The program in Windows that dials up a remote computer network is RAS, which is implemented through the DUN application

8. Answer C is correct. Dial-up Networking (DUN) is the client side of a remote access (RAS) connection. RAS is on the server, while DUN is on the client computer.

Answer A is incorrect. PPP is a line protocol that two hardware devices use to recognize each other in order to establish a connection.

Answer B is incorrect. Software that connects to a local printer is not related to RAS.

Answer D is incorrect. A modem is a device used by RAS and DUN.

9.   Answer B is correct. Winsock is an API that enables Windows programs to communicate with other computers by use of the TCP/IP protocol.

Answer A is incorrect. SMTP is Simple Mail Transfer Protocol. It is the standard method for passing electronic mail over the Internet. SMTP passes electronic mail messages between Internet mail servers. Each message has a standard header that identifies e-mail addresses of the recipients, the e-mail address and name of the sender, and the nodes on the network through which the message passed.

Answer C is incorrect. IMAP is an e-mail protocol that can perform a keyword search of a mail server and allows a person to do selective downloads of e-mail files.

Answer D is incorrect. POP3 is a popular electronic protocol used extensively by Internet Service Providers to provide e-mail service to their subscribers.

10. Answer B is correct. Cookies are used to collect information about visitors to a Web site. The data is often used by analysts in a company to determine the effectiveness of their Web site, its focus, and customer satisfaction.

Answer A is incorrect. A cookie cannot take remote control of a computer.

Answer C is incorrect. Information placed in a cookie often changes each time a Web visitor revisits the same Web site or any of its segments.

Answer D is incorrect. Cookies are not a network protocol, nor can they access remote servers. Cookies are information collection text files used to identify Web site visitors, and are often used to tailor and personalize a person's Web surfing experience.

Lesson 7: Web Page Creation

Although the Internet originated in the late 1960s, its popularity did not explode until the 1990s. This is due in large part to the Web and the Web's integral feature, the Web page.

Web pages are the result of two technologies blended together: HyperText and markup languages. The combination of HyperText, which interconnects documents and markup languages, and codes, which describe the meaning and formatting of text, created a technology that is truly greater than the sum of its parts.

Although this technology is amazingly powerful, the creation of Web pages is very straightforward. Even novice computer users can create a basic Web page in a short amount of time.

In this lesson, you will create a Web site with multiple interconnected pages. The Web site is for a technical support department at a large company. In the process, you will learn the basics of the language used to produce Web pages—HyperText Markup Language (HTML).

After completing this lesson, you should have a better understanding of the following topics:

- HTML
- Web Site Design
- HTML Tags
- Fonts and Colors
- Lists
- Tables
- Graphics
- Links
- Frames

HTML

A markup language is a collection of embedded codes that describe the meaning or formatting of text. The most popular markup language for creating World Wide Web (WWW) pages is HTML.

The two general categories of markup languages are:

- Physical markup language
- Semantic markup language

A physical markup language mainly describes how a document will look when printed. For example, you can use codes to indicate a 12-point character size, a Helvetica typeface, and an italic font style. The <B> HTML tag is a markup code and known as tags in HTML. The <B> tag is an example of a formatting code that marks text as bold. When you display the text in Figure 7.1 in a browser, "I like" will appear as normal text since there are no codes around it. The word "apples" has a <B> on either side to indicate that it should appear in bold.

Figure 7.1 Physical Markup Language

```
I like <B>apples</B>.
```

Although HTML has a few formatting codes to indicate bold, italics and so on, it is much more of a semantic markup language, than a physical markup language. This is seen through the example in Figure 7.2.

Figure 7.2 Semantic Markup Language

```
<H1>The Dawn of a New Day</H1>
```

The semantic markup language uses codes to mark the meaning of text rather than its physical appearance. The <H1> tag indicates that the text is a level-one heading. When this text displays in a Web browser, the browser decides how the text should appear on the screen. This semantic basis for HTML has both benefits and shortcomings.

On the plus side, it provides a lot of flexibility in displaying pages. Web pages are viewable on a UNIX, Macintosh, or PC Web browser. No special conversion process is necessary, unlike with many other types of files.

On the downside, different browsers tend to have their own way of physically displaying the logical meaning of text. You never know the precise formatting of a page unless you try it out in a variety of browsers.

Today, most browsers have a relatively consistent way of presenting HTML tags. Although there is some variation, a Web page looks similar in Microsoft, Netscape, or AOL browsers. If you are publishing a Web page, especially a complex one, it is a good idea to test it out in Internet Explorer and Netscape.

Besides having tags for elements such as headings, paragraphs, tables, and so forth, HTML has additional tags for creating hyperlinks that interconnect documents. HTML is also extensible, meaning that you can add new features to HTML without modifying previously created documents. This allows you to view a Web page created with an earlier version of HTML.

 Tip: The original standards for HTML were derived from a sophisticated markup language called the Standard General Markup Language (SGML). The current HTML standards are published by the World Wide Web Consortium (W3C), which is hosted by the Laboratory for Computer Science at the Massachusetts Institute of Technology (MIT), French National Institute for Research in Computer Science and Control (INRIA), and Keio University in Japan.

Web Site Design

Although you can jump in and immediately start writing Web pages with HTML, it is preferable to first plan the design of the Web site, especially if the site has multiple pages. In the end, a well-designed site saves time in subsequent modifications.

Site Plan

For the rest of this lesson, you are a Webmaster, the overall manager of a Web site. As Webmaster, keep in mind the following planning criteria:

Know your audience—Does your audience require numerous graphics that are time-onsuming to download or could you make better use of bandwidth by primarily using text?

Make navigation easy—Create a home page with links to major subcategories. Users should be able to navigate easily among the main pages, and they should always be able to jump back to the home page.

Use a consistent design throughout the Web site—Apply the same basic elements, such as logos, typefaces, and colors.

Sketch out your site on paper—You can get a bird's-eye view of how your users will navigate through your pages.

Develop a simple, consistent naming system—Use one-word folder and file names without any special symbols or punctuation for your Web pages, images, and other files.

Keep your files well organized on the disk—Group related files by topic and place them into their own folders.

 Note: To get a better idea of good site design, visit some major sites such as www.adobe.com, www.macromedia.com, or www.hotwired.com. Another great resource is The Non-Designer's Web Book: An Easy Guide to Creating, Designing, and Posting Your Own Web Site by Robin Williams.

Web Site Diagram

Assume that you need to create a Web site for a technical support center at a large company. The company uses three operating systems (OS): Windows 2000, Linux, and BeOS. When a company employee has a computer problem, he or she will connect to your site to get an answer. The main Web page, the site's home page, will have hyperlinks to three main subpages, one for each operating system. The subpages will be filled with technical support information.

A hierarchical design, one that employs a branching tree-like structure, works well for this type of site. It is a good idea to sketch out a Web site design, like the one shown in Figure 7.3.

Figure 7.3 Web Site Diagram

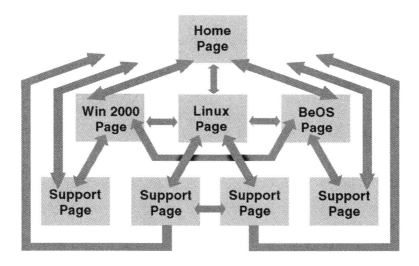

Every page connects to the home page. Do not be afraid to put plenty of hyperlinks in your pages. It is especially important to place a link in each page that takes the user back to the home page. No matter how deep a user drills into the Web site structure, he or she should always be able to easily return home.

In this lesson, you will create the main pages of the Web site. These include the home page and the Windows 2000, Linux, and BeOS pages. Just like the BeOS page above, every page in a Web site could have additional subpages.

Note: For more information about the BeOS operating system, link to the www.be.com site.

HTML Tags

Commands, or tags, in HTML are contained within less than (<) and greater than (>) symbols called angle brackets. Opening and closing tags often surround text. The closing tag contains a forward slash (/). Text with <B> and </B> around is marked as bold. Figure 7.4 has text marked for italics with the <I> tag. Notice that the opening and closing tags are identical except for the slash.

Figure 7.4 Opening and Closing Tags

```
Lisa recommends the book <I>Tale of Two Cities</I> by Dickens.
```

Tip: Although not a rule, you should type HTML tags in uppercase letters, which makes it easier to distinguish tags from other text.

Attributes

Many tags have attributes for delineating options. The <TABLE> tag, a tag for creating rows and columns of information, has several attributes including one for specifying a border. If you add the attribute <BORDER>, the resulting table will have lines separating the table's rows and columns. If you leave off the attribute, the table has no borders (Figure 7.5).

Figure 7.5 Table Border Attribute

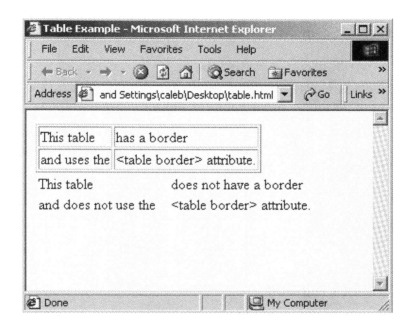

You use values to apply more control over the effects of attributes. For example, you can specify the width of a table border by adding an equal sign (=) followed by a number. The number represents the width of a border in terms of pixels (a pixel, or PICture ELement, is a small point on the screen). The first tag in Figure 7.6 specifies a border of two pixels.

The second tag in Figure 7.6 inserts a graphical image into a Web page. The SRC attribute identifies the filename of the image. The ALT attribute gives a text alternative for the image. If a Web browser cannot display images, the text specified by ALT will appear instead. Notice that the tag <IMG>, like most tags, can take multiple attributes.

Figure 7.6 Attribute Values

```
<TABLE BORDER=2>

<<IMG SRC="elvis.jpg" ALT="A picture of Elvis">
```

Some values, especially ones with spaces, need to be delineated with double-quotation marks (""). If the value contains simple digits (0 to 9) or letters (A to Z) you can omit the quotation marks. Many people put double-quotation marks around all values, just to be on the safe side.

Nesting Tags

What do you do if you have text that needs to be presented in a browser as bold, italics, and centered? You need to nest tags or put one set of tags inside of another.

The order for nesting tags is important. Figure 7.7 starts with the tags <CENTER>, <B>, and <I>. The closing tags are in a precise order. The innermost tag, in this case <I>, should be closed first. The next tag out, the <B> tag in this example, should be closed next, and so on.

Figure 7.7 Nested Tags

```
<CENTER><B><I>My Summer Vacation</I></B></CENTER>
```

Web Page Creation Programs

Many special applications, such as Microsoft FrontPage, Adobe PageMill, and Macromedia Dreamweaver, exist for generating Web pages. With little to no HTML knowledge, you can produce professional-looking pages. Commonplace programs such as WordPerfect and Excel allow you to save your work as Web pages. All of these programs take the images you compile on the screen and generate the underlying HTML for you.

If such capable programs exist, why bother with HTML? When problems arise, you need to know the code. Anomalies are common in complex Web pages. Something that works well under certain conditions can stop working correctly under different circumstances. Your skill at working with HTML code could someday make or break a Web site.

All you need in this lesson is a simple text editor such as Notepad on a Windows computer, SimpleText on a Macintosh, or vi on a UNIX system.

Web Page Structure

Web pages contain two main sections, the <HEAD> and the <BODY>.

The <HEAD> provides information about the Web page; the <BODY> contains the page's main content, including all text and graphics. The <HTML> tag embeds both the <BODY> and <HEAD> tags, and marks the beginning and end of a Web page (Figure 7.8).

Figure 7.8 Web Page Structure

```
<HTML>

<HEAD>

   . . .

</HEAD>

<BODY>

   . . .

</BODY>

</HTML>
```

The ellipsis, or three dots (…), indicates that more text or HTML tags can appear. The <HEAD> section is usually relatively small. Since it contains the main body of the Web page, the <BODY> section can grow to be quite large.

Creating the <HEAD> Section

Most of the <HEAD> will not display within the browser. Instead, the <HEAD> section specifies information about the Web page such as the title; the name of the person who authored the page; keywords that can be used for searching the page; external programs, or scripts, that run in the page; and style sheets that format the page. Figure 7.9 contains examples of all of these.

Figure 7.9 An Example of the <HEAD> Section

```
<HEAD>

<TITLE>Raging Bees</TITLE>

<META NAME="author" CONTENT="Carl Scharpf">

<META NAME="keywords" CONTENT="ant bee ladybug">

<SCRIPT SRC="bugs.js" TYPE="application/x-javascript">

<LINK REL="stylesheet" TYPE="text/css" HREF="styles.css">

</HEAD>
```

The only part of Figure 7.9 that appears in a browser is the text enclosed within the <TITLE> tag. The <TITLE> text, "Raging Bees" in this example, is placed in the title bar of the browser window.

 Tip: You can have only one TITLE in a Web page and it cannot contain any links or graphical images.

Within the <META> tag you place META information, (META is a computer science term meaning 'about.' HTML META tags describe the Web page document.) Although the <META> tag is optional, if you use it, you must follow <META> with NAME or HTTP-EQUIV and CONTENT. Figure 7.9 shows how to display the author of the Web page and several document keywords.

The keywords that follow CONTENT are important. Several search engines, such as Lycos and AltaVista, use keyword information to help users find your Web page. If you do not include keywords, a search engine uses the first few sentences of your Web page to keep track of its content.

The <SCRIPT> tag, which can also appear in the <BODY> section, defines internal or external programs used with your Web page. JavaScript and VBScript are the programming languages of choice for these types of scripts. The example in Figure 7.9 specifies an external Java script called BUGS.JS.

Style sheets enable you to define how different elements of your Web page appear in the browser. For example, if you always want paragraphs to be slightly indented, fully justified, and a certain color, you can specify all of these settings in a style sheet. The <LINK> tag in Figure 7.9 includes the TYPE of style sheet being used, a text-based Cascading Style Sheet (CSS), and the name of the file that contains the style, STYLES.CSS.

Web Page Header

As you recall, in this lesson you designed a sample Web site for a technical support center. You will now start creating the site by using a text editor and then entering the<HEAD> section of the site's home page.

To create the head section of a Web page, follow these steps:

1. Launch a text editor such as Microsoft Notepad, SimpleText on a Macintosh, or UNIX vi. To start Notepad, from the Start menu, choose Programs and from the Accessories menu, select Notepad.

2. Type the following text:

```
<HTML>

<HEAD>

<META NAME="author" CONTENT="Heather Kiwi">

<TITLE>Technical Support Center</TITLE>

</HEAD>


</HTML>
```

3. The CONTENT should have your name, not Heather's. Also leave a blank line below </HEAD> so that you can later insert the <BODY> information there.

4. Save the file as HOME.HTM

HTML files have the extension HTM or HTML. In this lesson, make sure that you save all files into the same directory on a floppy or hard disk.

 Note: Depending on how you have Microsoft Windows configured, Notepad appends the extension .TXT to your files. This can happen without your notice. If you have trouble viewing the Web pages that you create in this lesson, re-open the document in Notepad and then choose Save As from the File menu. Save the file again with double-quotation marks around the filename. For example, "HOME.HTM" instead of HOME.HTM.

Browser Web Page View

To view your web page in a browser, follow these steps:

1. Open a Web browser such as Netscape or Internet Explorer.

2. From the **File** menu, choose **Open**.

3. Navigate through your files until you find HOME.HTM and then open the file in the browser.

In Figure 7.10, HOME.HTM was found on Drive A. You should be able to see the title Technical Support Center in the title bar of your browser window. The main browser window is empty since you have not entered anything in the <BODY> section.

Figure 7.10 Blank Web Page with Title

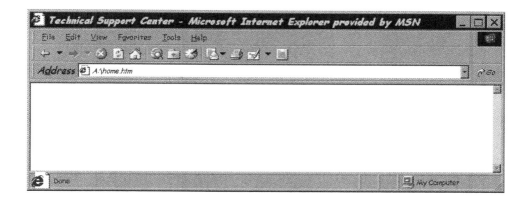

<BODY> Section

The <BODY> of your HTML document contains the substance of your Web page, including text and graphics. The <BODY> section fills the main browser window with content.

The rest of this lesson will deal primarily with tags that are contained between <BODY> and </BODY>. Since most pages have headings, the heading tag is a good place to start. Headings are different from the <HEAD> section of a Web page. Headings consist of the letter H followed by a number (1 to 6). The smaller the number, the larger the heading appears in the browser.

<BODY> Heading

You can use your text editor to add a heading between the body tags by following these steps:

1. Within your text editor, type the following text between the tags </HEAD> and </HTML>.

```
<BODY>

<H1>Home</H1>


</BODY>
```

2. Save your work using the same filename. (In Notepad, from the File menu, click Save.) Do not exit from the text editor, as you will enter more text soon.

3. Start your Web browser.

4. Within the browser, from the View menu, select Refresh. Using Refresh allows the browser to reload the page, enabling the changes. Compare your Web page with the one in Figure 7.11.

Figure 7.11 Browser View of Heading

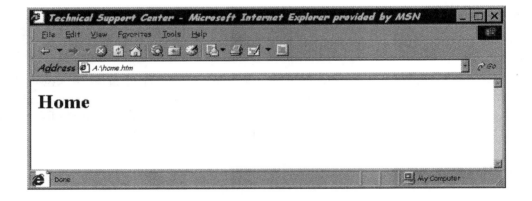

You should give some forethought to your headings. A consistent use of headings among your Web pages gives the site a more professional look.

The technical support site that you are creating has short, concise headings centered on the page. To center headings, use the ALIGN="center" attribute. You can also use ALIGN="left" and ALIGN="right" to left-align and right-align headings.

Centered Heading and Rule

You can now change the heading to center between the margins and add a thin line, called a horizontal rule (HR), below the heading to separate it from the main body of text. You can make a horizontal rule by placing an HR tag where you want the rule to appear.

Follow these steps to center a heading and add a rule line:

1. Change the heading line so that it reads like this:

   <H1 ALIGN="center">Home</H1>

2. Just below the heading **<H1 ALIGN="center">Home</H1>**, type the following text: **<HR>**

3. Save your work but do not exit the text editor.

4. Switch to the browser window and then from the View menu, select Refresh. Compare your Web page to the one in Figure 7.12.

Figure 7.12 Horizontal Rule

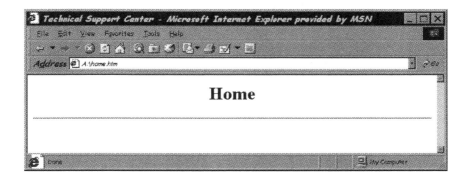

You are ready to start entering the main body of text. Although you do not have to mark your paragraphs, it is a good idea to use the <P> tag. The <P> tag provides a blank line before and after paragraphs. If you do not use paragraph tags, the text ends up running together.

Main Body Text

In the following steps, you enter text without paragraph tags. When you are done, the text will be in one long string. Use the <P> tag to insert a blank line between paragraphs.

1. In the text editor, type the following text between <HR> and </BODY>:

```
Welcome to the Technical Support Center. Our staff is working hard to
solve your problems as if they were our own.


We have developed step-by-step solutions to common technical prob-
lems. If you cannot find the answer at this web site, please fill out
a help form.
```

2. Save your work and then view it in the browser by selecting Refresh. Compare your Web page to the one in Figure 7.13.

Figure 7.13 Browser View of <BODY> Text

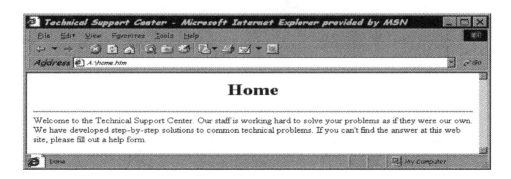

Paragraph Tags

Even though you enter text as separate paragraphs in the text editor, the browser runs the text together into one long string without any breaks. You can fix this with the <P> tag. Paragraph tags are applied to the paragraphs in Figure 7.14. Notice that there are both opening and closing <P> tags. Adding extra blank lines make it easier to read the HTML.

1. In the text editor, insert <P> tags as needed (you will enter <P> and </P> for each paragraph). Make sure that your document looks like the one in Figure 7.14.

2. Save your work and then view it in the Web browser. Remember to Refresh the browser. You should see two distinct paragraphs.

Figure 7.14 Text with Paragraph Tags

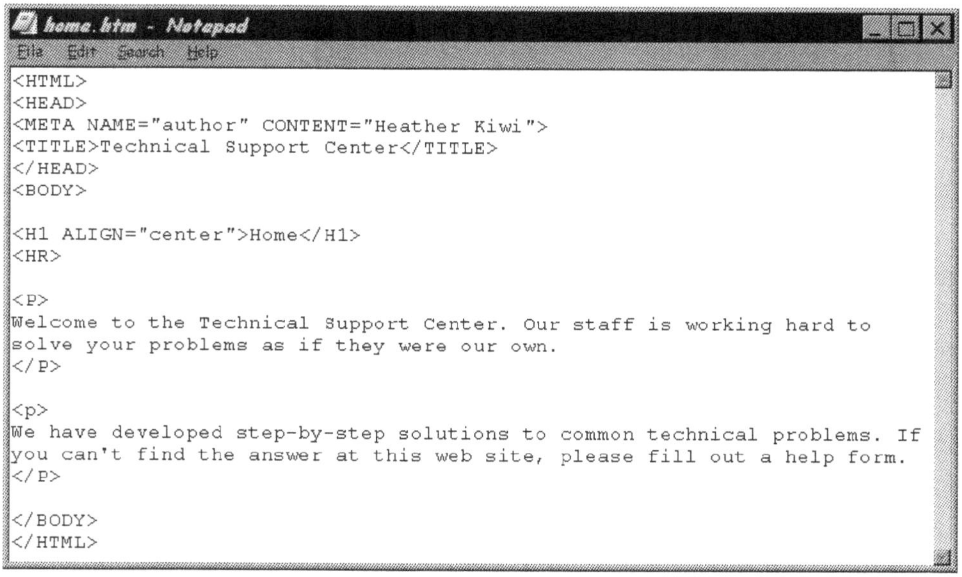

```
<HTML>
<HEAD>
<META NAME="author" CONTENT="Heather Kiwi">
<TITLE>Technical Support Center</TITLE>
</HEAD>
<BODY>

<H1 ALIGN="center">Home</H1>
<HR>

<P>
Welcome to the Technical Support Center. Our staff is working hard to
solve your problems as if they were our own.
</P>

<p>
We have developed step-by-step solutions to common technical problems. If
you can't find the answer at this web site, please fill out a help form.
</P>

</BODY>
</HTML>
```

Fonts and Color

So far, the home page for the technical support site is looking good. By applying a few formatting techniques, you can transform the home page into a professional-looking document. This section concentrates on two important aspects of HTML document formatting: fonts and color.

Fonts

All browsers have a default font with which they display text. Often the default font defaults to Times New Roman, which means that unless otherwise specified in HTML, all standard text appears in Times New Roman. You can change the default font from within the browser. For example, from the Internet Explorer menu bar, choose Tools and then select Internet Options, Fonts to specify a new default font.

To override the default browser settings use the HTML tags <BASEFONT> and <FONT>. The <BASEFONT> tag sets the font for the entire document; the <FONT> tag sets the font for a section of the document, such as a word or paragraph. Both tags have the following three attributes:

■ FACE

■ SIZE

■ COLOR

FACE Attribute

The FACE attribute accepts typefaces as its value. A typeface is a collection of characters that all have the same basic design shape. Examples of typefaces are Times New Roman, Courier, Vladimir, and Verdana. You might say that these are fonts, but technically speaking they are really typefaces. A font is the combination of the typeface, character style (for example bold or italics), and character size.

Figure 7.15 displays several examples of typefaces.

Figure 7.15 Typeface Examples

This is Times New Roman.

This is Vladimir Script.

This is Verdana.

`This is Courier.`

It is best to limit the number of typefaces in a document, otherwise, you get the ransom note effect. One or two typefaces per Web page should be plenty. Additionally, the entire collection of pages that make up a Web site should have a consistent use of typefaces. For precise control of typefaces, many professionals use style sheets.

You enter the <BASEFONT> tag at the beginning of a document, just below the <BODY> tag. If a typeface name has spaces, you must enter the spaces or the browser will revert to the default font. For example, <BASEFONT FACE="comic sans ms"> must have spaces in the name. You can also specify multiple fonts. In the example <BASEFONT FACE="arial", "helvetica">, if the user's computer does not have Arial, it will automatically use Helvetica. If it also does not have Helvetica, it reverts to the default font.

The <FONT> tag works similarly to <BASEFONT> except that you use it for small sections of text. You precede the affected text with <FONT> and then close the text with </FONT>. The rules for placing spaces in typeface names and for using multiple typefaces apply as they do for <BASE-FONT>.

SIZE Attribute

The SIZE attribute specifies the size of the font in either absolute or relative terms. The absolute font size ranges from 1 to 7 with 1 being the smallest and 7 the largest. The default size is 3. For example, <FONT SIZE="6"> sets the size of characters to a rather large size until another </FONT> tag is encountered. The relative size in the tag <FONT SIZE="-3"> reduces characters three sizes from its current size.

Numbers used in the SIZE attribute do not refer to pixel sizes or point sizes. It is up to the browser to render the characters in the right size. Figure 7.16 contains HTML code that changes font sizes.

Figure 7.16 Font Sizes

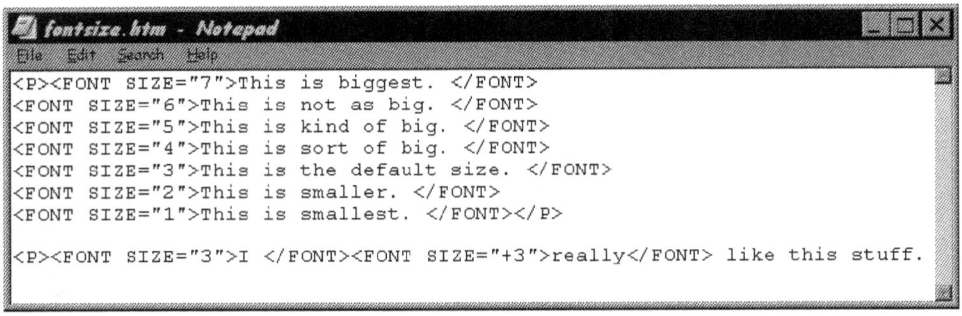


```
<P><FONT SIZE="7">This is biggest. </FONT>
<FONT SIZE="6">This is not as big. </FONT>
<FONT SIZE="5">This is kind of big. </FONT>
<FONT SIZE="4">This is sort of big. </FONT>
<FONT SIZE="3">This is the default size. </FONT>
<FONT SIZE="2">This is smaller. </FONT>
<FONT SIZE="1">This is smallest. </FONT></P>

<P><FONT SIZE="3">I </FONT><FONT SIZE="+3">really</FONT> like this stuff.
```

If you take the file that is displayed in Figure 7.16 and open it in a browser, you see the results that are displayed in Figure 7.17.

Figure 7.17 Size Attribute

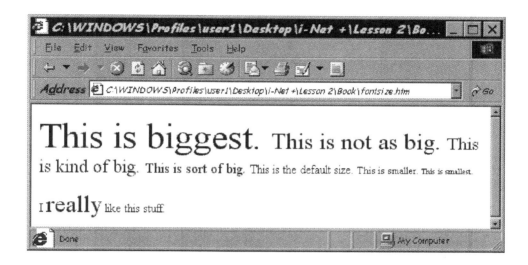

The technical support Web site will use a Microsoft typeface called Verdana. Since some computers might not have this typeface, you will give the alternatives of Arial and Helvetica.

<BASEFONT>HTML Document

To set the <BASEFONT> of an HTML document, follow these steps:

1. In the text editor, insert the following tag directly below the BODY tag:

    `<BASEFONT FACE="verdana","arial","helvetica">`

2. Save your work and then view it in the Web browser. Notice that all text, including the heading, has changed to the Verdana font.

Web Page Color

Depending on your video card and monitor, a Web page can generate millions of colors. Most professionals use only a few colors to give a Web site a consistent look. Too many colors make a site look busy, and older equipment often cannot handle a wide color spectrum.

Web Page Background Color

The colors available for Web page backgrounds are almost limitless. As you browse the Web, you will notice that many Web designers enjoy colorful backgrounds. A colorful background does not necessarily make a site better, and it often detracts from the site. Certain background colors make text difficult to read.

Many professional sites have a white background. Text on a red screen is as hard to read as text in a book of red pages. If you do change the color, you can use the BODY tag along with the BGCOLOR attribute. For example, <BODY BGCOLOR="green"> gives you a green background.

The BGCOLOR attribute accepts most conventional colors. If you want precise color control, you need to use hexadecimal numbers in the form #rrggbb. The 'rr' represents two hexadecimal digits for the color red, the 'gg' represents the color green, and 'bb' is blue. As the number increases, so does the intensity of the color.

For example, since hexadecimal numbers range from 0 to F, a value of #FF0000 represents a really intense red, as the highest value (F) is in both 'rr places (the first two places) and the lowest value (O) is in the 'gg' (middle two places) and 'bb' places (last two places). Therefore, the tag <BODY BGCOLOR="#FF0000"> gives you a red background.

By varying the amounts of red, green, and blue, you can represent almost any number. The color cyan is #00FFFF, yellow is #FFFF00, hot pink is #FF69B4, chocolate is #D2691E, and salmon is FA8072. If you combine all colors, #FFFFFF, you get white, and if you remove all color, #000000, you get black.

Note: For more information about hexadecimal color representations, see http://seurat.art.udel.edu/Site/Cookbook.html, http://www.bagism.com/colormaker/ or http://www.zoran.net/olu/picker_large.asp.

Blue Background Color

The following steps show you how to set the background color to blue. You can use either <BODY BGCOLOR="blue"> or <BODY BGCOLOR="#0000FF">. Since this effect is rather overpowering, the following steps also show you how to remove the blue background:

1. In the text editor, replace the current <BODY> tag with the following:

    <BODY BGCOLOR="blue">

2. Save your work and then view it in the Web browser. Do you like this effect?

3. Return to the text editor.

4. Modify the <BODY BGCOLOR="blue"> tag so that it is reads:

    <BODY>

5. Save your work.

Text Color

One place where you might find a little variety in color is text. Although black text works quite well, a particular text color can give your site a unique look. The COLOR attribute works with both the <BASEFONT> and <FONT> tags.

Blue Text Color

To give the technical support site a distinctive, consistent look, all text will be in blue. You can do this with either <BASEFONT COLOR="blue"> or <BASEFONT COLOR="#0000FF">.

To set the text color to blue, follow these steps:

1. In the text editor, replace the current <BASEFONT> tag with the following:

    <BASEFONT FACE="verdana","arial","helvetica" COLOR="blue">

2. Save your work and then view it in the Web browser. Do you like this effect? Notice that the heading has also changed to blue.

Note: An alternate method of changing the text color for an HTML document is with the TEXT attribute of the <BODY> tag. For example, <BODY TEXT="green"> produces green text.

Blue Horizontal Rule Color

While you are at it, change the horizontal rule to blue, too. The <HR> tag has a COLOR attribute, so you can use <HR COLOR="blue">, as follows:

1. In the text editor, replace the current <HR> tag with the following:

    <HR COLOR="blue">

2. Save your work and then view it in the Web browser.

Lists

HTML provides several methods for arranging items in a list. In this section, you will see Unordered Lists and Ordered Lists, the two most common methods.

Unordered Lists

An unordered list is essentially a bulleted list, a list in which each item is preceded by a bullet. Bullets are typically small circles or squares. Unordered lists work well when you do not want to number each item in a list. An unordered list indicates that no item in a list is more important than another or that no item in a list needs to be performed before another.

Each bullet is marked with an <LI> tag as displayed in Figure 7.18. The figure also has a heading that describes the contents of the list.

Figure 7.18 HTML Code for an Unordered List

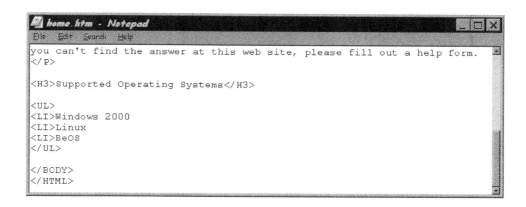

```
home.htm - Notepad
File  Edit  Search  Help
you can't find the answer at this web site, please fill out a help form.
</P>

<H3>Supported Operating Systems</H3>

<UL>
<LI>Windows 2000
<LI>Linux
<LI>BeOS
</UL>

</BODY>
</HTML>
```

Creating an Unordered List

Your home page needs to list the name of each operating system. An ordered list works well for this type of list. You enclose an unordered list within opening and closing <UL> tags, as follows:

1. In the text editor, insert the following HTML code within the </P> and </BODY> tags. Use Figure 7.18 as a guide.

   <H3>Supported Operating Systems</H3>

   <UL>

   <LI>Windows 2000

   <LI>Linux

   <LI>BeOS

   </UL>

2. Save your work and then view it in the Web browser. Your list should look like the one in Figure 7.19.

282   i-Net+

Figure 7.19 Browser View of Unordered List

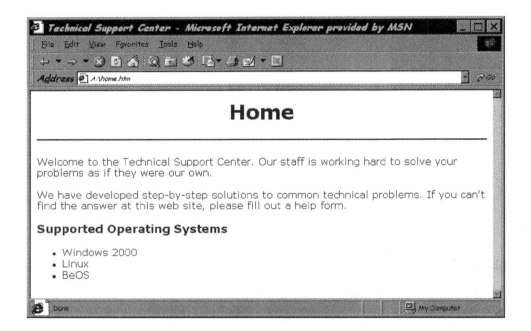

Ordered Lists

A number precedes each item in an ordered list. These lists are effective when you have numbered steps that need to execute in a certain sequence. Ordered lists are also useful when you want to apply some degree of importance to higher numbered items.

Your Web site needs a page dedicated to Linux technical support information. Within this page, include an ordered list that consists of numbered steps for installing Linux.

Creating an Ordered List

Enclose ordered lists within opening and closing <OL> tags. Each number is marked with an <LI> tag.

To create an ordered list, follow these steps:

1. In the text editor, create a new file. (In Notepad, from the File menu, choose New.) You should see a blank screen.

2. Type the following Web page code into the text editor. This page is the main page for Linux Help.

```
<HTML>
<HEAD>
<TITLE>Linux</TITLE>
</HEAD>
<BODY>
<BASEFONT FACE="verdana","arial","helvetica" COLOR="blue">
<H1 ALIGN="center">Linux</H1>
<HR COLOR="blue">


<P>
Welcome to the Technical Support Center Linux page.
</P>


<P>
We have had a lot of questions lately about installing Linux. The numbered steps below provide a general overview of the installation process.
</P>


<H3>Steps for Installing Linux</H3>
<OL>
```

<LI>Gather system hardware information.

<LI>Back up your old system.

<LI>Create a Linux partition.

<LI>Install the kernel.

<LI>Install software packages.

<LI>Configure the system.

<LI>Boot up a running system.

</OL>

</BODY>

</HTML>

3.   Save your work as LINUX.HTM.

4.   Within the browser, open LINUX.HTM. Your page should look like the one in Figure 7.20.

Figure 7.20 Browser View of Ordered List

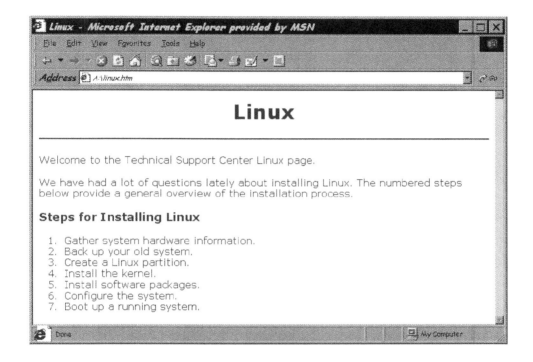

Tables

Tables provide a somewhat more complex, but much more powerful way to lay out data in a Web page. In fact, tables are one of the most flexible and commonly used tools for arranging data.

Like tables in a spreadsheet, Web page tables are arranged in rows and columns. Since using HTML tags in large tables can get rather tricky, many people use programs such as Microsoft FrontPage or Macromedia Dreamweaver to generate HTML tables. You can even use the latest versions of electronic spreadsheets such as Microsoft Excel or Lotus 1-2-3. To create a small table, a simple text editor such as Notepad or SimpleText is fine.

Table 7.1 describes the <TABLE> tag and some of its commonly used attributes. All attributes are optional.

The <TABLE> tag can and should contain tags for defining rows and columns. One of the main components of a table is a cell, the intersection of a row and column. Although there are no tags for cells, cells are integral parts of tables and are dependent upon how you define your rows and columns.

Table 7.1 <TABLE> Tag Attributes

Tag	Attribute	Purpose
<TABLE>		Defines the beginning and ending of a table
	ALIGN	Defines alignment of a table. Accepts a value of "center", "left", or "right".
	BGCOLOR	Defines the background color of a table. Uses same syntax as the <BODY> BGCOLOR attribute.
	BORDER	Defines a line around each cell in a table. Accepts a number (number of pixels) as the value.
	CELLPADDING	Defines the space between the cell border and the cell contents. Uses a number (number of pixels) as the value.
	WIDTH	Defines the width of a table, either in pixels or as a percentage of the browser window. Accepts a number or percentage as the value.

Some of the main tags and attributes associated with building tables are shown in Table 7.2. All attributes are optional.

Table 7.2 Table-Building Tag Attributes

Tag	Attribute	Purpose
<CAPTION>		Defines a caption for a table.
<TR>		Defines a row in a table.
	ALIGN	Defines the horizontal alignment of the contents of each cell in a row. Accepts a value of "center", "left", or "right".
<TH>		Defines a column heading in a table.
<TD>		Defines a column in a table.
	ALIGN	Defines the alignment of the contents of a cell. Accepts a value of "center", "left", or "right". Overrides the TR ALIGN attribute. Used with <TH> and <TD>.
	COLSPAN	Defines the number of columns spanned by a cell. Accepts a number (the number of columns) as the value. Used with <TH> and <TD>.
	ROWSPAN	Defines the number of rows spanned by a cell. Accepts a number (the number of rows) as the value. Used with <TH> and <TD>.
	WIDTH	Defines the width of a column, either in pixels or as a percentage of the browser window. Accepts a number or percentage as the value. Used with <TH> and <TD>.

Tables and Data

Tables are extremely flexible at presenting data. You use them without borders to arrange text and graphics on the screen. Figure 7.21 is an example of HTML source code that uses table-building tags and attributes. Indenting some lines makes the HTML code easier to read.

Figure 7.21 HTML Table Tags and Attributes

```
<HTML>
<BODY>
<<BASEFONT> FACE="verdana","arial","helvetica">

<TABLE ALIGN="center" BORDER WIDTH="50%" CELLPADDING=4>
  <TR>
    <TH COLSPAN=4>Team Records</TH>
  </TR>
  <TR>
    <TH ALIGN="center">School</TH>
    <TH>Team</TH>
    <TH ALIGN="right">Won</TH>
    <TH ALIGN="right">Loss</TH>
  </TR>
  <TR>
    <TD ALIGN="center" rowspan=2>USC</TD>
    <TD>Men</TD>
    <TD ALIGN="right">12</TD>
    <TD ALIGN="right">4</TD>
  </TR>
  <TR>
    <TD>Women</TD>
    <TD ALIGN="right">15</TD>
    <TD ALIGN="right">3</TD>
  </TR>
  <TR>
    <TD ALIGN="center" rowspan=2>UCLA</TD>
    <TD>Men</TD>
    <TD ALIGN="right">9</TD>
    <TD ALIGN="right">6</TD>
  </TR>
  <TR>
    <TD>Women</TD>
    <TD ALIGN="right">10</TD>
    <TD ALIGN="right">5</TD>
  </TR>
</TABLE>

</BODY>
</HTML>
```

If you take a close look at the source code, you can see how it generates the table in Figure 7.22. Notice that the <TH> tag automatically centers and bolds text. In addition, the text Team Records spans four columns. Every occurrence of <TR> and </TR> represents one row and every <TD> and </TD> is one column.

Figure 7.22 Browser view of HTML Table

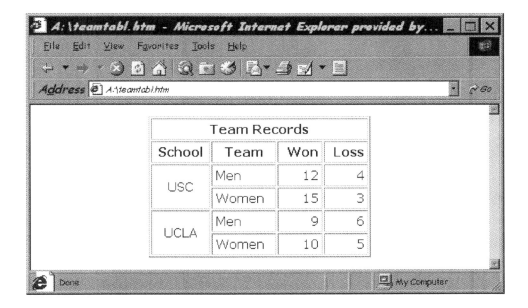

Creating A Table

You are ready to create a table for the technical support Web site. Use the following steps to create a table that lists the compatibility of Windows file systems on dual-boot computers.

1. In the text editor, create a new file. (In Notepad, from the File menu, click New.) You should see a blank screen.

2. You can create a Web page by entering the following into a text editor. This page is the main page for Windows 2000 Help.

```
<HTML>
<HEAD>
<TITLE>Windows 2000</TITLE>
</HEAD>

<BODY>
<BASEFONT FACE="verdana","arial","helvetica" COLOR="blue">
<H1 ALIGN="center">Windows 2000</H1>
<HR COLOR="blue">

<P>
Welcome to the Technical Support Center Windows 2000 page.
</P>

<P>
We have been receiving a lot of questions lately on the compatibility of Microsoft Windows operating systems with different file systems, especially on dual-boot computers.
</P>

<TABLE BORDER ALIGN="center" CELLPADDING=4>
<CAPTION>Windows File Systems</CAPTION>
```

```
<TR>
<TH>OS</TH><TH>FAT-16</TH><TH>FAT-32</TH><TH>NTFS</TH>
</TR>
<TR>
<TD>Windows 95</TD><TD>Yes</TD><TD>No</TD><TD>No</TD>
</TR>
<TR>
<TD>Windows 95 OSR2</TD><TD>Yes</TD><TD>Yes</TD><TD>No</TD>
</TR>
<TR>
<TD>Windows 98</TD><TD>Yes</TD><TD>Yes</TD><TD>No</TD>
</TR>
<TR>
<TD>Windows NT 4</TD><TD>Yes</TD><TD>No</TD><TD>Yes</TD>
</TR>
<TR>
<TD>Windows 2000</TD><TD>Yes</TD><TD>Yes</TD><TD>Yes</TD>
</TR>
</TABLE>

</BODY>
</HTML>
```

3. Save your work as WIN2000.HTM

4. Within the browser, open WIN2000.HTM. Your page should look like the one in Figure 7.23.

Figure 7.23 Another HTML Table

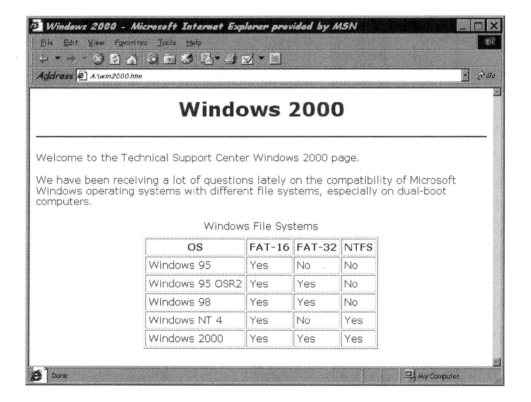

Graphics

You can use graphical images in two ways, either as a stand-alone image or as a background for the entire Web page. Stand-alone images, also called inline images, are the same as hyperlinks within a Web page. These images can consist of company logos, maps, pictures (photos of family pets seem to be popular), or just about anything else.

Acquiring Images

One of the most common methods for acquiring images is scanning photographs. Any scanned photograph can be placed into a Web page. Now that optical color scanners are under $100, they seem to be everywhere.

If you do not have a scanner, there are several other alternatives. For example, many photo shops develop your pictures directly onto a Compact Disc (CD) or other type of disk. Since graphical image files tend to be huge, CDs are currently the medium of choice for image files. If you feel that your photographic skills are lacking, you can buy CDs full of pictures taken by professional photographers. Professional photographs are great for brochures or catalogs.

If you can afford it, a digital camera might be your best bet. You take a series of pictures and then download them directly into your computer. This process eliminates the intermediate step of having your pictures developed. If you are unsatisfied with any image, you can take it again and then download it straight into your computer.

Acquiring pictures from the Web is another popular method for obtaining images. On a PC, you first display the desired Web page in your browser, you right-click the image and then save it in your computer. Of course, you need to check copyright information associated with the image before using it in your own page.

Once you have acquired an image, you may want to edit it with an image-editing program such as Abode Photoshop or PaintShop Pro. These programs allow you to seamlessly alter your images. For example, if someone in your photo has red eyes caused by a camera flash, you can change this into a natural eye color. You can even remove entire objects, including people, from images.

Regardless of how you obtain or alter an image, save it as a Joint Photographic Experts Group (JPG or JPEG) or Graphic Interchange Format (GIF) file. Most modern browsers also accept Portable Network Graphics (PNG) files. Table 7.3 describes some of the differences between JPG and GIF files. Some image features, such as the maximum number of colors, are dependent upon your video adaptor and monitor. Also, there are two main types of GIFs, GIF87A and GIF89A.

GIF89A files are much more feature-rich than GIF87A files.

Table 7.3 JPG and GIF Image Features

Feature	JPG	GIF87A	GIF89A
Maximum number of colors.	16.7 million	256	256
Can be animated.	No	No	Yes
Can be transparent.	No	No	Yes
Can be interlaced.	No	No	Yes
Compression	Lossy	Lossless	Lossless

Files saved with a GIF89A format can be animated, transparent, and interlaced. Animated images seem to be everywhere on the Web. Examples are bouncing balls or revolving logos. You can see through some images. These are transparent files. Have you ever seen an image that slowly comes into focus? It is probably interlaced.

Since graphics files tend to be quite large and take much longer to download than text, it is a good idea to compress them. With some files, such as JPGs, you can control the amount of compression. Often a JPG can be compressed to one-forth of its original size or smaller without too much of a loss in image quality. JPG compression uses a lossy compression method that eliminates data that the eye does not normally perceive.

GIF files use a lossless compression method that does not diminish the quality of the image, but they are typically not as compressed as JPGs. Logos or images with just a few colors usually use a GIF format. Pictures with multiple colors look better as JPGs.

 Note: A good site for getting help with your GIFs is www.gifwizard.com.

Inline Image

The <IMG> (or image) tag along with several of its attributes, controls the appearance of images. The <IMG> tag has many attributes, but the ones you will most likely use are ALT, BORDER, SRC, HEIGHT, and WIDTH. You can even use them all at once such as in Figure 7.24. The only attribute that is required is SRC.

Figure 7.24 <IMG> Tag Attributes

```
<IMG SRC="elvis.jpg" ALT="Elvis" BORDER=0 HEIGHT=50 WIDTH=30>
```

The ALT attribute specifies a text string that displays in browsers that do not support graphics. Instead of an image appearing, text appears. In a graphical environment, the text in the ALT attribute shows up on top of the graphical image whenever you leave the mouse pointer perched on the image for more than a second.

Browsers place a thin border around images. You can remove the border with the BORDER=0 attribute, or you can increase the border by entering a larger number.

You specify the name of the image with the SRC, or source, attribute. Values can range from a simple filename to a complete Uniform Resource Locator (URL). Examples are SRC="emu.jpg" and the fictitious site SRC="http://www.phlogiston.com/emc/fire.gif."

The HEIGHT and WIDTH attributes use numeric pixel values to specify the size of an image. Though often omitted, there is a good reason to include these attributes. Due to the mechanisms that browsers use to display Web pages, when you include a height and width for an image, it can speed up the loading of a Web page.

Tip: The latest specifications for HTML recommend that you use style sheets instead of these attributes. This makes sense, since HTML should deal with structure rather than presentation. However, since millions of Web pages already exist with the <IMG> tag and its attributes, you need to know how these elements are used.

Figure 7.25 shows an example of the <IMG> tag with text.

Figure 7.25 The <IMG> Tag

```
<IMG SRC="fireman.gif" ALT="Fireman">

This is fireman Bob. Hi fireman Bob.
```

The HTML code from Figure 7.25 displays rather strangely in the Web browser (Figure 7.26). Notice that the image renders as very tall text.

Figure 7.26 A Simple <IMG> Tag in a Browser

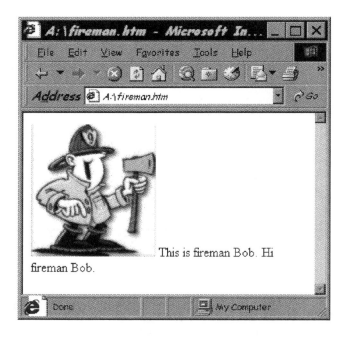

All well-seasoned HTML authors have learned to place images within tables. The code from Figure 7.25 is better when written as Figure 7.27. Notice that the <TABLE> tag has no BORDER attribute. If you do not specify a border, no border is used.

Figure 7.27 +HTML Table

```
<TABLE>

<TR>

  <TD><IMG SRC="fireman.gif" ALT="Fireman"></TD>

  <TD>This is fireman Bob. Hi fireman Bob.</TD>

</TR>

</TABLE>
```

The image in Figure 7.28 looks more professional since the text wraps around on the right. Use of tables is common for page layout. Later in this lesson, you will use them again when you create frames.

Figure 7.28 Image within a Table

Inserting an Image

You are ready to add an image to the technical support site. You will create a new page, the BeOS technical support page, which will have an image that was copied from the real BeOS Web site, www.be.com. If you cannot find this image at that site, use a different one or draw an image in a paint program, such as Microsoft Paint. Then save it as BEOS.GIF. No matter how you acquire the image, make sure that it saves into the same directory as your other Web pages.

To insert an image into a Web page, follow these steps:

1. In the text editor, create a new file. (In Notepad, from the File menu, click New.) You should see a blank screen.

2. Type the following Web page into the text editor. This page is the main page for BeOS help.

```
<HTML>

<HEAD>

<TITLE>BeOS</TITLE>

</HEAD>

<BODY>

<BASEFONT FACE="verdana","arial","helvetica" COLOR="blue">

<H1 ALIGN="center">BeOS</H1>

<HR COLOR="blue">


<P>

Welcome to the Technical Support Center BeOS page. BeOS is a great
operating system.

</P>


<P>

Our tech experts are still ramping up their BeOS skills. To get the
latest information on BeOS, click the image below to jump to the BeOS
Web site.

</P>


<IMG SRC="beos.gif" ALT="Go to BeOS" BORDER=0>


</BODY>

</HTML>
```

3. Save your work as BEOS.HTM

4. Within the browser, open BEOS.HTM. Your page should look like the one in Figure 7.29.

Figure 7.29 Image with Wrapped Text

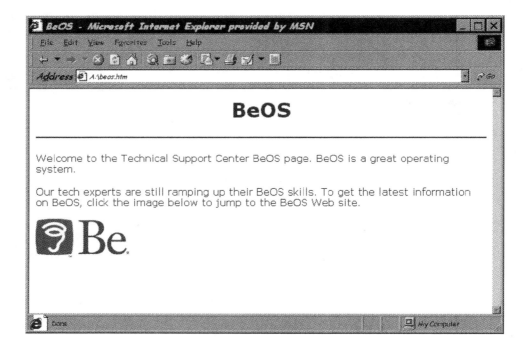

Later you will alter the BeOS Web page so that you can click on the image and go directly to the BeOS Web site.

Tip: The most common image problem is when images do not appear when they should. Varieties of reasons cause this: the image is deleted, the image has been moved, or the HTML code that points to the image is incorrect. When having image problems, look closely at the value of the SRC attribute and then navigate very carefully through the specified path to find the image file.

Background Images

Have you ever been to a Web page that has a strong image in the background, an image that is so busy and full of color that you cannot read the text on the page? Most professionals avoid using graphical images as Web page backgrounds, unless there is a need to have a very faint, watermark-like background. You should also avoid background images unless necessary.

You use the BACKGROUND attribute of the <BODY> command to place a background image on a Web page (Figure 7.30). When the page appears in a browser, the image is tiled, or repeated, across the background until it fills the entire browser window. The technical support Web site will not have a background image.

Figure 7.30 Background Attribute
```
<BODY BACKGROUND="waves.gif">
```

Links

I link, therefore I am. Almost as important as the actual content of a Web page, are the connections between the page and the rest of the Web. You can have the greatest content in the world, but if no one can link to it, it is not of much use.

A link has two main parts: a destination and label. The destination can be another Web page, an e-mail address, a video clip, a sound clip, an executable program, or perhaps something else. The label is a block of text or an image that a user clicks to reach a destination.

Link Use

The <A>, or anchor, tag defines a hyperlink destination and label. The <A> tag can have many attributes, but one is always necessary, either NAME or HREF. The NAME attribute marks a location within a Web page. If you have a large Web page, you can name different parts of the page so that links can point directly to a named location. This combined with HREF will jump to any point in a page.

Use the HREF attribute to specify a hyperlink destination. The destination can be within the same Web page, within the same Web site, or somewhere across the world. The HREF attribute uses a URL as its value. Figure 7.31 has several examples of the <A> tag along with the NAME and HREF attributes.

Figure 7.31 <A> Tag

```
<HTML>


<HEAD>

</HEAD>


<BODY>


<A NAME="intro">

The rain in

<A HREF="http://www.spain.com">Spain</A>

 falls mainly on the
```

```
<A HREF="http://www.plain.com">plain.</A>


<P>

<A HREF="http://www.tourspain.es"><IMG SRC="spain.gif" ALT="Spain"></A>

</P>


<A HREF="spain.htm#intro">Go to top</A>


</BODY>

</HTML>
```

Figure 7.32 shows the HTML code results. In this example, as in most Web pages, the hyperlinks are underlined. That is, everything between the <A> and the </A> represents the label that you click to go to a destination.

The top of the <BODY> section has the name "intro." At the bottom of the BODY section, the HREF value "spain.htm#intro" points to the top of the page. The pound symbol (#) separates the filename from "intro." If you click the label "Go to top," you will go to the name "intro." In short pages like this one, links within a page are usually unnecessary. These types of links can be indispensable in longer pages.

The label "Spain" points to the site www.spain.com, a discount travel agency. The label "plain" points to an Internet software company.

The tag <IMG SRC="spain.gif" ALT="Spain"> represents a graphical hyperlink. If you click the image "spain.gif," you go to www.tourspain.es, the Spanish tourism office located in Spain (the .es in the URL indicates a site in Spain). If you do not want a border around the image, use the <IMG> attribute BORDER=0.

Figure 7.32 Browser View of <A> Tag

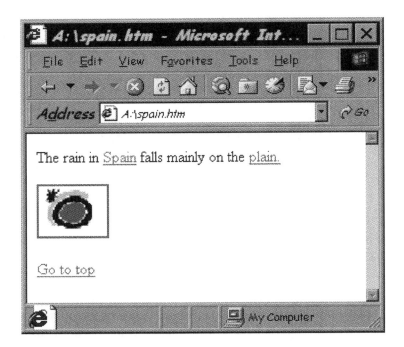

Adding Links to a Web Page

You are ready to add hyperlinks to the technical support Web site. The home page should point to each subpage: Windows 2000, Linux, and BeOS. Each subpage should point back to the home page. In addition, the BeOS page has a graphical image that should point to the real BeOS Web site.

To add hyperlinks to your Web page, follow these steps:

1.   In the text editor, open HOME.HTM.

2.   Change the unordered list to the following:

```
<ul>

<li><a href="win2000.htm">Windows 2000</a>

<li><a href="linux.htm">Linux</a>

<li><a href="beos.htm">BeOS</a>

</ul>
```

3. Save your work and then view it in the Web browser. Try out each link. To get back to the home page, click the browser's Back button.

Adding a Link Back to the Home Page

At the bottom of each subpage, you should have a link back to the home page. The following steps show you how to do this and how to center a hyperlink with the CENTER tag. Anything enclosed in a CENTER tag ends up centered on the screen.

1. In the text editor, open WIN2000.HTM.

2. At the bottom of the page (just before </BODY>), insert the following:

    ```
    <CENTER>

    <P>

    <A HREF="home.htm">Home</A>

    </P>

    </CENTER>
    ```

3. Save the file WIN2000.HTM.

4. In the text editor, open LINUX.HTM.

5. At the bottom of the page (just before </BODY>), insert the following:

    ```
    <CENTER>

    <P>

    <A HREF="home.htm">Home</A>
    ```

```
</P>

</CENTER>
```

6. Save the file LINUX.HTM.

7. In the text editor, open BEOS.HTM.

8. At the bottom of the page (just before </BODY>), insert the following:

```
<CENTER>

<P>

<A HREF="home.htm">Home</A>

</P>

</CENTER>
```

9. Save the file BEOS.HTM.

10. In the browser, test out all your links. All subpages should link to the home page and vice versa.

Adding a Link to a Graphical Image

You have one more link to add to the technical support site. The BeOS page has a graphical image that should link to the main BeOS Web site.

1. In the text editor, open BEOS.HTM.

2. At the bottom of the page, before <CENTER><P>**<A HREF="home.htm">Home</A>**, change the <IMG> tag to the following:

```
<CENTER>

<A HREF="http://www.be.com">

<IMG SRC="be.gif" ALT="Go to BeOS" BORDER="0">

</A>

</CENTER>
```

3. In the browser, test the graphics link to make sure it connect to the location you specified.

Frames

Using frames, you can display more than one Web page within the browser window. Just as a regular window divides into separate sections called panes, a browser window can be divided into separate sections called frames. Although many Web site designers question the usefulness of frames, if used properly, frames can be useful tools in easing navigation through a site.

Frame Use

Figure 7.32 displays several ways in which you can divide a browser window. Each frame should contain a different Web page.

Figure 7.32 Window Divided into Frames

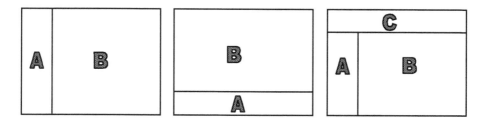

Within a collection of frames known as a frame set, one Web page is usually set up for navigation. One frame, or Web page, consists of hyperlinks. As each hyperlink is clicked, the target Web page shows up in a designated frame. For example, in Figure 7.32, each frame labeled "A" could contain hyperlinks. When a user clicks a hyperlink in A, the target Web page would appear in "B." The frame labeled "C" could contain company information, an ad banner, or perhaps more hyperlinks.

It is best not to have too many frames. More than three can make your site look confusing. The technical support site has a frame set with just two frames. A frame across the top contains hyperlinks, and a large frame on the bottom holds the target pages. The completed frame set will look like the one in Figure 7.33.

Figure 7.33 Tech Support Frame Set

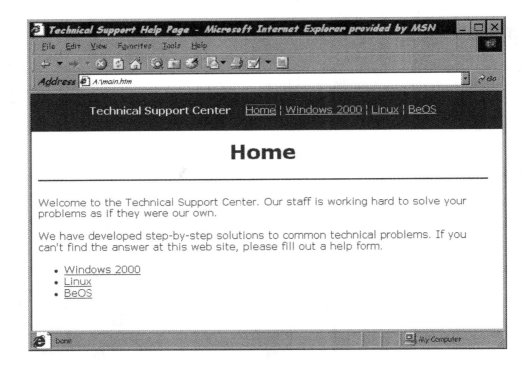

All of the target pages are created. You need to create the top page that will contain hyperlinks. You also need to create a special page that defines the frame set. Start with the frame set page.

Creating a Frame Set

To create a frame set, follow these steps:

1.   In the text editor, create a new file. You should have a blank screen.

2.   Type the following:

```
<HTML>

<HEAD>

<TITLE>Technical Support Help Page</TITLE>

</HEAD>

<FRAMESET ROWS="60,*" BORDER=0>

<FRAME SRC="links.htm" NAME="links">

<FRAME SRC="home.htm" NAME="content">

</FRAMESET>

</HTML>
```

3. Save your work as MAIN.HTM.

The frame set HTML file has several interesting new tags. In a Web page with frames, a <FRAME-SET> tag replaces the <BODY> tag. <FRAMESET> defines the layout of the frames in the browser window.

Within <FRAMESET>, the ROWS attribute specifies the size of horizontal frames in terms of pixels or percentages. The example ROWS="60,*" defines two horizontal frames: the first is 60 pixels high and the second is defined as an asterisk (*). The asterisk indicates that the second frame or row should fill up the rest of the browser window.

The first <FRAME> tag defines the first frame, in this case, the first row. The SRC attribute specifies a source file called "links.htm," that you will create. It consists of hyperlinks. The NAME attribute gives the first frame a name. In essence, the content of this frame is "LINKS.HTM," the name of the frame is "links."

The second <FRAME> tag defines the second frame or row. In this frame, the contents or SRC is "HOME.HTM;" the name of the frame is "content." The second frame will hold the main contents of the Web site.

The last thing you need to create is the HTML file for the first frame. This file called "LINKS.HTM" consists of a table with hyperlinks. The links point to the main subpages of the Web site, that is, Windows 2000, Linux, and BeOS. Is also puts the subpages into the "content" frame.

Creating a Page of Hyperlinks

To create a Web page that contains hyperlinks, follow these steps:

1. In the text editor, create a new file.

2. Type the following:

```
<HTML>


<BODY   BGCOLOR="blue"   TEXT="white"   VLINK="white"   ALINK="white"
LINK="white">

<BASEFONT FACE="verdana","arial","helvetica">


<TABLE ALIGN="center">
  <TR>
    <TD><B>Technical Support Center    </B></TD>

    <TD><A HREF="home.htm" TARGET="content">Home</A></TD>

    <TD>&brvbar;</TD>

    <TD><A HREF="win2000.htm" TARGET="content">Windows 2000</A></TD>

    <TD>&brvbar;</TD>

    <TD><A HREF="linux.htm" TARGET="content">Linux</A></TD>

    <TD>&brvbar;</TD>

    <TD><A HREF="beos.htm" TARGET="content">BeOS</A></TD>
  </TR>
</TABLE>


</BODY>

</HTML>
```

3. Save your work as LINKS.HTM.

4. Open the file LINKS.HTM in the Web browser. Test out all your links.

 Note: If something does not work, more often than not, it is because of a typing error. Go back into your HTML files, make any necessary changes, save your work and then Refresh LINKS.HTM in the browser.

This new HTML file has several attributes and other features that you have not seen before. The <BODY> tag uses four new attributes: TEXT, LINK, ALINK, and VLINK. The TEXT attribute sets the default color for all text in the page. As you recall, the <BASEFONT> tag and COLOR attribute can also set the default text color. Additionally, the text color for a section of the document can be set with the <FONT> tag and COLOR attribute.

The next three attributes, all of which have a color as their value, set the default color of text links. To set the color of links not yet visited, use LINK followed by a color. Use VLINK to change the color of visited links and ALINK to set the color of a link that is being clicked. In this example, they have all been set to white to help define this site's unique look and feel.

Many characters exist, including foreign ones, which are not on the keyboard. For example, how do you place the Norwegian character "Å" into a document? HTML has a special mechanism for entering these types of characters. You type an ampersand (&) followed by a special number or special text string that corresponds to the character. The letter Å is entered as Å or Å. The copyright symbol (©) is © or ©.

In the Web page that you created above, you have two of these special characters. You probably have noticed that extra spaces in a Web page do not display in the browser. For example, "Steve Austin is so   quick." would display with only one space between so and quick. If you want an extra space, you must use the code   (nbsp comes from "nonblank space").

Another special character that appears in your HTML code is a broken vertical bar (¦), which separates links in the top frame. You enter this character with the code ¦ or ¦.

Tip: For a complete list of character codes, visit the site: http://www.utoronto.ca/web-docs/htmldocs/book/Book-3ed/appa/en_test.html

Comments

Professionals often add comments to their HTML documents to describe what results they are trying to achieve. It is a good idea to include comments when you know that other people will be updating your HTML code later. Since Web pages, like programs, can get quite complex, good comments are indispensable in helping others understand what you were trying to achieve with your use of tags.

Using the Comment Tag

Comments will not display in a browser, but they are read in a text editor like any other tag. Although your Web page should include many comments, the following steps show you how to add just one. If you want to add a complete set of comments, you can add them later on your own.

To add a comment to an HTML document, surround the comment with a <!-- and a -->. Since the technical support Web site uses the color blue to create a distinctive, consistent look, it would be a good idea to describe this within a comment. Within the HOME.HTM file, you will find the place where you first start using color, the <BASEFONT> tag, and then add the comment.

Adding a Comment

To add a comment, follow these steps:

1. In the text editor, open HOME.HTM.

2. Create a blank line between the <BODY> tag and the <BASEFONT> tag.

3. Type the following comment:

4. `<!—The color blue is used to create a distinctive, consistent look for the technical support Web site-->`

5. Save your work and then view it in the Web browser. The comment should not be visible.

Vocabulary

Review the following terms in preparation for the certification exam.

Term	Description
animated image	A GIF file that moves on the screen is an animated image.
attribute	An add-on to a tag that is used to specify tag options.
comment	Text that appears in the text editor, but not in the browser window. Adds explanations for using HTML.
frame	A rectangular section of a Web browser window. Multiple frames can exist simultaneously.
GIF	Graphics Interchange Format. A graphics standard used on the Web.
heading	Darker and larger text that marks a section of a Web page.
hexadecimal	A base-16 numbering system.
horizontal rule	A narrow line across a Web page.
interlaced image	An image that slowly comes into focus as it appears on the screen.
JPG	Joint Photographic Experts Group. A graphics standard used on the Web. Also known as JPEG.
nested tag	A tag that appears within another tag.
ordered list	A numbered list of items.

Term	Description
physical markup language	A markup language that describes how a document looks when printed.
semantic markup language	A markup language that uses codes to mark the meaning of text rather than its physical appearance.
SGML	Standard General Markup Language, from which HTML was derived, provides structure definitions and tags to denote documents.
table	A collection of rows and columns used for laying out data in a Web page.
tag	An HTML command, always enclose in angle brackets (<>).
transparent image	A GIF file that you can see through.
typeface	A collection of characters that all have the same basic design.
unordered list	A bulleted list of items.
value	Numeric or string data used to quantify attributes.
W3C	World Wide Web Consortium. An Internet organization that publishes the current standards for HTML.
Webmaster	The overall manager of a Web site.

In Brief

If you want to...	Then do this...
Create a Web site	Sketch out a Web site diagram on paper.
Type an HTML tag	Use upper case to distinguish it from surrounding text.
Add attributes and values to a tag	Separate the attribute and value with an equal sign.
Nest tags	Close the innermost tag first and then systematically close outer tags.
Quickly create a Web page	Use a Web page creation program such as Microsoft FrontPage or Adobe PageMill.
Create a Web page by typing your HTML tags from scratch	Use a text editor and then save your work as an HTM or HTML file.
Specify style sheets and scripts for a Web page	Define them in the < HEAD> of the page.
Apply precise color control to Web page elements	Define your colors with hexadecimal numbers instead of text.
Create a bulleted list	Define an unordered list.
Create a numbered list	Define an ordered list.
Acquire graphical images	Use a scanner, have your photos developed onto a CD, buy third-party photos, use a digital camera, or grab your photos off the Web.
Use a graphical image in your Web page	Save it as a JPG or GIF file.
Lay out your text and images more precisely	Use tables.
Display multiple pages simultaneously in a Web browser window	Use frames.

Lesson 7 Activities

Complete the following activities to prepare for the certification exam.

1. Explain how HTML is much more of a semantic markup language than a physical markup language.

2. Explain why you should sketch out a Web site on paper before you start writing HTML code.

3. Describe the purpose of Web page creation programs.

4. Describe the importance of knowing HTML.

5. Describe the difference between the Head and Body sections of a Web page.

6. Describe how a typeface is different from a font.

7. Explain the difference between absolute and relative values of the SIZE attribute in the <FONT> tag.

8. Explain why many professional Web sites use a white background rather than a colorful one.

9. Describe why digital cameras are an effective means for acquiring images.

10. Describe the purpose of comments.

Answers to Lesson 7 Activities

1. HTML has many tags that describe the meaning of text. Examples are paragraph, table, frame, and heading tags.

2. By creating a Web site diagram, you can get a bird's-eye view of how your pages interconnect. This makes it easier to get a feel for how people will navigate through your site.

3. Web page creation programs such as FrontPage and PageMill enables users with little to no HTML knowledge to quickly create a Web page. FrontPage or PageMill generates all HTML code for you.

4. Although Web page creation programs can generate all HTML for you, knowing HTML is indispensable for troubleshooting Web page problems.

5. The Head provides information about the Web page such as the name of the author, style sheets, or programs. The Body contains the main contents of the Web page including text, graphics, and all links.

6. A typeface is a collection of characters that all have the same basic design. The typeface is one component of the font. A font includes the typeface, character size, and character style (e.g., bold, italics, etc.) In everyday usage, the terms typeface and font are interchangeable.

7. The SIZE attribute can use absolute values that range between 1 and 7 (1 is the smallest; 7 the largest). Preceding relative values, a plus (+) or minus (-) sign, can be used. Relative values increase or decrease the font size based on the current value.

8. Usually, a white background makes the foreground text much easier to read. A colorful background can detract from the main content of a Web page.

9. Photographs from digital cameras require no intermediate steps. That is, you do not need to develop film or scan images; the pictures download directly into the computer.

10. Comments describe what you were trying to achieve with your use of HTML codes. This makes it much easier for others to update your work.

Lesson 7 Quiz

These questions test your knowledge of features, vocabulary, procedures, and syntax.

1. Which of the following is a correct example of nested tags?

    A. <I><B>One Thousand Years of Solitude</I></B>

    B. <I><B>One Thousand Years of Solitude<B><I>

    C. <I><B>One Thousand Years of Solitude</B></I>

    D. <I></I>One Thousand Years of Solitude<B></B>

2. Which of the following tags are found in the Body section?

    A. <TITLE>

    B. <TABLE>

    C. <META>

    D. <HEAD>

3. What extension can a Web page have?

    A. JPG

    B. GIF

    C. RPG

    D. HTM

4. Which if the following is a <FONT> attribute?

    A. FACE

    B. SRC

    C. BOLD

    D. <TD>

5. Which of the following specifies a blue the background for a Web page?

A.   <BODY BACKGROUND="blue">

B.   <BACKGROUND COLOR="blue">

C.   <BODY COLOR="blue">

D.   <BODY BGCOLOR="blue">

6.   Which of the following tags is necessary to create a bulleted list?

A.   <UL>

B.   <OL>

C.   <BULLET>

D.   <LIST>

7.   Which of the following is not a table-building tag?

A.   TR

B.   <TD>

C.   TG

D.   <CAPTION>

8.   Which of the following is correct?

A.   Tables can center in the browser window.

B.   By default, tables have a narrow border.

C.   The Head section defines tables.

D.   Tables can only include text; they cannot include graphical images.

9.   Which of the following graphics standards support animation, transparency, and interlacing?

A.   GIF87A

B.   GIF89A

C.   JPEG

D.   JPG

10. Which of the following tags correctly uses the comment tag?

    A. <COMMENT>This is a test. </COMMENT>

    B. <REMARK>This is a test. </REMARK>

    C. <!- This is a test -->

    D. <!>This is a test. </!>

Answers to Lesson 7 Quiz

1. Answer C is correct. Inner tags must close before outer tags.

    Answer A is incorrect. It closes the outer tag before closing the inner tag.

    Answer B is incorrect. Closing tags must include a forward slash (/).

    Answer D is incorrect. Opening and closing tags must surround the text that they affect.

2. Answer B is correct. Tables are defined in the Body section.

    Answer A is incorrect. The Head section defines titles.

    Answer C is incorrect. <META> tags are found in the Head section.

    Answer D is incorrect. The <HEAD> tag always precedes the <BODY> tag; it is not embedded within the <BODY> tag.

3. Answer D is correct. A Web page typically has the extension HTM or HTML.

    Answer A is incorrect. JPG is an extension for a JPG graphics file.

    Answer B is incorrect. GIF is an extension for a GIF graphics file.

    Answer C is incorrect. RPG is the name of a programming language, not an extension for any type of file associated with the Web.

4. Answer A is correct. The FACE attribute sets the typeface.

    Answer B is incorrect. The SRC attribute defines an image source.

    Answer C is incorrect. There is no BOLD attribute. There is a <B> tag, but it is not used within the <FONT> tag as an attribute.

    Answer D is incorrect. The <TD> tag defines tables.

5. Answer D is correct. The BGCOLOR attribute sets the background color.

    Answer A is incorrect. The BACKGROUND attribute sets the background to a graphical image.

    Answer B is incorrect. There is no BACKGROUND tag.

    Answer C is incorrect. The correct attribute is BGCOLOR, not COLOR.

6. Answer A is correct. The <UL> tag specifies an unordered list, which is the same as a bulleted list.

    Answer B is incorrect. The <OL> tag specifies an ordered list. Ordered lists use numbers, not bullets.

    Answer C is incorrect. There is no BULLET tag.

    Answer D is incorrect. There is no LIST tag.

7. Answer C is correct. There is no TG tag.

    Answer A is incorrect. The <TR> tag is for defining table rows.

    Answer B is incorrect. The <TD> tag is for defining table columns.

    Answer D is incorrect. The <CAPTION> tag is for defining table captions.

8. Answer A is correct. You center a table with <TABLE ALIGN="center">

    Answer B is incorrect. You need to use the BORDER attribute to get a border.

    Answer C is incorrect. The Body section defines tables.

    Answer D is incorrect. Tables can include text and graphics.

9. Answer B is correct. The GIF 89A standard supports all of these features.

    Answer A is incorrect. This GIF 87A standard does not support any of these features.

    Answer C is incorrect. Standard JPEG files do not support any of these features.

    Answer D is incorrect. Standard JPG files do not support any of these features.

10. Answer C is correct. The <!- tag is the correct tag for comments.

    Answer A is incorrect. There is no COMMENT tag.

    Answer B is incorrect. There is no REMARK tag.

    Answer D is incorrect. There is no <!> tag.

Lesson 8: Interactive Web Page Construction

HyperText Markup Language (HTML) documents provide a great way for distributing information over the Web, but HTML is lacking when it comes to Web page layout or interactive content. This lesson takes you beyond HTML into a realm with many exciting Web technologies.

After completing this lesson, you should have a better understanding of the following topics:

- Style Sheets
- Web Programming
- Web Scripting Languages
- Database Access
- Extensible Markup Language (XML)
- Plug-in, File Formats, and Extensions
- Finishing Touches

Style Sheets

Although HTML has several tags that define the physical appearance of a page, HTML's strength lies in marking the meaning of text rather than its format. HTML supports the classification of various parts of your page; the browser is responsible for displaying the contents onscreen.

Many HTML authors have gone to great lengths to create precise page layouts for a particular browser. Often they are disappointed when they view the same page in a different browser, or when they load the page in a text-to-speech system or handheld computer. HTML is designed to control substance, not appearance.

HTML 4.0, the latest recommendation of the World Wide Web Consortium (W3C), reinforces the separation of Web page content from Web page presentation. The W3C is a consortium of Internet professionals who propose recommendations for Web standards. A recommendation indicates that the consortium members have reached a consensus that a specification is appropriate for widespread use. A W3C recommendation is for all practical purposes an Internet standard.

HTML 4.0 has many valuable features, which include the following:

- Support for style sheets

- Greatly expanded foreign-language support

- New features for accessibility

- New tools for creating tables and forms

- Advanced multimedia support

- New scripting support

Although HTML allows you to use any type of style sheet, Cascading Style Sheets (CSS) have by far the most support. A W3C recommendation in December of 1996 established Cascading Style Sheets, level 1 (CSS1) as the industry standard. In May of 1998, a W3C recommendation for CSS2 added support for downloadable fonts, element positioning, and tables. Although you can specify different output devices in CSS1, it is primarily concerned with the onscreen appearance of Web pages. CSS2 has extensive support for system-specific style sheets, that is, style sheets for printers, projectors, text-to-speech devices, and so on.

Note: To view information on CSS1, CSS2, and other W3C recommendations, go to the site www.w3c.org.

Cascading Style Sheets (CSS)

The term cascading refers to the fact that multiple style sheets apply to one Web page. Users who are getting starting with style sheets usually create and apply just one. You can define the style sheet within the Head section of the Web page or you can create it in a separate external file.

CSS uses a different syntax from HTML. For example, to specify blue text on a white background, you enter the HTML tag <BODY TEXT="blue" BGCOLOR="white">. To specify the same formatting in a style sheet, you enter BODY { color: blue; background: white; }.

In Figure 8.1, you can see the standard syntax and terminology of a CSS rule. Rules define formatting in a style sheet.

Figure 8.1 CSS Rule

A selector is the element for which you are defining a format. Any Web page that uses this rule will have blue text in the H1 headings. Therefore, when you use the H1 tag anywhere in a Web page, the property and value defined in the rule are applied.

The property of a selector refers to a distinguishing feature of the selector. In addition to text color, H1 headings use a particular typeface, point size, background color, and so on. The value is the current setting of the property. You can specify multiple properties and values separated by semicolons (;).

The easiest way to see the effects of a style sheet is to use one. Figure 8.2 displays the results of a style sheet that is embedded into the Head section of the Web page. Defined are two different heading styles and paragraph styles. In the next couple of pages, you create this Web page and its embedded style sheet.

Figure 8.2 Web Page-Embedded CSS

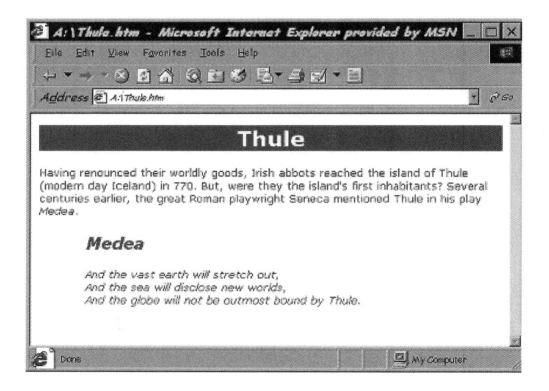

Creating an Embedded Style Sheet

To create an embedded style sheet, follow these steps:

1. Launch a text editor such as Microsoft Notepad, SimpleText on a Macintosh, or UNIX vi. To start Notepad, choose Programs from the Start menu and then from the Accessories menu, choose Notepad.

2. Enter the following information for the style sheet:

```
<HTML>

<HEAD>

<STYLE TYPE="text/css">

<!--

H1   {text-align:center;

     background:blue;

     color:white;

     font:bold 20 pt "verdana","arial","helvetica"}


H2   {margin-left:10%;

     text-align:left;

     color:#083194;

     font:bold italic 15 pt "verdana","arial","helvetica"}


P.normal {text-align:left;

     color:blue;

     font:normal 10 pt "verdana","arial","helvetica"}
```

```
P.passage{margin-left:10%;

        text-align:left;

        color:#083194;

        font:italic 10 pt "verdana","arial","helvetica"}

-->

</STYLE>

</HEAD>
```

3. Save your work, give it the name THULE.HTM and then stay in the text editor.

Although it is not necessary, indenting the rules for each selector make the style sheet easier to read. In addition, the style sheet has been commented out so that it will be ignored by older browsers that do not recognize style sheets. Comment tags (<!-- and -->) surround the style sheet so that older browsers see the style sheet merely as a comment and not as some undecipherable text.

The TYPE attribute sets the style sheet type to CSS. Although there are other types of style sheets, you will usually specify CSS.

Two heading styles are defined: H1 and H2. When you write the content of the Web page, wherever you enter an H1 or H2, the rules associated with these headings will apply. H1 provides a characterized style that is bold, white, and 20-point text centered on a blue background. H2 specifies bold, italic, left-aligned text with a 10% indent, and a unique shade of blue, #083194.

Two paragraph styles are defined: P.normal and P.passage. Both of these are examples of style sheet classes. Classes enable you to apply precise control over an HTML element. To create a style sheet class, enter an HTML element, such as a P, and then type a period followed by the class name. As a style sheet author, you will devise class names based on their function.

Applying an Embedded Style Sheet

The Web page that you create has two types of paragraphs: normal paragraphs and paragraphs that are passages from plays or poems. As you can see, a normal, left-aligned text style defines normal paragraphs. An italic text style that indents by 10% defines paragraphs that derive from passages in a play. Like H2 headings, the P.passage style sheet class uses a unique shade of blue, #083194.

To apply an embedded style sheet, follow these steps:

1. Within the text editor, go to the bottom of the file THULE.HTM just below the </HEAD> tag.

2. Type the following HTML content.

```
<BODY>

<H1>Thule</H1>


<P CLASS=normal>Having renounced their worldly goods, Irish abbots
reached the island of Thule (modern day Iceland) in 770. But, were
they the island's first inhabitants? Several centuries earlier, the
great Roman playwright Seneca mentioned Thule in his play
<I>Medea</I>.</P>


<H2>Medea</H2>


<P CLASS=passage>And the vast earth will stretch out,<BR>

And the sea will disclose new worlds,<BR>

And the globe will not be outmost bound by Thule.</P>


</BODY>

</HTML>
```

3. Save the file again as THULE.HTM.

4. Load THULE.HTM into your browser. Compare your work to the Web page in Figure 8.2.

Notice that you use the CLASS attribute, such as <P CLASS=normal>, to apply a class. In addition, even though you have a style sheet, you still use HTML tags the style sheet does not define. The <I>

tag, which is used for italics, and the <BR> tag, which is used to set a line break, are not defined in the style sheet.

Embedded style sheets have one major limitation—they can only apply to the Web page in which they are defined. If you want to use the same style sheet in a different page, you must either retype it or copy-and-paste it into the other page.

External style sheets provide much more flexibility because they are applicable to multiple Web pages. For example, if you were creating a Web site with numerous pages that resemble chapters in a book, you could create an external style sheet called CHAPTER.CSS.

The embedded style sheet that you created for THULE.HTM can be used for the Web page displayed in Figure 8.3. The page in Figure 8.3, which looks like a chapter from a book, describes problems with the Japanese stock market. It consists of two files: JAPAN.HTM and CHAPTER.CSS.

Figure 8.3 External CSS Web Page

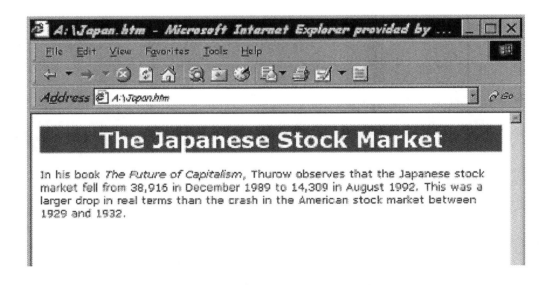

Creating an External Style Sheet

In the steps below, you use a text editor to create an external style sheet and then a Web page.

1. Within a text editor, create a new file. Your screen should be blank.

2. Enter the following text. Since this style sheet is exactly the same as the one used in THULE.HTM, you could copy it from that file.

```
H1   {text-align:center;
     background:blue;
     color:white;
     font:bold 20 pt "verdana","arial","helvetica"}


H2   {margin-left:10%;
     text-align:left;
     color:#083194;
     font:bold italic 15 pt "verdana","arial","helvetica"}


P.normal {text-align:left;
     color:blue;
          font:normal 10 pt "verdana","arial","helvetica"}


P.passage{margin-left:10%;
     text-align:left;
          color:#083194;
          font:italic 10 pt "verdana","arial","helvetica"}
```

3. Save the file as CHAPTER.CSS.

Applying an External Style Sheet

To apply an external style sheet, follow these steps:

1. Within a text editor, create a new file. Your screen should be blank.

2. Enter the following Web page information:

```
<HTML>

<HEAD>

<LINK REL=stylesheet TYPE="text/css" HREF="chapter.css">

</HEAD>

<BODY>

<H1>The Japanese Stock Market</H1>


<P CLASS=normal>In his book <I>The Future of Capitalism</I>, Thurow
observes that the Japanese stock market fell from 38,916 in December
1989 to 14,309 in August 1992. This was a larger drop in real terms
than the crash in the American stock market between 1929 and 1932.</P>


</BODY>

</HTML>
```

3. Save the page as JAPAN.HTM in the same directory as CHAPTER.CSS.

4. View JAPAN.HTM in your Web browser. It should resemble the Web page in Figure 8.3.

The <LINK> tag sets up a relationship between a Web page and an external file; the type of external file is specified by the REL attribute. In the above example, the value of REL is style sheet. The HREF attribute, which is always mandatory, contains as its value the file name of the external file.

The topic of style sheets is a large one. Entire books exist on CSS. It is worthwhile becoming familiar with CSS, especially since the W3C has set CSS as a Web standard. In fact, the W3C now considers standard HTML tags such as <FONT> to be harmful. They strongly discourage Web page designers from generating fancy page layouts by performing tricks with <FONT>, BR, , and other HTML features. Structure documents around items such as paragraphs, headings and lists, which style sheets should define.

Web Programming

In its early days, the Web was a collection of HTML pages with static content. Web pages sat on Web servers waiting for someone to download and display them. Unless their author made modifications, the content was always the same.

Although many sites remain static, dynamic content is the current trend, especially at professional sites. For example, assume that you worked at a company that wanted to allow users to search one of its databases. Once the desired data is found, you could automatically have it placed into a Web page and returned to the user. To achieve this level of interactivity, you need to add a programming component to your Web site.

Programming Languages

Computer programming has been around as long as computers. Early programmers used the complex, low-level machine language of computers, 0s and 1s, to develop step-by-step instructions to control a computer. Today we can program in English-like, high-level languages, such as C++, Practical Extraction and Report Language (Perl), and Visual Basic, which the computer translates for us into machine language.

Programming languages divide roughly into two broad groups: compiled languages and interpreted languages. Compiled languages use a compiler to convert the original program, called the source code, into a machine-language version called the executable code. On a PC, the executable code usually has an .EXE or .COM extension.

If you find that you have an error in your executable code, you must go back to the source code, make the correction, re-compile the program, and then test it again. C, C++, Visual C++, Visual Basic, FORTRAN, and COBOL are examples of compiled programming languages.

Interpreted languages use a different method to translate high-level source code into low-level executable code. When you run an interpreted program, an interpreter reads one instruction and then translates and executes it. If that instruction translates and executes successfully, the interpreter reads, translates, and executes the next instruction. This process continues until the end of the program. When it encounters an error, the translation process ceases. At this point, you can fix the problem in the original source code and then restart the interpretation process. QBasic and scripting languages, such as Perl, JavaScript, and VBScript, are examples of interpreted languages.

Because an interpreted program works on a line-by-line basis, they take much longer to execute than a compiled program. On the other hand, interpreted programs tend to be easier to develop because you can get much more immediate feedback on errors.

Another way of categorizing programs is by looking at how they solve problems. In a procedural language, programs consist of a series of step-by-step instructions called statements, which execute in a relatively linear manner. Program execution starts at the top, proceeds through a set number of instructions and then ends at the bottom. FORTRAN and COBOL are classic examples of procedural languages.

Object-oriented programming languages use objects or entities, to control the flow of program execution. Programs typically run in a window object. Within the window are buttons and other objects that a mouse controls. For example, by a choosing a button, you could sort a list of numbers or print out a graph. While procedural languages implement the solution to a problem through a series of linear steps, object-oriented languages solve a problem through the interaction of objects.

Object-oriented languages have many other concepts and features that are difficult to learn. Many procedural programmers have made the switch to object-oriented languages because, in the end, object-oriented languages offer much more power in the development of applications. For example, many C programmers have switched to C++. C++ has all of the features of C, a procedural language, plus all the tools of a modern object-oriented language. Languages such as Microsoft Visual C++ and Visual Basic go a step further by providing a graphical Integrated Development Environment (IDE) for quickly laying out and writing applications.

Related to object-oriented programs are dynamic link library (DLL) files. These files contain pre-existing objects, which programmers can access and use in their programs. A large part of the Windows operating system consists of DLLs.

You can even write your own DLLs to extend the capabilities of an application. For example, you can write a DLL in C++ that connects to a Web server and then expands the power of the Web server. What is nice about DLLs is that they use memory efficiently because they can be loaded and unloaded as needed.

Programming on the Web

In the world of Web programming, you are always dealing with more than one computer. A client computer, where an end user sits and opens a Web browser, connects to a server computer that serves up content. Often you have a scenario where a user on the client side enters data, such as the name of a product, and then a program processes the input and returns relevant information.

You can write programs that run on the client side or server side. To write client-side programs, use Java or a scripting language such as JavaScript or VBScript. For server-side programs use Perl, C, C++, or even one of the popular scripting languages in use for client-side programming.

So far, Web programming might sound straightforward. Confusion arises when you try to answer some of the following questions:

■   Under what circumstances is it better to have your programs run on the client side? When is it better to have them run on the server side?

■   Should the programs be physically stored on the client, the server, or both?

■   If you are sitting on the client end, should you let any program run on your computer? Could a rogue program attack your computer and do unimagined damage?

■   Should you compile or interpret your programs?

■   Will your clients need any special software or equipment to run your programs on the client side?

■   Are there any methods to speed up the processing of programs?

The remainder of this lesson addresses these questions. In short, as long as the client has a Web browser that is compatible with a particular programming language, there should be no problems on the client side. For example, if a client has a browser that is configured correctly to run Java applets, Java applets will run. The same applies to scripting languages such as JavaScript.

On the other hand, if you are using a Web browser that is not configured for a particular language, you will have problems. For example, many people use versions of Netscape Navigator that are not compatible with Microsoft VBScript.

When you look at server-side programming, often the issue is not compatibility, but efficiency and ease of development. To write interactive applications that run on the server side, you have a few options:

The Common Gateway Interface (CGI)—CGI is a traditional way for a server and browser to interact. CGI is not a programming language, but an interface that defines communication standards that a server program and a client browser must follow.

Application Programming Interface (API)—A program can directly communicate with another program through an API. For example, when you write a program that accesses the Microsoft Excel API, you are directly communicating with the chunks of code, called functions, that make up Excel.

Active Server Pages (ASP)—Active Server Pages are server-side scripts that specifically work on Microsoft Web servers by using ActiveX.

Netscape's Web server has a large, complex API called NSAPI. Microsoft has their own Web server, called Internet Information Server (IIS), and their own API, called ISAPI. Web programmers typically use C or C++ to access these APIs. For example, a programmer can write a DLL that can be loaded and used with IIS. The DLL could employ user input to pull data out of a database and then send the results back to the user.

Applications that use the APIs, such as ISAPI, are much more complex to write then CGI scripts, and consequently take more development time. However, they execute much faster because they run in the same address space as IIS and have access to all the resources available to the Web server.

CGI scripts on the other hand, run in a separate address space each time they are loaded. This means that if ten users simultaneously submit the same form, a CGI script will create ten different processes in memory to handle the ten forms. Ten forms submitted to a program that uses APIs will create only one process to handle the ten forms.

Entire books have been written on CGIs and APIs. To truly understand these concepts, you need to spend some time writing these types of programs. This lesson gives a general idea about them.

Forms

The most common way for a Web author to gather information from a Web user is through a fill-in HTML form. A client-side or server-side program processes the collected data. For example, if you create Web pages for an E-commerce site, you can design a form that asks a customer to enter his or her name, address, product information, and credit card number. The user could then choose a button to submit the form's data to a server-side Perl script that processes the order.

Forms are in use for questionnaires, surveys, complaints, or for soliciting just about any kind of information. Figure 8.4 displays a form that you will create in the following few pages.

You start a form with the <FORM> tag, which requires at least one attribute: ACTION. Since an HTML <FORM> does no processing of data, you must specify what to do with the collected data. When the user chooses the Submit button (renamed to Send Question in this example), the data transmits to the program specified by ACTION.

For example, <FORM ACTION=http://www.someplace.com/cgi-bin/survey.pl> indicates that user data should be submitted to a Perl script called SURVEY.PL which is in the CGI-BIN directory on a computer at the www.someplace.com Web site.

Figure 8.4 HTML Form

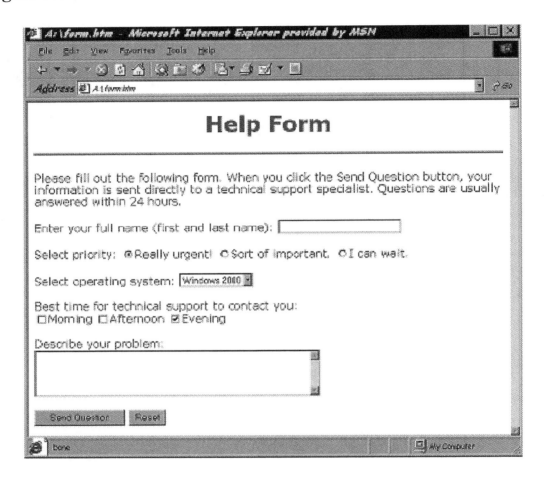

Another important attribute is METHOD, which has two values: "get" and "post." The difference between the two is how data transmits to the server. When you use "get," user data from the form appends to the destination Uniform Resource Locator (URL) of the program specified in the ACTION attribute.

For example, assume that you have a form that asks for a user's age and gender, and the user enters 34 and female, respectively. This gets sent to the server as http://www.someplace.com?age=34&gender=female. The URL is separated from the form data by a question mark (?); the data is separated from each other by an ampersand (&).

The post method does not append data to a URL. Instead, data is packaged as separate items when it transmits to the program specified by ACTION.

The difference between these two methods can be confusing. In the next few pages you will get practice working with both methods: you use "get" with a Perl script and "post" with an Active Server Page (ASP) script. Afterward, things should become clearer.

Creating and Viewing an HTML Form

Before creating any scripts, you should create a form. The following steps describe how to create the one in Figure 8.4. In the process, you will use many HTML tags associated with forms.

To create and view an HTML form, follow these steps:

1. Within a text editor, create a new file. Your screen should be blank.

2. Enter the following form:

```
<HTML>

<HEAD>

</HEAD>


<BODY LINK="blue" VLINK="blue" ALINK="blue">

<BASEFONT FACE="verdana","arial","helvetica" COLOR="blue">

<H1 ALIGN="center">Help Form</H1>

<HR COLOR="blue">


<P>
```

Please fill out the following form. When you click the Send Question button, your information is sent directly to a technical support specialist. Questions are usually answered within 24 hours.

```
</P>


<FORM METHOD="post" ACTION="mailto:somebody@somewhere.com">


<P>

Enter your full name (first and last name): <INPUT TYPE ="text"
NAME="fullname" SIZE="24">
</P>


<p>

Select priority:

<INPUT TYPE="radio" NAME="priority" VALUE="1" CHECKED>Really urgent!

<INPUT TYPE="radio" NAME="priority" VALUE="2">Sort of important.

<INPUT TYPE="radio" NAME="priority" VALUE="3">I can wait.

</P>


<P>

Select operating system:

<SELECT NAME="os">

  <OPTION SELECTED>Windows 2000

  <OPTION>Linux

  <OPTION>BeOS
```

```
</SELECT>

</p>


<p>

Best time for technical support to contact you:<br>

<INPUT TYPE="checkbox" NAME="contact" VALUE="morning">Morning

<INPUT TYPE="checkbox" NAME="contact" VALUE="afternoon">Afternoon

<INPUT TYPE="checkbox" NAME="contact" VALUE="evening" CHECKED>Evening

</p>


<p>

Describe your problem:<BR>

<TEXTAREA NAME="comments" ROWS=4 COLS=50>

</TEXTAREA>

</p>


<P>

<INPUT TYPE="submit" VALUE="Send Question"> <INPUT TYPE="reset">

</P>


</FORM>

</BODY>

</HTML>
```

3. Save the Web page as FORM.HTM.

4.   View your form in the browser. It should look like the form in Figure 8.4.

One of the first things you notice in this form is that the ACTION attribute points to an e-mail address. The word mailto: followed by an e-mail address can be used as the value of the ACTION attribute and can also be used as the hyperlink in an <A> tag. For example, <A HREF="mailto:somebody@somewhere.com">.

It is possible to put text into the subject line of an e-mail address. You add a question mark followed by the word "subject=" and some text. For example, to put the words, "Technical question" into the subject line, you use <FORM METHOD="post" ACTION="mailto:somebody@somewhere.com? subject=Technical question">. You are welcome to use it, even though it will not be a part of this exercise.

Using an e-mail address as the value of the ACTION attribute does not work with some e-mail clients. For example, the AOL e-mail client will produce some unexpected results. Outlook and Outlook Express will work.

Forms often utilize the <INPUT> tag. Its TYPE attribute specifies a type of input. A text type allows the user to enter a short amount of text, like a name, city, phone number, and so on. A radio type generates radio buttons in a form. Within a group of radio buttons, also called option buttons, users can select just one item.

A checkbox type puts small boxes in a form. Users can select one or more items by placing a check mark next to each one. To automatically select a check box or radio button, use the CHECKED attribute.

The submit type places a command button on the form. When the user chooses the button, the form data transmits to the program or e-mail address specified in the ACTION attribute. The reset type clears all user input in a form.

The <SELECT> tag with OPTION creates a drop-down list box. You can pre-select an item by using the SELECTED attribute. The <TEXTAREA> tag is similar to the text input type except that it allows a much larger text box.

Instead of specifying an e-mail address as the value of the ACTION attribute, most Web site developers use a program. The Perl programming language is a good choice for writing programs that process user input. These programs use a special interface called CGI.

CGI

A CGI program is any program designed to accept and return data using the CGI communication standards. A CGI program always resides on the server side and can be written in almost any programming language, including Perl, C, or Visual Basic.

Although other methods are gaining in popularity, CGI programs remain the most common way for Web servers to interact dynamically with users. Using CGI standards, a Web server communicates with applications that you have written or other applications such as database management systems. In the next section, you will write a program that interfaces with a Web server through CGI.

Perl

Perl is one of the most popular programming languages for writing CGI scripts. Perl does an excellent job at processing text, text manipulation is important for any program using CGI. As with all CGI programs, Perl runs on the server side.

Perl has many other assets. Any simple text editor can create a program; you do not need a sophisticated graphical development environment. A lot of code already exists for Perl; if you need a program, someone has probably already written it and posted it on the Web. Perl scripts are very portable; a program written on a PC runs on a UNIX or Linux system with few or no modifications. In addition, like most modern programming languages, Perl has object-oriented programming support.

Using existing UNIX tools, a linguist/programmer named Larry Wall developed Perl to solve UNIX administrative tasks. Today, in addition to being a powerful UNIX administrative tool, it is in use for many other applications. For example, many Windows NT administrators use it to write short programs for managing an NT server. You will be using Perl to process data gathered from a Web page form.

Perl is ideal for short programs, such as ones that parse through user input and then initiate a database search. In the following steps, you will write a Perl script that accepts user input from an HTML form and then returns data to the user in the form of a Web page. In a real scenario, the returned data would be the result of a Web search or some similar operation.

Your Perl script will simply send back to the user a confirmation of the data that he or she has entered. Although this is a brief example, you will gain a basic understanding of the process of writing and executing a Perl script. To gain anything more than a casual acquaintance with Perl, you will need to invest more time and energy in studying the language.

Perl is an interpretive language, which makes it easy to build and test simple programs. To run a Perl program you must have a Perl interpreter. PC users can download a free interpreter from the site www.ActiveState.com. UNIX and Linux users also have free Perl interpreters available to them on the Web. Although you can find Perl compilers, Perl interpreters for CGI are preferred.

If you are going to write Perl programs that function as CGI scripts, you also need to install Web server software on your computer. Windows 95 and 98 users can use the program Personal Web Server, which Microsoft distributes free. Windows NT Server 4 and Windows 2000 come with a popular Web server called Internet Information Server (IIS). UNIX and Linux users will probably want to use the Apache Web server.

 Note: You can find a lot of Perl resources at Usenet newsgroups like comp.lang.perl, at Web sites like www.perl.com or through a Web search by using a search engine such as Yahoo!

Modifying an HTML Form

The following steps assume that you have already installed a Perl interpreter and a Web server. In the following steps, you will start by changing the value of the ACTION attribute in your form and then saving the form into the default directory of your Web server.

To modify an HTML form, follow these steps:

1. Within a text editor, open the file FORM.HTM.

2. Change the FORM tag so that it looks like the one below. Make sure that you use the "get" method.

   ```
   <FORM METHOD="get" ACTION="/cgi-bin/procform.pl">
   ```

3. Save your file into the default directory of your Web server and give the file the new name PERL-FORM.HTM. For example, in Notepad from the File menu, you would choose on Save As. Next, you would change directories to WWWROOT and then you would type PERLFORM.HTM as the file name.

The modified form should be in the root directory of your Web server.

Creating a Perl Script

You now need to create the Perl program that will process the form. Name the program PROC-FORM.PL. It will be saved in the CGI-BIN directory beneath the default Web server directory. Notice that the ACTION attribute specifies the path and filename for the Perl program called PROC-FORM.PL. Create a Perl script with the following steps:

1. Within a text editor, create a new file. Your screen should be blank.

2. Enter the following Perl script:

```perl
#!/perl/bin/perl


#procform.pl


$QS = $ENV{'QUERY_STRING'};


@NameValuePairs = split (/&/, $QS);


print "<HTML>", "\n\n";
print "<HEAD>", "\n\n";
print "<TITLE>Technical Support</TITLE>", "\n\n";
print "</HEAD>", "\n\n";


print "<BODY TEXT='blue'>\n";
print "<H1>Thank you.</H1>\n";
```

```
print "<HR COLOR='blue'>\n";


foreach $NV (@NameValuePairs)
{
    ($N, $V) = split (/=/, $NV);
    print "$N = $V<BR>\n";
    }


print "</BODY>\n";
print "</HTML>\n";
```

3.   Save your file into the CGI-BIN directory that exists right below the default directory of your Web server (create CGI-BIN if you need to). Give the file the name PROCFORM.PL. For example, in Notepad, from the File menu you would choose Save As. Next, you would change directories to CGI-BIN, and then you would type PROCFORM.PL as the file name.

The Perl script has a few lines with which you should become familiar. First, the line #!/perl/bin/perl indicates the path (/perl/bin) of your Perl interpreter and the name of the Perl executable (perl). The path on your computer may be different. Also, be sure to use the appropriate case because many of Perl's elements are case-sensitive.

The line #procform.pl indicates the file name of the Perl script. The pound sign (#) in this line and the previous one is the comment symbol.

The string 'QUERY_STRING' is an environment variable that contains the actual data, or query string, that was sent to the Perl script. The data in 'QUERY_STRING' is assigned to the variable $QS so that it can be manipulated by the program.

The print statements generate the HTML code that the Perl script sends back to the browser. The group of lines below each statement breaks up the original query string into its constituent parts and then prints them into the Web page that transmits back to the browser.

Now comes the fun part of trying out your program.

Running a Perl Script

Within your browser, you will open the form and then fill in some data. Next, you will choose Send. If everything works correctly, your Perl script will process the data and then generate a Web page that contains the data that you entered.

To run a Perl script, follow these steps:

1. Within the Web browser, open the file PERLFORM.HTM by typing **127.0.0.1/perlform.htm** in the address bar.

2. Fill out the form and then choose Send Question. You should see a screen like the one in Figure 8.5.

Figure 8.5 Results of Perl Script

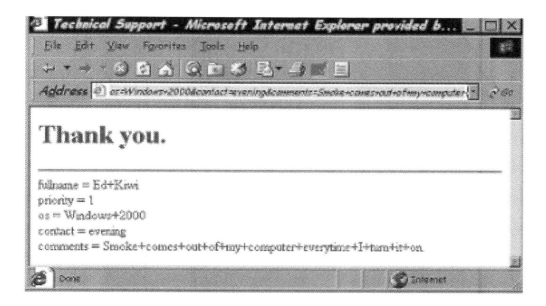

The address 127.0.0.1 is a loopback address. Its use is for testing a computer's Internet connection to make sure that it is working properly. Here you are using it to call PERLFORM.HTM on the default

Web server. An alternative method is to use your actual IP number (if you know it). This example assumes that you have completely installed TCP/IP.

Notice that spaces render as plus signs (+). If you are skilled at Perl, you can write additional lines of code that eliminate these plus signs.

Look closely at the address bar and you can see the entire contents of the query string. The query string appears here because you used the get method in your <FORM> tag. If you use a put method, you would not see the query string in the address bar, and you would have to rewrite the Perl program for it to process the data correctly.

All of this may look like a foreign language to you. The main goal here is to get you familiar with how Perl scripts operate and not to make you a Perl expert. To become a Perl guru, you should spend some time on the Web checking out Perl resources.

Using C and C++

C and C++ are the most popular programming languages for developing both system and application software. C, which was originally created to develop the UNIX operating system, places very few restrictions on a programmer. It provides high-level commands and low-level access to hardware. C++ is a superset of C. It adds object-oriented features to C.

There is no rule that states that CGI programs must be written in Perl. Perl is effective because it parses text well, it can very readily take a query string and break it up into its constituent parts. C and C++, power users' programming languages, can also parse text, but unfortunately, manipulating text strings in C or C++ takes many more lines of code than Perl. A CGI program that takes a few lines of code in Perl can end up being a large application in C.

CGI programmers also like the way Perl scripts interpret because they translate into machine code on the fly. This means that a programmer does not have to go through the cumbersome process of compiling every time there is a modification to a program.

On the other hand, compiled C and C++ programs run much faster than Perl scripts. This is an important factor at a busy Web site with multiple simultaneous connections. Furthermore, fast execution times can be critical for large complex programs.

Another reason why you should not dismiss the possibility of using C or C++ is the vast collection of useable code that already exists. Companies like Microsoft have made it easy to produce new code. Microsoft Visual C++ comes with features such as code wizards and ActiveX components. Wizards ask you questions and then use your feedback to quickly generate custom applications. ActiveX components are pre-existing chunks of code that you can insert into your programs.

If you are going to create ISAPI programs (ISAPI provides an alternative to writing CGI applications) then Visual C++ is a good choice. Visual C++ even comes with a wizard for creating DLL programs that extend the capabilities of an ISAPI-compliant Web server. Microsoft IIS, which runs on Windows NT Server 4.0 or Windows 2000, is one of the few ISAPI-compliant Web servers.

Visual C++ is also perfectly suited for writing ActiveX applications. Visual C++ can both use and produce ActiveX components.

Writing C and C++ applications is beyond the scope of this book. You can get a feel for a CGI program written in C by perusing the C source code in Figure 8.6. Notice that it generates a Web page by using PRINTF statements that are similar to Perl's print statements. You can see that Perl has its roots in C.

Figure 8.6 CGI Program Written in C

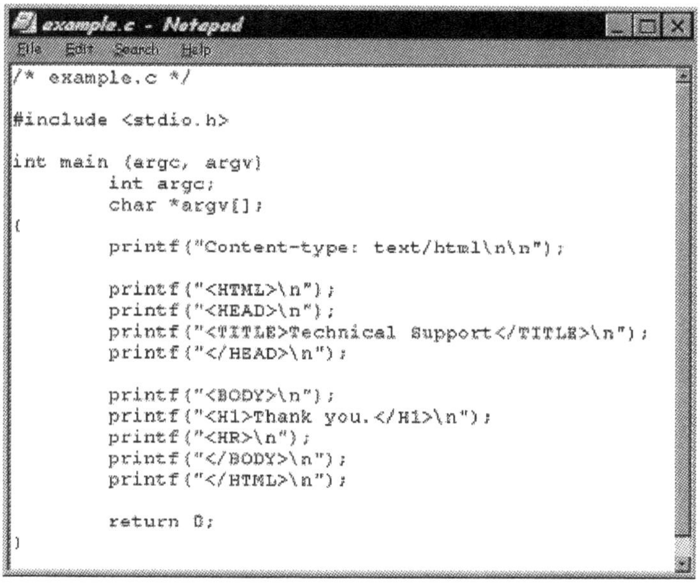

```
/* example.c */

#include <stdio.h>

int main (argc, argv)
        int argc;
        char *argv[];
{
        printf("Content-type: text/html\n\n");

        printf("<HTML>\n");
        printf("<HEAD>\n");
        printf("<TITLE>Technical Support</TITLE>\n");
        printf("</HEAD>\n");

        printf("<BODY>\n");
        printf("<H1>Thank you.</H1>\n");
        printf("<HR>\n");
        printf("</BODY>\n");
        printf("</HTML>\n");

        return 0;
}
```

Visual Basic

Visual Basic is one of the fastest ways to develop applications for Microsoft Windows. It excels in enabling programmers to quickly develop event-driven applications that have a Graphical User Interface (GUI).

Because of its ease of use and rapid application development features, Visual Basic is a viable alternate for CGI programming. The constraints of working only in a Windows environment can be a big drawback. Porting a Visual Basic application to UNIX or Linux is nearly impossible.

If you are using Microsoft Windows NT Server 4.0 or Windows 2000, you can use Visual Basic to build ISAPI programs that are designed for Microsoft Internet Information Server. These types of applications physically reside on the server, but, on the client-side, they can run within any modern browser on any hardware platform.

Like Visual C++, you can create and use ActiveX components with Visual Basic.

Java and Visual J++

Java is a general-purpose, object-oriented programming language that is well suited for creating small Web programs called Java applets. Applets are sent from a Web server to an end user's computer. To run the applet, the user must have a Java-compatible browser, such as Internet Explorer or Netscape, and a Java runtime environment called a Java Virtual Machine (VM). An applet will run on any computer that meets these requirements.

Java, which was developed by Sun Microsystems, was originally designed for small intelligent devices, such as set-top boxes. It is similar to, but simpler than, C++. Java has no pointers like C++ (pointers point to memory addresses), and the Java VM manages memory instead of the program itself. This means that the program cannot affect the underlying operating system, which could create a security hole.

To create a Java program, you can use a standard text editor to type the source code. Figure 8.7 displays a simple program whose sole purpose in life is to print onscreen "Hello, crime fighters." Notice that this program, like all Java programs, has the extension JAVA.

Before you use a Java applet, you must compile it with a program such as Symantec Visual Café. Compiled Java programs, which acquire the extension "CLASS," are the actual applets sent out by a server. These applets execute on the client computer, which is different from CGI scripts, which run on the Web server.

Figure 8.7 Short Java Program

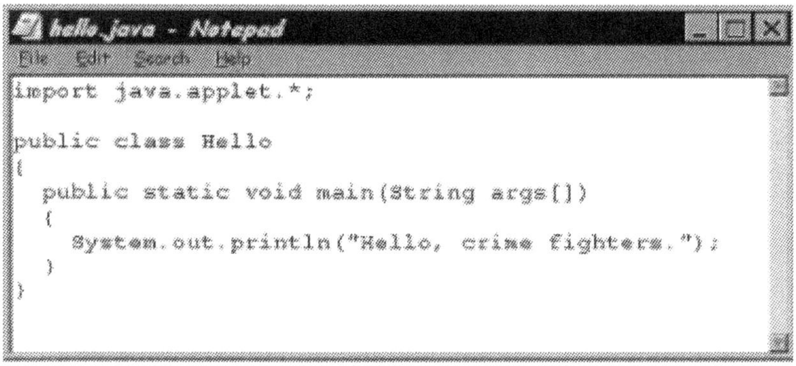

To use a Java program like the one in Figure 8.7, you must complete the following tasks:

1. You create the Java source code and save it with a JAVA extension. For example, HELLO.JAVA.

2. You translate the source code into a special compiled format called bytecode. Files in bytecode have the class extension, such as HELLO.CLASS. Class files have 70% to 80% of the information needed to run the applet; the runtime environment provides the rest. Runtime environments delineate how the applet will run on a specific platform.

3. You create an HTML file that specifies the name of the applet within an <APPLET> tag. The CODE attribute contains the name of the Java file and the CODEBASE attribute specifies the file's location on the server. The location can range from a simple directory to a complete URL. The following example illustrates this:

```
<HTML>

<HEAD>

<TITLE>The Crime Fighters Home Page</TITLE>

</HEAD>

<BODY>
```

```
<APPLET CODE="hello.class" CODEBASE="\java">

</APPLET>

</BODY>

</HTML>
```

4. A user requests the Web page.

5. The Web browser receives the page and displays it.

6. The Web browser reads the <APPLET> tag and then requests the specified Java applet from the server.

7. The browser receives the applet and then executes the code.

Some Java applets depend upon other applets. All dependent applets must be downloaded from the server for the program to work properly.

Microsoft Visual J++ is a visual development environment for creating and compiling Java-compatible programs. Microsoft has thrown in a bunch of tools, including an application wizard, to facilitate applet development. Both Java and J++ can create ActiveX controls, which are described below.

Time will tell if Java lives up to all its hype. It definitely has strong support in all major browsers. If you are looking for an inexpensive way of developing and distributing platform-neutral applications, Java is hard to beat.

Microsoft ActiveX

Microsoft has recognized the value of a platform-independent, object-oriented programming system. Java is a great tool, but Microsoft is not satisfied with just creating its own version of Java called J++; it has developed an entirely separate competing technology known as ActiveX.

Descriptions of ActiveX range from simple explanations such as "a Windows-based system for developing and distributing Internet applications" to complex descriptions that require entire books to fully understand.

Here, we will aim for some middle ground. ActiveX has three main elements:

■   ActiveX controls, formerly called Object Linking and Embedding (OLE) controls, are objects that insert into Web pages or any other ActiveX-compatible application. The control can reside on the client side or download from a server. Examples range from simple buttons to stock tickers, charts, and complex systems that use interconnected controls.

■ ActiveX documents display within Web browsers or other document viewers. Before ActiveX, embedded objects such as Word documents were limited to a small section of the screen. With ActiveX technology, documents can occupy the entire browser window. You can try it yourself by loading a Word document into the latest version of Internet Explorer.

■ ActiveX scripting languages, such as VBScript, can connect controls and add interactive functionality to Web pages. With scripting, you can move processing from the server to the client. For example, an HTML form can be pre-processed at the client to validate data entries before the form data transmits to the server.

ActiveX grew out of Microsoft OLE technology, which created a framework for interconnecting different applications. OLE gave users more of a document-centric view of computing, in which a user could create a document that employed the functionality of many different applications. For example, a report written in Word could have a chart generated with Excel and a database created with Access.

The foundation of OLE is the Component Object Model (COM). COM defines a paradigm for almost any type of software to interact, including application software, system software, and programming libraries. In theory, regardless of the language in which they were created, COM components can readily interact with each other on single computer. With DCOM (D stands for Distributed), components can communicate across a network, even across the Internet.

A competing standard called CORBA (Common Object Request Broker Architecture) is backed by Sun Microsystems, IBM, Hewlett-Packard and many other important software developers. Both standards are trying to solve the problem of allowing object-oriented applications to share data by employing reusable software components.

Thousands of ActiveX controls are available free or for a price. You could write your own controls, but if one exists that provides you with the desired functionality, it is easier and faster to use the existing control.

Note: For more information on COM, ActiveX, and related technologies, go to http://www.microsoft.com/com.

Choosing ActiveX or Java

ActiveX and Java are two technologies that enable people to attach programs to Web pages. Although ActiveX controls and Java applets seem to have a lot in common, they are very distinct technologies. ActiveX is not a programming language, but rather a set of rules that specify how applications should communicate. Visual C++, Visual Basic, or some comparable language creates ActiveX controls. Java writes Java applets.

Java applets run on the client side within a sandbox, an area that acts as an envelope surrounding the program in main memory. In theory, if you accidentally download a malicious Java applet, it stays contained in the sandbox, and your important computer data remains secure. There have been cases of Java programs breaking out of the sandbox, but overall, the average user is pretty well protected.

Unlike Java applets, ActiveX controls have the capability to access any part of your computer, including the inner sanctuaries of the Windows operating system. Although this gives you the ability to create more powerful applications than Java, in the wrong hands, the potential for damage is enormous. To contain this risk, Microsoft uses a registration system that validates the integrity of ActiveX controls through a system of digital signatures.

Mirosoft Internet Explorer supports running ActiveX controls. If you are on a Windows platform, you can also configure Netscape for ActiveX. To use an ActiveX control, point the Web browser to a page that contains the control. Your browser checks the system registry to see if the control is registered and available on the local computer. If the control lists are in the registry, the control activates.

If he control is not on the local computer, your browser finds the control in the place specified by the HTML document. The location of an ActiveX control is defined in the CODEBASE attribute of the <OBJECT> tag. Before the control downloads, you see a message onscreen that lets you cancel the download. If the control has a digital signature, you see a message stating that the control comes from a trusted source. Typically, you should only download digitally signed controls.

Although ActiveX controls give you more power in controlling a Windows-based computer than Java, that power creates a greater security risk. You can lower your risk by using only controls from trusted vendors. It is a good idea to download security patches for your browser whenever they become available.

Web Scripting Languages

Scripting languages are programming languages that excel at performing certain kinds of tasks. They were originally designed to automate repetitive tasks that a system administrator would perform at the command line of an operating system. DOS batch files and UNIX AWK scripts reflect these origins.

Although scripts might not be as powerful as programs written in industrial languages like C++, you can find scripts running mission-critical applications such as controlling scientific equipment, supervising railroad operations, and administering computers.

In addition to performing administrative tasks, scripts are used to process user input from Web pages. As you saw earlier in this lesson, Perl is a scripting language that runs on a server. It does a great job at processing text strings.

JavaScript and VBScript are languages that are well suited for writing scripts that run on the client side. The scripts insert directly into a Web page. When a user opens the page, the Web browser executes the script on the user's local computer. Client-side processing can go a long way toward relieving an over-burdened server. It also lessens network congestion because a certain amount of the data that previously would have traveled back to the server for processing can now remain at the local computer.

A scripting language is often a subset of a complete programming language. For example, VBScript is a subset of Visual Basic. In addition, a scripting language usually has restricted access to a client's Operating System (OS). However, even with this limited access to core sections of a computer, many users have been victims of malicious scripts. Some users have gone as far as disabling client-side script execution on their computer.

Using JavaScript and JScript

In 1995, Netscape renamed its existing scripting language from LiveScript to JavaScript. This was done in large part because of a partnership with Sun Microsystems, the makers of Java. Although they have different origins, Java and JavaScript share a lot of features, such as the same security precautions.

JScript is Microsoft's version of JavaScript. It is much more compatible with ECMAScript, the Web's only standard scripting language. In 1997, the European Computer Manufacturers Association (ECMA), which was staffed with representatives from Netscape, Microsoft, Sun, and others, established standards for Web scripting languages and called the result ECMAScript.

Creating a JavaScript Program

In the steps below, you create a JavaScript program that embeds in a Web page. The program, which is within the <SCRIPT> tags in the Head section of the Web page, greets the user with "Good morning," "Good afternoon," or "Good Evening." The <SCRIPT> tag also specifies the script language. To run the script, you simply open the page in a Web browser.

To create an embedded JavaScript, follow these steps:

1. Open a text editor such as Notepad or SimpleText.

2. Create the Web page by typing the following HTML code:

```
<HTML>

<HEAD>

<TITLE>Technical Support</TITLE>

<SCRIPT LANGUAGE="JavaScript">

<!--


   // A greeting based on the current time.


   var hours = new Date().getHours()


   if (hours < 12)

     document.write("Good morning. ")
```

```
    else if (hours < 17)

       document.write("Good afternoon. ")

    else

       document.write("Good evening. ")


//-->

</SCRIPT>

</HEAD>

<BODY>

   We'll take care of it immediately!

   <FORM>

     <P><INPUT TYPE="Button" NAME="TimeButton" VALUE="Show me the time"
ONCLICK=alert(Date())>

    </FORM>

</BODY>

</HTML>
```

3. Save the Web page as JAVAGREETING.HTM.

4. Open JAVAGREETING.HTM in your Web browser. If you want to see the current time, choose the button labeled "Show me the time."

Notice that the entire script is contained within HTML comment tags. This allows browsers that are not JavaScript-enabled to ignore the script. Also, notice that JavaScript writes text into the browser window with the DOCUMENT.WRITE statement. If you have a keen eye, you will also see that the numbers used in the IF statement use a 24-hour clock to check the current time.

In the next section, you will see a VBScript program that performs the same operations as this JavaScript program.

Note: The JavaScript Source is an excellent JavaScript resource with many "cut and paste" scripts. Point your browser to www.javascriptsource.com.

Using VBScript

VBScript derives from Microsoft Visual Basic. Like JavaScript, you can embed your scripts into a Web page, the scripts run on the client side, and the browser interprets the script code. Unlike JavaScript, VBScript works with Internet Explorer, but not Netscape. Netscape users need a special plug-in to run VBScript programs.

Creating a VBScript Program

Like the JavaScript program that you wrote earlier, the VBScript program below generates a greeting based on the current time. Create a VBScript with these steps:

1. Open a text editor such as Notepad or SimpleText.

2. Create the following Web page:

```
<HTML>

<HEAD>

<TITLE>Technical Support</TITLE>

<SCRIPT LANGUAGE="VBScript">

<!--

    ' A greeting based on the current time.

    Dim hours

    hours = Hour(Now)
```

```
    If hours < 12 then

    Document.Write "Good morning. "

    ElseIf hours < 17 then

        Document.Write "Good afternoon. "

    Else

        Document.Write "Good evening. "

    End If

-->

</SCRIPT>

</HEAD>

<BODY>

    We'll take care of it immediately!

    <FORM>

        <P><INPUT TYPE="Button" NAME="TimeButton" VALUE="Show me the
time" ONCLICK="MsgBox Date() & ' ' & Time()">

    </FORM>

</BODY>

</HTML>
```

3. Save the Web page as VBGREETING.HTM.

4. Open VBGREETING.HTM in a VBScript-compatible Web browser. If you want to see the current time, choose the button labeled "Show me the time."

One of the first things that you notice is that VBScript and JavaScript have many more similarities than differences. If you were to write longer samples of code, you would see more distinctions between the two.

You might be wondering which scripting language to use. If you are comfortable with Java or C++, you might want to use JavaScript since it is based on those two languages. If you already know Visual Basic or Visual Basic for Applications (VBA), you will probably choose VBScript. You also have to think about your target audience. Do they have a VBScript-compatible browser? If not, JavaScript is your best solution.

Dynamic HyperText Markup Language (DHTML)

DHTML is a set of features that gives Web pages interactive capabilities without having to rely on server-side processing. For example, with DHTML you can hide images and then make them appear at the click of a button. You can make objects such as images and text glide across the screen. You can create a form that responds instantly to user input without any data having to travel back to a server.

To achieve these results, DHTML combines three technologies:

- HTML
- CSS
- Scripting Languages

Both Netscape and Microsoft have defined their own standards for achieving the same results. Netscape relies on the <LAYER> tag to segment a Web page into layers that can overlap, move across the page, and be manipulated in a variety of ways with JavaScript.

In Microsoft's version of DHTML, you can segment a Web page with the <DIV> tag. You can also use JavaScript, JScript, or VBScript as the scripting language.

Creating a Simple DHTML Document

The following steps guide you through a simple example of DHTML. Using Microsoft's standard, you will create some headings whose text color changes as a mouse pointer moves over them.

To create a simple DHTML document, follow these steps:

1. Open a text editor such as Notepad or SimpleText.

2. Create the following Web page:

```
<HTML>

<HTML>

<HEAD>

<STYLE TYPE="text/css">

<!--

H1   {text-align:left;

     background:blue;

     color:white;

     font:bold 20 pt "verdana"}

-->

</STYLE>


<SCRIPT LANGUAGE="VBScript">

<!--

sub Option1_onMouseOver

   Option1.Style.Color = "red"

end sub


sub Option1_onMouseOut

   Option1.Style.Color = "white"

end sub


sub Option2_onMouseOver

      Option2.Style.Color = "red"
```

```
    end sub

sub Option2_onMouseOut
    Option2.Style.Color = "white"
end sub


sub Option3_onMouseOver
    Option3.Style.Color = "red"
end sub


sub Option3_onMouseOut
    Option3.Style.Color = "white"
end sub
-->
</SCRIPT>
</HEAD>
<BODY>


<H1 ID=Option1>Welcome</H1>
<H1 ID=Option2>To</H1>
<H1 ID=Option3>DHTML</H1>


</BODY>
</HTML>
```

3. Save the Web page as DHTMLTEST.HTM

4. Open DHTMLTEST.HTM in Internet Explorer 4.0 or higher. When you move the mouse pointer over the headings, the text color should change.

Each heading (H1) has a unique ID tag. Based on these ID tags, several blocks of VBScript code, called subroutines, are written. Each subroutine checks to see if the pointer is either over or off the heading and then it changes the heading's color.

You can change more than just the color of text. For example, if you change the statement Option1.Style.Color = "red" to Option1.Style.Textalign = "right", the text alignment changes instead of the color. If you make this change, you should also change Option1.Style.Color = "white" to Option1.Style.Textalign="left".

DHTML is a large topic. For more information, fire up your favorite Web search engine or look up DHTML on the Microsoft and Netscape sites.

Active Server Pages (ASP)

You have seen several examples of scripts running on the client side. Active Server Pages (ASP) create a good framework for developing scripts that run on the server side. ASP works especially well with programs that pull data out of a database and then produce HTML pages based on that data.

The Web server is responsible for generating HTML pages that transmit to the client when your scripts run on the server side. HTML pages created with ASP are viewable on any browser, however, on the server side, ASP needs to run on an ASP-compatible Web server. The following Web servers, all from Microsoft, support ASP:

■ IIS, which runs on Windows NT Server 4.0 and Windows 2000.

■ Peer Web Services, which runs on Windows NT Workstation 4.0.

■ Personal Web Server, which runs on Windows 95 and 98.

ASP files have the extension .ASP. They save to a Web publishing directory such as WWWROOT on a Microsoft Web server. An .ASP file is a text file and can contain any combination of the following:

■ Text

■ HTML tags

■ Script commands

ASP is similar to gateway interfaces such as CGI or ISAPI because, like these interfaces, the associated Web applications run on the server side. However, with ASP, you do not need a separate interpreter or compiler to convert your programs into machine language. ASP has built-in script engines for VBScript and JScript that run on an ASP-compatible server. That means you can enter your text, HTML tags, and script commands all together in one file. You can also add sophisticated functionality by incorporating pre-written ActiveX server components.

In ASP, if you do not specify a scripting language, VBScript is used by default. Also, you must enclose script commands within the delimiters <% and %>. For example, the command <% tree = "ginkgo" %> assigns the value ginkgo to the variable tree.

Creating an ASP File

The steps below guide you through the creation of an ASP page that processes an HTML form. The page takes user input and generates an HTML page as a response. The results are very similar to the results from the Perl script that you created earlier in this lesson. In fact, the steps below use the same HTML form as input. For these steps to work properly, run an ASP-compatible Web server.

1. In a text editor such as Notepad, open the file PERLFORM.HTM that you created eariler in this lesson.

2. Change the <FORM> tag <FORM METHOD="get" ACTION="/cgi-bin/procform.pl"> to the one below:

    ```
    <FORM METHOD="post" ACTION="procform.asp">
    ```

3. Save the file into the default Web directory on your server (probably WWWROOT). Use the filename ASPFORM.HTM

4. Choose New from the File menu to create a new file.

5. Create the following ASP page:

    ```
    <HTML>


    <HEAD>

    <TITLE>Technical Support Confirmation</TITLE>
    ```

```
</HEAD>

<BODY>

<H2>Thank you.</H2>
<HR>

<P>
   fullname = <%= Request.Form("fullname") %><BR>
   priority = <%= Request.Form("priority") %><BR>
   os = <%= Request.Form("os") %><BR>
   contact = <%= Request.Form("contact") %><BR>
   comments = <%= Request.Form("comments") %>
</P>

<% If Time < #12:00:00 PM# Then %>
   <P>Good morning.
<% ElseIf Time <= #17:00:00 PM# Then %>
   <P>Good afternoon.
<% Else %>
   <P>Good evening.
<% End If %>

<% If Request.Form("priority") = 1 Then %>
```

```
We'll take care of it immediately!
<% Else %>
  We'll get to it eventually.
<% End If %>


</BODY>

</HTML>
```

6. Save the file into the default Web directory on your server. Use the filename PROCFORM.ASP

7. In your Web browser, to open the file ASPFORM.HTM, type in the address bar **127.0.0.1/aspform.htm**

8. Fill out the HTML form with some sample data and then choose Send Question. You should see a Web page similar to the one in Figure 8.8.

Figure 8.8 ASP Response

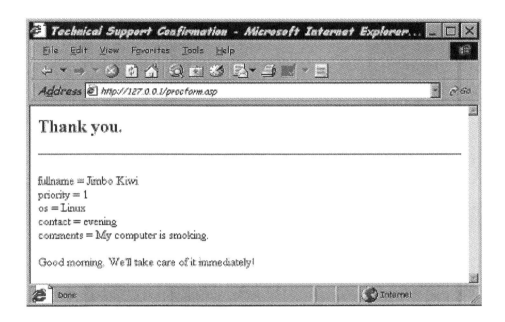

Since we specified no scripting language with a <SCRIPT> tag, the scripting language is the ASP default—VBScript. The "If" statements in this ASP page work just like the VBScript statements you created in the VBScript section earlier.

Like most topics in this lesson, learning ASP cannot be accomplished in just a few pages. If this taste of ASP whets your appetite for more, this is a good beginning.

Database Access

A database is a highly structured collection of data—facts, figures, and various other pieces of information. The example that most people are familiar with is a telephone directory. All data are stored in a uniform format: last name, first name, address, and phone number lists for each person. Other examples of databases are card catalog systems at libraries or lists of products at an E-commerce Web site.

Relational Databases

Relational databases are collections of tables or lists of data that interact with each other. The term relational database refers to that fact that you have to create relationships among tables for them to interact with each other. The Structured Query Language (SQL) is a popular language for defining, querying, modifying, and controlling the data in a relational database. Figure 8.9 displays a SQL query that, when executed, will list data from two tables: Company and Customer. Only companies from the state of California will be listed.

Figure 8.9 SQL Command

```
SELECT Company.CompanyName, Company.State, Customer.LastName, Company.Phone

FROM Company INNER JOIN Customer ON Company.ITPSNumber = Customer.ITPSNumber

WHERE ((([Company]![State])="CA"));
```

APIs

Java Database Connectivity (JDBC) and Microsoft Open Database Connectivity (ODBC) are two database APIs that provide a uniform interface for most relational databases. Both enable you to use SQL to request and process information from a remote database. JDBC specifically supports Java; ODBC supports a wider variety of languages, including Visual C++.

Extensible Markup Language (XML)

XML is a language for creating new markup languages that are geared toward a particular type of content. XML is a META-markup language, a language that describes and defines other markup languages.

Understanding XML

XML goes beyond HTML for document markup. HTML's simple yet powerful design enabled it to quickly become a global standard. Its widespread usage also reveals some of HTML's limitations. For example, mathematical and chemical formulas are difficult to display.

Could not the W3C, the consortium that develops many Web standards, just expand HTML or design a special markup language for each discipline, business, or other endeavor? Can they not just make new mathematical tags or create a special mathematical markup language? Yes, but expanding HTML would make it extremely unwieldy. Designing a markup language for every diverse group would be just as impractical.

In XML, any developer can write their own Document-Type Definition (DTD) that describes sets of tags and attributes. The DTD for a markup language defines the rules of that language. Essentially, W3C has wisely concluded that the development of markup languages should be handled by developers who know exactly what they are looking for.

XML is also a good platform for structuring data so that languages such as C++, Java, and VBScript can process it. This allows a certain degree of database management within a Web page.

The W3C provides a good example of XML, which is displayed in Figure 8.10. This example uses XML tags designed for marking up addresses.

Figure 8.10 XML

```
<customer-details id="AcPharm39156">

    <name>Acme Pharmaceuticals Co.</name>

    <address country="US">

        <street>7301 Smokey Boulevard</street>

        <city>Smallville</city>

        <state>Indiana</state>

        <postal>94571</postal>

    </address>

</customer-details>
```

Tip: W3C has standards for the Extensible Stylesheet Language (XSL) for expressing style sheets. For more information on XML and XSL, choose www.w3c.org/XML or www.ucc.ie/xml.

Plug-ins, File Formats, and Extensions

The average Web browser does a great job at displaying HTML files but falls short when presenting animation, audio, video, and other multimedia content. If you produce multimedia content with programs such as Macromedia Director or Adobe Acrobat, you will need to extend the viewing capabilities of your browser.

Since the early 1990s, hundreds of Web browser plug-ins and file formats have emerged. Following are a few you should know.

Animated Graphics Interchange Format (GIF)

File formats for Web graphics include Joint Photographic Experts Group (JPG or JPEG) and GIF. The GIF standard enables you to save multiple images into one file. When the GIF file is loaded into a Web browser, the images are displayed one after another to create an animated effect. There is no special plug-in needed for these types of files. A good program for creating animated GIFs is the GIF Constructor Set, which is available at http://www.mindworkshop.com/alchemy/alchemy.html.

QuickTime Multimedia Viewing

Available free from Apple Computer, the QuickTime player is a cross-platform multimedia system. With QuickTime installed on your computer, you can open files from most major multimedia formats. QuickTime opens graphics files such as JPG, GIF, Portable Network Graphics (PNG). It plays synthesized music files in the Musical Instrument Digital Interface (MIDI) format. QuickTime also plays digital video files such as Audio Video Interleave (AVI) and Moving Picture Experts Group (MPEG), and plays sound files such as Audio (AU) and WAV.

QuickTime also supports its own virtual reality (VR) standard and streaming audio and video. For more information, select www.apple.com.

Viewing Documents with Acrobat

Adobe Systems has developed a system that enables you to view over the Web almost any document created with almost any type of application software. Not only do you see both text and graphics, but the document also retains its original layout. You do this by using Adobe Acrobat to convert your original document into a special format called the Portable Document Format (PDF). To view a PDF file, you need Acrobat Reader, which is available free from Adobe. For more information, refer to www.adobe.com.

Shockwave Presentations

Shockwave technology enables you to play Macromedia Director multimedia presentations over the Web. With Director, you can create interactive content that includes graphics, sound, animation, text, and video. The free Shockwave player allows you to view it in your browser. For more information, refer to www.macromedia.com and www.shockwave.com.

Flash Plug-ins

Using Macromedia Flash and drawing programs such as Macromedia FreeHand, you can create small, low-bandwidth multimedia presentations that you can view from within a Web page with the Flash Player. Your presentations can include morphing, animations, and other current graphics technologies.

RealAudio and RealVideo

Using advanced compression techniques, RealNetworks has developed streaming technology for transmitting live audio and video over the Web. To hear or see this type of content within a Web page, you need RealPlayer, which is built-in to many Web browsers and is available free from www.realnetworks.com.

Windows Media Player

Windows Media Player is Microsoft's answer to RealPlayer. Media Player, which is available for all versions of Windows and for the Macintosh, can play many multimedia file types, including WAV, AVI, and MP3 (MPEG, audio layer 3). It can also handle streaming audio and video. See www.microsoft.com for more information.

Finishing Touches

Once you have a Web site up and running and have tested it thoroughly, you are going to want people to visit. You could give the URL of your home page to your friends and family, but you are probably going to want wider exposure than that.

Web Site Tests

All it takes is one misspelled word or one misplaced angle bracket to mess up your Web page. Fortunately, many programs such as FrontPage and PageMill help you find misspelled tags or missing brackets. Sometimes the only way to find errors is to carefully go through your page with a fine-toothed comb.

Be sure to try out each Web page in as many browsers as possible but, at least, check them in Microsoft Internet Explorer and Netscape Navigator. If you have access to other browsers such as Opera, use those as well. Also, be sure to try all associated programs.

If you are creating a Web site for a business or other organization, be sure to connect to the site from the outside. Many organizations have firewalls that restrict access by remote users. At the very least, if you want Web visitors from outside the organization, go home and try connecting to the site through your ISP.

Web Search Engines

Many people discover Web pages by using search engines. To get your home page and its subpages indexed at a search engine like AltaVista, you really do not need to do anything. Search engines like AltaVista use little programs called spiders and robots that search the Web for new and updated pages. If your site has at least one link to the rest of the Web, AltaVista should be able to find it. If you cannot wait for AltaVista to find your page, you can send its URL to them directly. You go to www.altavista.com and then follow the instructions for submitting a URL. You can also do this with other search engines such as Lycos, Yahoo, and Excite.

After a search engine knows about your URL, people who perform a search that matches the contents of your Web page will see a short description of your page. AltaVista uses the first few words of the document as a short abstract. As you can see in Figure 8.11, it is possible for you to control the page's description and how it indexed by using <META> tags. You can use a combined 1,024 characters within the description and keywords. All words from the description and content are used in the searches.

Figure 8.11 Search Engines and METAs

```
<META NAME="description" CONTENT="We specialize in olive trees.">

<META NAME="keywords" CONTENT="gnarled trunk, Mediterranean, olive oil">
```

 Tip: To exclude your page from being listed by a search engine, use <META NAME="robots" CONTENT="noindex, nofollow">

Vocabulary

Review the following terms in preparation for the certification exam.

Term	Description
ActiveX	Microsoft's all-encompassing solution for developing and distributing Internet applications. In many ways, a competing product with Java.
ASP	Active Server Page is a framework for developing server-side scripts.
C	A compiled, procedural programming language.
C++	An object-oriented superset of the C programming language.
CGI	Common Gateway Interface is not a programming language, but an interface that defines how programs can interact on the Web.
class	In a style sheet, categories into which you can divide HTML elements in order to assign styles to them more selectively.
COM	Component Object Model is a Microsoft specification that defines standards for interaction among programs, including application software and operating systems.
compiled programming language	A programming language in which source code converts in one fell swoop into machine code to create an executable file.
CSS	Cascading Style Sheet is a type of style sheet that lets you assign several properties at once to a particular tag.
DHTML	Dynamic HyperText Markup Language is a set of tools, including HTML, CSS, and scripting languages, that enable client-side interactivity.

Term	Description
DTD	Document-Type Definition is an XML feature for defining the rules—tags, attributes and so on—of a markup language.
ECMAScript	A standard Web scripting language developed by the European Computer Manufacturers Association (ECMA).
embedded style sheet	A style sheet that embeds into an HTML document.
external style sheet	A style sheet that is defined in separate file from an HTML document.
interpreted programming language	A programming language in which source code converts into machine code and executes line-by-line.
ISAPI	The API for Microsoft's Web server called Internet Information Server (IIS).
Java	A general-purpose, object-oriented programming language that is well suited for creating small Web programs called Java applets.
JavaScript	A scripting language developed by Netscape.
Jscript	Microsoft's version of JavaScript.
NSAPI	The API for Netscape's Web server.
object-oriented programming language	A programming language in which solutions to problems derive from the interaction of objects.

Term	Description
procedural programming language	A programming language in which solutions are derived from linear, step-by-step instructions.
property	In a style sheet, a distinguishing feature of a selector for which you can set a value.
script	In Web programming, a short, interpreted program that is relatively easy to debug. In general, Perl scripts run on the server side and JavaScript and VBScript programs run on the client side.
selector	A style sheet element for which you define a format.
SQL	Structured Query Language is a language for manipulating relational databases.
value	In a style sheet, the current setting of a property.
VBScript	Microsoft's Web scripting language based on Visual Basic, which supports Internet Explorer.
Visual Basic	An object-oriented programming language that grew out of QBASIC. Includes an Integrated Development Environment (IDE) and many other tools such as wizards.
Visual J++	Microsoft's version of Java.
VM	A Virtual Machine is software that mimics hardware device performance, such as a Java program that allows applications written for an Intel processor to run on a Motorola chip.

In Brief

If you want to...	Then do this...
Separate Web page content from presentation	Use a Cascading Style Sheet.
Apply more precise control over HTML elements	Use CSS classes for precision control over HTML elements.
Use an external style sheet	Create it in a text editor, save it with a .CSS extension, and then specify it in the Web page with the < LINK> tag.
Write CGI scripts	Use Perl, C, or C+ + on the server side.
Enable a Web page to accept user input	Use an HTML form.
Use Perl scripts	Acquire a Perl interpreter.
Use C or C+ +	Acquire C or C+ + compilers.
Use Java applets	Make sure your browser is set up with a Java Virtual Machine.
Write server-side scripts	Use JavaScript, JScript, or VBScript to write the code and then include it in the HTML file or in an attached file.
Include client-side interactivity	Use DHTML.
Access data in a relational database	Use SQL commands.
Define your own markup language	Use XML.

Lesson 8 Activities

Complete the following activities to prepare for the certification exam.

1. Explain why you should use style sheets.

2. Describe how to connect an external style sheet to an HTML document.

3. Identify the purpose of Web programming.

4. Describe the difference between interpreted programs and compiled programs.

5. Describe the difference between procedural programming languages and object-oriented programming languages.

6. Identify why you would use an HTML form.

7. Describe what is necessary for you to use a Perl script.

8. Describe what you need to do to include your Web pages in a search engine.

9. Identify a potential problem with using VBScript on the client side.

10. Explain why you should add Adobe Acrobat Reader to the client side.

Answers to Lesson 8 Activities

1. W3C recommends that you should use style sheets because they separate Web page content from presentation.

2. You use the <LINK> tag. The REL attribute defines type of linked file, the TYPE attribute defines the type of style sheet, and the HREF attribute specifies the external file name.

3. Web programming enables you to create an interactive Web experience. Users can input data through a form and then a program can create a unique response based on the user input.

4. Interpreted programs translate into machine code and are executed line-by-line. Compiled programs translate into machine code in one fell swoop to produce an executable file. The executable file then runs.

5. Procedural languages define a solution to a problem through a series of linear steps; object-oriented languages define a solution to a problem through the interaction among objects.

6. HTML forms allow for user input within a Web page.

7. You need to have a Perl interpreter loaded on the server side. Your Perl source code files saves on the server side within their own directory.

8. You do not need to do anything. Search engines like AltaVista use little programs called spiders and robots that search the Web for new and updated pages.

9. VBScript is not compatible with some browsers such as Netscape Navigator.

10. Acrobat Reader enables you to read .PDF files, which are used to retain the original format of a document.

Lesson 8 Quiz

These questions test your knowledge of features, vocabulary, procedures, and syntax.

1. What is the name of Microsoft's version of Java?

    A. JavaScript

    B. VBScript

    C. Cappuccino

    D. Visual J++

2. What are Java programs called?

    A. Applets

    B. Programmites

    C. Scripts

    D. Javettes

3. Which of the following is not one of the three technologies combined into DHTML?

    A. HTML

    B. CSS

    C. Scripts

    D. Loopback addresses

4. Which of the following is a programming language?

    A. CGI

    B. API

    C. ASP

    D. Perl

5. Which of the following attributes is used to specify the name of the program that processes an HTML form?

A. ACTION

B. LINK

C. METHOD

D. CGI

6. What organization defined standards for Web scripting languages?

A. W3C

B. EMCA

C. Sun

D. CERN

7. After Java programs compile into byte code, what extension do they have?

A. .ASP

B. .JAVA

C. .CLASS

D. .BYTE

8. What application is used to play Macromedia Director multimedia over the Web?

A. Adobe Acrobat Reader

B. RealPlayer

C. Shockwave

D. QBASIC

9. Within an HTML document, which tag describes a Web site for a search engine?

A. DESCRIPTION

B. META

C. CONTENT

D. LINK

10. Which of the following Web servers is ASP-compatible?

   A. IIS

   B. CGI

   C. JavaScript

   D. UNIX

Answers to Lesson 8 Quiz

1. Answer D is correct. Visual J++ is Microsoft's version of Java.

    Answer A is incorrect. JavaScript is a scripting language that was developed independently from Java.

    Answer B is incorrect. VBScript is a scripting language unrelated to Java.

    Answer C is incorrect. Cappuccino is a style of Italian coffee.

2. Answer A is correct. Applets are small Java programs.

    Answer B is incorrect. Programmites do not exist.

    Answer C is incorrect. Java programs are compiled, whereas scripts are interpreted.

    Answer D is incorrect. Javettes do not exist.

3. Answer D is correct. A loopback address has nothing to do with DHTML; it is used mainly for testing a TCP/IP configuration on a host computer.

    Answer A is incorrect. HTML is a key part of DHTML.

    Answer B is incorrect. CSS is a key part of DHTML.

    Answer C is incorrect. Scripts are a key part of DHTML.

4. Answer D is correct. Perl is a programming language for server-side scripting.

    Answer A is incorrect. CGI is not a programming language; it is an interface.

    Answer B is incorrect. API is not a programming language; it is an interface.

    Answer C is incorrect. ASP is not a programming language; it is an environment for creating and executing server-side scripts.

5. Answer A is correct. The value for the ACTION attribute contains the name of the program that processes an HTML form.

    Answer B is incorrect. < LINK> is a tag that connects files.

    Answer C is incorrect. The METHOD attribute specifies the method, either "get" or "post," used to process a Web program.

Answer D is incorrect. There is no CGI attribute.

6.   Answer B is correct. The European Computer Manufacturers Association defined scripting standards and produced the scripting language ECMAScript.

Answer A is incorrect. W3C is responsible for many standards including HTML, CSS, and XML, but not scripting.

Answer C is incorrect. Sun is a company that produces Java, among many other things.

Answer D is incorrect. CERN is the particle research lab where the Web was invented.

7.   Answer C is correct. The .CLASS extension is used for compiled Java code.

Answer A is incorrect. The .ASP extension is used for ASP files.

Answer B is incorrect. The .JAVA extension is used for Java source code.

Answer D is incorrect. There is no .BYTE extension

8.   Answer C is correct. Shockwave plays multimedia produced by Director. Both products are from Macromedia.

Answer A is incorrect. Acrobat Reader reads and displays .PDF files.

Answer B is incorrect. RealPlayer plays RealAudio and RealVideo, among other things.

Answer D is incorrect. QBASIC is an interpreted programming language.

9.   Answer B is correct. The <META> tag is correct. For example,

<META NAME="description" CONTENT="We specialize in olive trees.">.

Answer A is incorrect. The word "description" is a value for the NAME attribute.

Answer C is incorrect. CONTENT is an attribute not a tag.

Answer D is incorrect. <LINK> is used to connect files.

10.   Answer A is correct. Microsoft Internet Information Server is ASP-compatible.

Answer B is incorrect. CGI is an interface not a Web server.

Answer C is incorrect. JavaScript is a programming language not a Web server.

Answer D is incorrect. UNIX is an operating system, not a Web server. UNIX has a good Web server, which you can load, called Apache.

Lesson 9: Internet Security

Internet security is a growing concern. Intranets, accessible only internally, have their own security issues. Breaches usually result from accidentally deleted files, lack of training or perhaps disgruntled employees. When you connect your intranet to the Internet, you open your secure Web up to a score of potential dangers.

After completing this lesson, you should have a better understanding of the following topics:

- Internet Security Overview

- Authentication

- Access Control

- Encryption

- Auditing and Tracking Suspicious Internet Activity

- Virtual Private Networking (VPN)

- Cookies

- Internet Viruses

Internet Security Overview

Connections with the public Internet are like a street with traffic able to flow in both directions. Without strict controls, a connection to the Internet can be a threat to a business. An Internet connection may permit attackers to gain access to valuable company data and may even cause damage by stealing, erasing, or corrupting files to render the data useless.

One method to keep potential intruders at bay is to have a standalone Web server that does not connect to any internal networks (Figure 9.1). This assures that no one will steal sensitive information. Only information that is available for public consumption is placed on the Internet Web server. Data may consist of the company history, consumer and product information, public relations information, and advertising, but never any sensitive data.

An intranet is similar to the Internet. Companies use intranets to allow their employees to share information in a secure Internet-like environment. Web page servers present information for people to use and stay informed. It is common practice to not connect intranets to the public Internet. This helps to prevent hackers from gaining access to the intranet and any sensitive information stored on those servers. Strict hardware and software controls are designed to keep potential intruders outside a company's networks.

Figure 9.1 Standalone Web Server

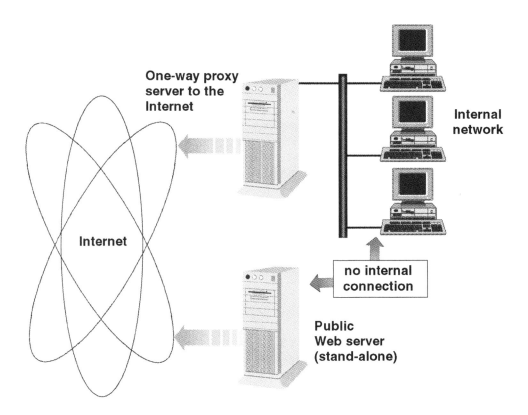

One-way proxy server to the Internet

Internal network

no internal connection

Internet

Public Web server (stand-alone)

Another method to keep intruders out is to use a network computer installed with two network cards (double-homed system). One network card attaches to the internal company network and the other card connects to the public Internet. Implementation of security systems keep unauthorized people out of the internal network. Methods can include protocol isolation, firewalls, IP address filters, and proxy services.

Extranets

An intranet that is set up to be partially accessible to people from outside the company is an extranet. Firewalls protect most intranets, making access available only to those inside the organization. Extranets are an alternative way of setting up access, based on usernames and passwords, which provide select individuals from outside the organization various levels of access. Extranets are a popular way for cooperating businesses to exchange information.

Network administrators audit the firewall for suspicious activities that may indicate hacker or cracker attacks from the Internet. On the inside of the firewall, the company intranet is monitored for potential unauthorized access attempt activities. For example, an employee of a trusted partnered business may try to gain unauthorized access to sensitive or confidential information to steal or destroy it by using the extranet. Sometimes hackers gain access by obtaining an authorized password or by discovering a path to the internal network from another network or backdoor.

The network administrator needs to determine if an attack is coming from outside the firewall or from inside. Knowing the source and type of attack aids the network administrator in determining the kind of attack taking place and what counter-measures to use. Counter-measures may include closing a firewall port or locking out internal access to another internal network gateway, a directory, or a file.

Authentication

Authentication is the means by which a system identifies a person and confirms that they are who they say they are. Authentication is typically based on a form of username and password security. Do not confuse authentication with authorization. Authorization is a process where the system will, based on the identity confirmed with the authentication process, grant or deny access to system or network objects and resources.

Usernames and Passwords

Usernames and passwords are forms of access control that use authentication to grant or deny access to a user's account. To gain access to these accounts, a person must provide the correct username and password, called a challenge-response method or Challenge Handshake Authentication Protocol (CHAP). The user account security feature identifies and validates (or denies) users against a database of authorized people.

Similar challenge-response authentication methods access Web sites and file transfer servers.

One method to protect against a hacker getting the password to a Web site account is not to cache passwords. Some Web sites offer free memberships to their site. The site software allows you to choose a username and password and creates a user account.

The next time you visit, the site requests you to log on with your username and password. If a dialog box requests to have the system save your user I.D. and password, decline. Hackers use tools to find and extract this kind of information from Web sites and networks so they can break into a legitimate user's account and start searching the network for sensitive data.

File-Level Security Practices

Access controls restrict what people can do with objects. An object in this context refers to anything that you can select and manipulate individually, such as files and folders. You can secure the files and subdirectories that you create in your home directory. This level of file protection provides personal control and is one of the best tools to use to prevent unauthorized people from accessing your data.

Authentication Certificates

Electronic Message (e-mail) attachments also have the means to be secure. This is similar to sending a coded message in a locked box with a trusted courier. Certificates of Authority (CA) (the trusted courier) issue digital certificates (the locked box) that confirm that a person who sends an encrypted (coded) message is the person they claim to be and provide the recipient with the means to make an encrypted reply.

Digital certificates are encrypted and contain the CA public key. The CA makes its public key available on the Internet. The recipient will first decrypt the digital certificate (unlock the box) and then open the message using the CA public key to confirm that the CA truly issued it. Once confirmed, the recipient can obtain the sender's public key to decrypt (decode) the message. The recipient can then send back an encoded message using the sender's information

Non-Repudiation

Non-repudiation takes the idea of a secure package one step further. Suppose that not only would you receive your package, knowing both that it is from whom it says it is (trusted courier), and that it is intact (locked box), but you could prove to a trusted third party that you received it? Non-repudiation allows both the sending party and the receiving party to prove that the sender did send and the recipient did receive the exact same transmission.

It takes considerably more effort to set up non-repudiation, but in certain industries, the value can offset the expense. All non-repudiation organizations and individuals are identified, authenticated, and authorized to perform the transaction. Transactions are audited and must remain intact throughout the process. It becomes obvious how this enables the high level of security required by E-commerce.

 Note: X.509 is currently the most common standard for digital certificates.

Access Control

Access controls protect objects. Remember that an object is a printer, a file, a directory, or anything that you can select. Whether you can manipulate it or not depends on your level of access control. Access controls and user account rights represent two different aspects of a system security.

Authentication is the process of identifying individuals based on username and password, ensuring that each person is who he or she claims to be. In security systems, authentication is distinct from authorization. Security systems use a

two-step process combining both authentication with authorization. Authorization

is the process of giving individuals access rights to system objects based on their identity, which is based on the authentication findings.

This section describes the following Internet security concepts:

- Access Control Lists (ACLs)
- Firewalls and proxy servers
- Packet filters

ACL

An ACL holds identity and permission level information about users and groups and determines who has permission to access the objects. Every object has its own ACL. Objects have different types of permissions that are used to grant or deny access and to determine the granted or denied access level.

All objects have a security descriptor that contains their security attributes. A person who has read-only permission to a file based on their user account may also have read/write permission based on membership in a particular group.

Directory and file object ACLs grant or deny specific permissions, for example to read, write, or execute a file. Permissions for print queues can be set to grant or deny a person other privileges, such as to manage, delete, and print documents.

Owners of objects make entries in the ACL using built in Operating System (OS) tools or by setting properties for files and folders.

Access Control with Firewalls

Firewalls are defense mechanisms for Web networks that act as a choke point for all internal and external traffic entering or leaving an intranet. Actually, any device that controls network traffic for security purposes can be called a firewall. Firewalls require continuous monitoring to ensure attackers do not break through. A company's intranet system administrator can monitor all the traffic into or out of the intranet at the firewall.

Packet Filters or Screening Routers

The addition of packet-filtering routers (screening routers) to firewalls boosts intranet security. These routers are programmed by systems administrators who define the filtering rules that tell how to inspect packets and when to grant or deny access to the network based on those rules.

Packet filtering routers have built-in filters, and they work at the lower layers of the network protocol stack. These routers may be stand-alone devices or computers that contain two or more Network Interface Cards (NIC) (multi-homed system) which connect two networks and perform packet filtering to control traffic between the two networks. Packet filtering routers combined with gateways build multi-level defensive systems.

However, packet-filtering routers by themselves are not considered adequate protection for connections between an internal network and the Internet. By themselves, the routers expose internal network IP addresses to the Internet. Hackers can monitor the packet stream that emanates from the internal network and capture the IP addresses of those computers. (Figure 9.2) Hackers use these IP addresses to identify and target computers on the internal network for attack.

Figure 9.2 Packet-Filtering Routers

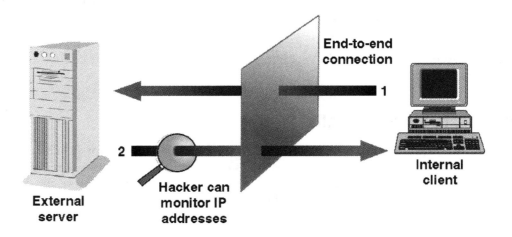

Other disadvantages of these routers are that most do not generate attack alerts, and they cannot detect or log a network break-in. However, proxy servers can overcome many of these problems. Proxy servers hide all the internal network IP addresses from the Internet and provide numerous monitoring and alert methods.

To increase security, many companies use several firewalls made by different vendors. This reduces the chances that an intruder who gains access through the first firewall will be able to use the same tactics to get through the next one. Continuous monitoring allows an administrator to take countermeasures to stop unauthorized accesses, such as blocking access to a port that leads through the firewall.

Access Control with Proxy Servers

A proxy server provides a controlled, virtual network connection between the internal and external network systems through the proxy server. Internet requests can go through the network to the proxy server, and the proxy server delivers those requests to the Internet after changing the IP address. External users only see the IP address of the proxy server. The proxy server then receives all responses and sends the appropriate response back through the circuit to the internal client. While internal traffic travels through to the intranet, people on the public Internet never see the company's internal systems. This type of connection is often used to connect internal Web network users to the public Internet (Figure 9.3).

Figure 9.3 Firewall Security

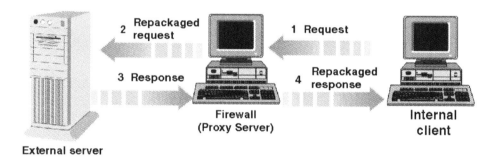

To protect a company from unauthorized access by people using the public Web, a system administrator can put proxy servers on the company's Web server. Proxy servers act as relay agents for employees who make requests to the public Internet. The employees may need to access the Internet for company business, and yet the management may want to limit access to other types of sites or certain protocols.

The proxy passes approved internal user requests and an external server replies from the Internet across the company's protective firewall. This provides security to the internal network, yet allows employees behind the firewall to have access to the Internet.

High-end proxy servers use the upper levels of the protocol stack, such as the application layer. These provide proxy services on external networks for internal clients. They can also perform advanced monitoring and traffic control by looking for certain information inside packets.

Application-level proxy servers provide the highest level of protection and access control through a firewall (Figure 9.4). These proxy servers understand the protocols of the applications that are allowed to pass. Screening routers operate at lower layers because they cannot operate at this high level. The proxy server manages both inbound and outbound traffic. Advanced filtering uses rules to permit only specified traffic to flow. Authentication is also possible using these proxy servers. Specific users pass through the firewall based on their identity.

Figure 9.4 Proxy Server Gateway

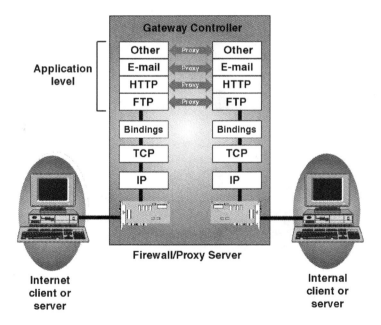

Proxy servers allow network administrators to track all the sites a person accesses on the Internet. Records, or logs, of site visits are made and kept. These records can be mailed to users on a periodic basis to remind them that they are being monitored. Proxy servers can also block specific hosts and Web site addresses to restrict the sites from access by internal users. Web pages that are viewed repetitively can be cached at the proxy server to reduce requests and responses to the Internet and to reduce the load on the Internet connection.

To address the tremendous volume of packets inspected, a new class of firewall that uses a technique called stateful inspection is on the rise.

Stateful inspection does not examine the contents of each packet like a standard proxy. Instead, the bit patterns of the packets are compared to packets that are already known and trusted. For instance, if access is made to a site outside the firewall, the server saves a copy of the original outgoing state of the request like the port number, the source address, and destination address. The response to the request returns and the firewall server compares the return packets to the copy of the original outgoing saved state to determine if they should be granted or denied access to the internal network.

Despite the improved speed and transparency of stateful inspection, one of the major problems is that packets from the internal network can travel to the outside network where their original internal host IP addresses are available for view by potential hackers. To combat this problem, several firewall vendors are deploying products that use both stateful inspection and proxies to improve security.

Another innovation on the upswing is that a few router vendors are now putting firewalls into their products. This may encourage the purchase of inexpensive hardware-based router devices over expensive application-level servers. Talk to the product vendors and read the reviews when shopping for a firewall product. In the meantime, the debate over proxies and stateful inspection techniques continues.

Encryption

Encryption is the protection of information by transforming or encrypting it into an unreadable format called cipher text. Only those who possess a secret key can decipher or decrypt the message into plain text. Although modern cryptography techniques are virtually unbreakable, expert code-breakers using highly sophisticated algorithms and ever-increasing computing power can sometimes decipher encrypted messages.

Electronic security is becoming more important as the Internet, and other forms of electronic communication, become common. Cryptography is used to protect e-mail messages, credit card information, corporate and other sensitive data. One of the most widely used cryptography systems on the

Internet is Pretty Good Privacy (PGP). Not only is it effective, but it is also free because the inventor of PGP, Philip Zimmerman, released it into the public domain.

Cryptography systems are broadly classified into two systems. One is the symmetric key and the other is the public key system. The symmetric key (or private key) system is where the sender and recipient each have a copy of the same key. The public key system uses two keys, a public key available to everyone and a private, secret key known only to the recipient of the public key encoded messages.

Encoded Data with Keys

Public key cryptography was invented in 1976 by Whitfield Diffie and Martin Hellman and is sometimes known as Diffie-Hellman encryption. It is also called asymmetric encryption because it uses two keys instead of a single key (symmetric encryption) for encryption/decryption.

The public and the private keys perform separate tasks; only the public key can be used to encrypt messages and only the corresponding private key can be used to decrypt them. It is virtually impossible to create another private key, even if you know the public key (Figure 9.5).

Figure 9.5 Public-Key Cryptography System

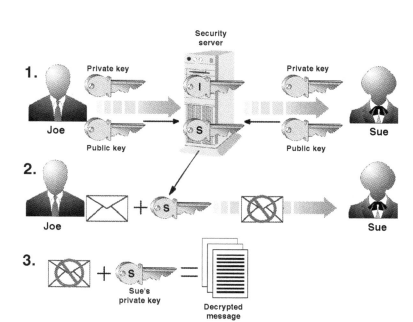

Public-key systems, such as Pretty Good Privacy (PGP), are popular for transmitting information via the Internet. They are considered very secure and relatively easy to use. The only difficulty with public key systems is that you need to know the recipient's public key to encrypt a message for them. The best method is to simply send a copy of the public key to anyone who wants to send you encrypted information.

Messages encrypted with the public key can only be decrypted with the matching private key. For example, if a sender encrypts their message with your public key that message will only be deciphered with your private key.

A person, who wants to send a secure message to a friend uses the friend's public key to encrypt the message and sends the message to the private key holder. The private key holder uses the corresponding private key to decrypt the message. The sender and receiver must both have the same mathematical encoder and decoder. The sender encrypts using the algorithm and the receiver decrypts using the reverse.

In public key encryption, the public key is given to anyone who wants it. In private key encryption, a single private encryption and decryption key is given only to trusted parties.

Encoding Data with Private Keys

To encode data with private keys, the sender and receiver must both have the same mathematical encoder and decoder. The sender encrypts using the algorithm and the receiver decrypts using the reverse.

There are several problems with this approach. First, there is the need to exchange keys safely. You cannot just send the private key to the receiver over the network. If someone gets hold of the private key, all communication can be decoded.

Unfortunately, use of the private key encryption system is vulnerable because there is little assurance the key will not be compromised, unless you first deliver the matching key in person. What if you exchange your key with someone who is less than dependable or some third party steals it? The primary reason that people have largely adopted the public-key system of encryption is that it avoids these problems of the private-key system.

Secure Socket Layers (SSL) with HTTPS

Web browsers that connect with Internet Web servers often need secure connections to ensure privacy for business transactions and transmission of sensitive data. A secure channel service provides this in the form of SSL to establish a secure session.

Netscape developed SSL for sending secure transmissions over the Web through the Internet. SSL uses the private key type of transfer. Many Web sites, Internet Explorer, and Netscape, all support SSL. Web sites that use HTTPS: in the beginning of their URL instead of HTTP: require SSL.

Another complementary protocol for secure data transmission over the World Wide Web is Secure HyperText Transfer Protocol (S-HTTP). S-HTTP is an application level protocol designed to encrypt individual messages, such as parts of documents, for transmission using HTTP. SSL creates a secure connection between a client and a server, over which any amount of data can be sent securely.

Private Communication Technology (PCT) is a newer protocol that is considered a more secure and efficient protocol than SSL. Although PCT is similar to SSL, it separates authentication from encryption and allows applications to use authentication that is stronger than the 40-bit key limit for encryption allowed by the U.S. Government for export. Microsoft's implementation is backward compatible with SSL. A Certificate Authority is required to use these protocols.

Transport Layer Security (TLS) is a new Microsoft security protocol that incorporates both SSL and PCT into one standard that supports both certificates and password authentication. The client and server establish a level of security, and once a session begins, it encrypts all the data sent between the two.

Secure Multipurpose Internet Mail Extensions (S/MIME)

RSA Data Security, Inc. is credited with developing the Secure/MIME protocol. RSA stands for Rivest, Shamir, and Adelman, the inventors of the technique. The protocol is a version of Multipurpose Internet Mail Extensions (MIME) that can support the encryption of messages for transmission using e-mail. S/MIME is based on RSA's public-key encryption technology. The data format for the encrypted message is based on the RSA Public Key Cryptography Standards (PKCS #7), and the format for certificates is based on Version 3 of the X.509 standard.

The inventors based their algorithm on the fact that there is no efficient method for factoring very large numbers. As a result, figuring out an RSA key requires extraordinary time and computer processing power. It is the standard for sending encrypted e-mail over the Internet and is built into several software products, including Eudora and the Netscape Communicator and Microsoft Internet Explorer Web browsers.

Digital Signatures

Digital signatures are used to authenticate the sender of an electronic message. The creation of digital signatures involves two processes, one performed by the signer of the message and the other by the receiver of the message with the digital signature.

A digital signature is a mathematically created code that attaches to an electronically transmitted message that uniquely identifies or authenticates the sender. Like a written signature, the purpose of a digital signature is to guarantee that persons sending a message really are who they claim to be. E-commerce often uses digital signatures. A one-way hash function creates a digital signature, and these signatures are almost impossible to forge.

The one-way hash function uses an algorithm that turns messages or text into a fixed-length string of digits called a message digest. Encrypting the message digest with a private key creates the digital signature and becomes an electronic means of authentication of the sender of a digitally transmitted message. Use of one-way hash functions means that it is almost impossible to determine the original text from the string of digits.

One-way hash functions include MD2, MD4, and MD5 from RSA Data Systems. Another one-way function (created by the National Security Agency) is the Secure Hash Algorithm (SHA), which is part of the U.S. Government Digital Signature Standard (DSS).

Encryption Transmission Standards

Bits of information make up computer keys, and these binary units can have a value of either a (1) or (0). To decipher an encrypted message by brute force, every possible key combination needs to be tried. This means the longer the encryption key, the more computing power and time required to break a code.

The two most used and recognized encryption standards today are the 128-bit key and the limited 40-bit key versions. Both were developed by RSA Data Security, Inc. The strongest version uses the 128-bit encryption key.

A French programmer was recently successful in breaking a 40-bit key and used it to decrypt a single secure Netscape transaction. The people at Netscape estimated the effort took the equivalent of 64 Million Instructions Per Second (MIPS) to correctly decipher it.

A comparison of key lengths starts with an 8-bit key. 8-bit keys have 256 possible values (2 to the eighth power), while a 56-bit key has 72 quadrillion possible values.

A 128-bit key is the equivalent of a 16-character message on a personal computer, and requires a brute-force attack that is 4.7 sextillion (4,700,000,000,000,000,000,000) times more difficult to break than a 56-bit key. This means a 56-bit key can be broken, but 128-bit key cannot. This type of security is the reason why the 128-bit key is valued and becoming the new electronic encryption standard.

One of the most important advances in cryptography is the invention of public key systems. These systems use algorithms that encrypt messages with one key (a public one) and permit decryption only by use of a different key (a secret, private key). A person can openly distribute his or her public key. If someone uses it to encrypt a message, the only person who can correctly decrypt it is the owner of the private key. Anyone else who tries to decipher the message gets unusable gibberish.

Secure Electronic Transactions (SET)

The SET standard is a new protocol that is in joint-venture development by Microsoft, GTE, Netscape, MasterCard, and Visa. Plans are for support by all major financial institutions to encrypt all credit card transactions and integrate it into the credit card processing system.

It will use digital signatures to authenticate credit card holders, merchants, and financial institutions like banks. Encryption will protect all the transaction information, which will transmit directly to the affected financial institutions to prevent theft of credit card information and keep payment data confidential (Figure 9.6). Protocols are in development to include support for debit cards, electronic cash, and check payments.

Figure 9.6 SET

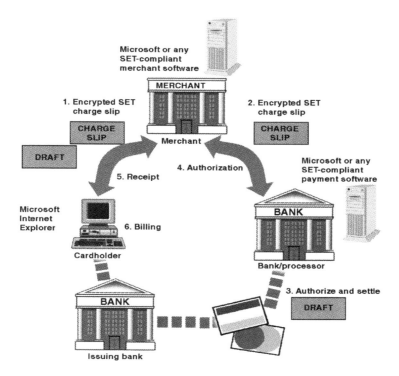

SET will require digital signatures to verify that the customer, merchant, and financial institution are legitimate. Plans are to use encrypted multi-party messages that go directly to financial institutions. Encryption and direct messaging will be designed to keep credit card numbers secure. It will work in conjunction with several other protocols and transports.

Suspicious Internet Activity Auditing and Tracking

The Internet is a great place to find information; unfortunately, it is also a playground for intruders who seek out computers and networks to attack. The following centers on several common types of attacks administrators need to know about, how to detect them and what countermeasures are available:

- Denial of service attacks

- Multiple logon failures

- Packet Internet Groper (PING) attacks

- Spamming and mail floods

- SYN floods

- Using intrusion detection utilities

Denial of Service Attacks

Denial of service encompasses a general category of attacks aimed at networks connected to the Internet, where the attackers do not try to steal information, but try to disable a computer or network. These attacks take several forms, but they all try to overwhelm a network with superfluous traffic.

Packets contain both source and destination addresses that hackers can change using easy-to-get tools. Denial of service attacks often use IP-spoofing to target a host on a network. IP-spoofing makes a packet appear as coming from a trusted node on another network by making false addresses in the IP packets. The falsified packets transmit to the target network. Alterations of the actual IP source addresses prevent tracing the attackers (Figure 9.7).

Figure 9.7 IP Address Spoofing

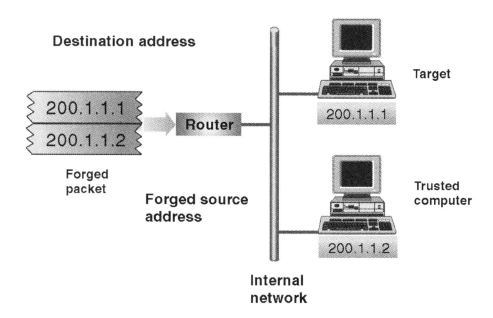

Multiple Logon Failures

When an administrator sees multiple logon failures, either live or recorded in an audit log, it is an indication that a hacker is attempting to break into the system. OSs have a default number of logon failure attempts, for example, Windows NT has a default of allowing only three logon failures before it revokes logon permission to an account. Revocation of logon requires the authorized user of the account to contact the system administrator and have the logon reset. The administrator will authenticate the service requestor using several means to make certain the request is from the authorized user.

E-Mail Spamming

Sending hundreds or thousands of unsolicited electronic mail messages to an e-mail server to overload the system is a spam attack.

Most are traceable to the source IP address. It takes some time and skill to determine which lines in a spam are fake and which are real, but it is possible. Once determined, an administrator can block out those messages that have the source IP address in the header.

PING Floods

Another denial of service attack is a PING flood or smurf. Here, a network connected to the Internet is swamped with replies to Internet Control Message Protocol (ICMP) echo requests (PING uses ICMP). A smurf attacker sends PING requests to an Internet broadcast address. These addresses send all the received messages to the hosts connected to the subnet.

Each broadcast address can support up to 255 hosts which means that a single PING request can multiply up to 255 times. The return address of the request itself is a fake and is actually the IP address of a host on the network under attack. All the hosts receiving the PING request reply to this victim's IP address instead of the address of the real sender. A single attack that sends hundreds or thousands of PING messages per second can fill the victim's connection line with PING replies and disable the entire Internet service.

SYN Floods

A SYN attack is a type of denial of service ploy designed to crash the target network. It occurs when a hacker sends hundreds or thousands of SYN start-connection messages to an ISP system and never completes the connection process. The ISP computer takes the connection requests and waits almost 60 seconds for them to complete. These continuous incomplete connections and automatic delays create an overload on the ISP system and disable it from responding to legitimate connection requests. When these half-open connections fill the ISP's server memory, the server crashes.

SYN attackers use fake source IP addresses in the requesting packets. Since each packet contains a different fake return address, it makes them extremely difficult or impossible to determine the actual source of the attack. Packet filtering cannot stop a SYN attack because it requires knowing the true source IP address. Any system connected to the Internet that provides TCP-based network services (such as a Web server, FTP server, or mail server) is open to this type of attack.

Detecting a SYN attack is not easy. Users of the attacked server system may not notice anything unusual, since the IP-spoofed connection requests may not stop the system from establishing outgoing connections. Only the clients trying to make a legitimate connection to the ISP's service under attack are likely to notice the problem.

Current technology is not able to eliminate IP-spoofing packets, so it is almost impossible to stop this kind of attack. The best method an administrator can use to reduce the number IP-spoofed packets is to install incoming and outgoing packet filters. The incoming filter can restrict the input by not allowing packets through if they have a source address from your internal network. The outgoing packet filter is set so that packets have source addresses that are different from those on the internal networks. The outgoing packet filter is often used to prevent a source IP spoof attack originating from the ISP's own site (Figure 9.8).

Figure 9.8 Normal SYN Request and ACK Response

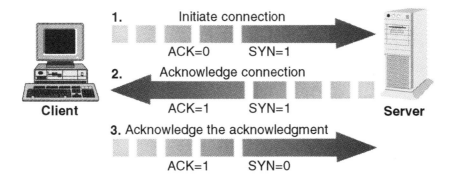

Using Intrusion Detection Utilities

Several software manufacturers make security packages that can detect suspicious activity, identify and record it for analysis, trace the sources of attacks, and block threats. Manufacturers design auditing software to log the activities and processes to files for analysis. People who visit a Web site leave a trail that system administrators can trace and determine if a visitor attempted any unauthorized activities.

Monitoring can focus on anything or everything. The decision of which network segments, programs, servers, firewalls, and other items to monitor can be staggering. Concentrate the majority of your efforts on those networks with sensitive data. Concentrated monitoring minimizes performance hits caused by the auditing process of recording events to the hard disk.

Tip: A properly configured incoming packet filter always knows when an incoming packet is a spoof. It is a fake when the packet that arrives on the external port has a source address that corresponds to an IP address from its own internal network.

Active attacks are those where data changes during transmission or while stored. Passive attacks are those when someone collects information without anyone's knowledge. Electronic eavesdropping is often used to get information to make an attack on a computing system.

Real-time monitoring of an attack that is in progress enables taking countermeasures. Administrators need to avoid detection of their monitoring activity because an intruder may lock out the administrator or damage information before an attack is stopped.

Countermeasures may include immediate blocking of an attacker or setting false files to lure the attacker to another system that does not contain sensitive data. Do not mount counterattacks because the attacker can hide his activities and record yours to accuse you in court of being the attacker.

Note: Remember, it is not legal to monitor the activity of intruders unless logon notices are posted on network systems telling potential users that they must log on to valid accounts and that all activities may be monitored. This legal precaution protects network administrators from hackers who are caught. If a hacker is caught and taken to court, this notice prevents the hacker from accusing the administrator of being the attacking party.

A successful attack can result in alteration of audit logs, administrative accounts, and security configurations. It is always good practice to keep backups of logs to see if an attacker made changes or follows a pattern every time he breaks in.

Tracking attackers from outside your networks may require you to ask for the assistance of telecommunications companies and law enforcement agencies.

Virtual Private Network (VPN)

Creating encrypted communication channels over the public Internet is the core idea of VPNs. It saves the costs of long distance charges by employees who would normally access their company network from remote locations using long-distance telephone lines. VPNs also save the costs of leasing dedicated lines that stretch the entire distance to branch offices (Figure 9.9).

Figure 9.9 VPN

Leased-line costs increase with distance, as illustrated here:

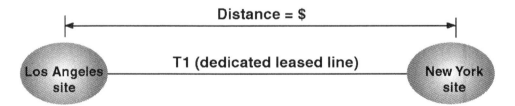

However, the Internet can be used to provide the long-distance part of the connection and dramatically reduce the cost of your WAN links, as shown here:

Point-to-Point Tunneling Protocol (PPTP) provides encryption, while RAS authentication protocols validate user logons. VPN is a ready-made encrypted Wide Area Network (WAN) that connects employees and offices to their corporate networks through the Internet using PPTP servers. This kind of connection usually requires connection to a local ISP for Internet access and a separate connection to the VPN tunnel server.

A key is required at each end of the tunnel to encrypt and decrypt the data.

VPN for Encrypted Communications

While logon information is not encrypted in Windows 9x computers, logons are encrypted on Windows NT Workstations. If you are using a Windows 9x client to log into an ISP account, you can encrypt this data using software from several vendors that make security software products. PPTP servers are used by a VPN to create a secure encrypted connection with your computer, the VPN, and your company network over the public Internet. Once you establish a connection, it is like dialing directly into the PPTP server, but you are using the Internet in a secure connection to access your company's server with its file and printer resources.

Connecting Two Sites with an Internet VPN

Most companies find that dedicated telephone lines are expensive to lease and often several are required to efficiently connect distant sites. The costs may increase according to the distance between locations. The use of VPNs to create virtual connections to remote sites via the Internet can dramatically reduce these connection costs.

A local high-capacity line, like a T1, is used at each remote office to connect to the local VPN. The long distance communication is made over the public Internet using the VPN to provide the encryption channel.

Connecting Remote Users to a VPN Site

VPNs can also securely connect remote employees to their corporate networks using local phone lines and the Internet. To make this kind of connection requires a regular connection to an ISP and a separate connection to the VPN tunnel server. However, if you are using the PPTP protocol to connect directly to a PPTP server through the Internet, only one connection is necessary.

Installing the Microsoft VPN Networking Dial-Up Adapter

To install a VPN dial-up adapter in Windows 95, follow these steps:

1. From the **Start Menu**, choose **Control Panel** and then select **Network**.

2. Locate the **Dial-Up Adapter** in the installed components list, and then choose **Add**.

3. Choose **Adapter** and then select **Add**.

4. Choose **Microsoft** from the **manufacturer's list**.

5. Choose **Microsoft Virtual Private Networking Adapter** and then select **Add**.

6. Click **OK** and reboot the computer if prompted.

VPN as an Extranet

To use a VPN as an extranet requires the use of digitally encrypted electronic tunnels. A company's remote users and remote branch offices connect to the Internet using a designated ISP that uses PPTP dial-in servers. Any Point-to-Point Protocol (PPP) client can establish an encrypted PPTP connection to a PPTP server. PPTP supports multiple protocols on Windows and non-Windows computers. The only requirement is that the remote computers have a PPTP connection to the Internet. The drawbacks to this kind of networking are the performance issues: slow connection speeds of modems that people use to connect to the local ISP and additional traffic loads on the Internet.

Cookies

Companies and organizations place information on Web servers for public use. This gives them exposure to inform, provide goods and services, and garner the goodwill of those who visit the site. The object is often not only to share information that may benefit the visitor but also to gain information about visitors to the site.

Web sites capture this information about visitors in text files called cookies. There are two parts to every cookie. One part loads on the hard disk of the client computer and the other portion resides on the visited server in a user profile database. Each cookie contains a unique identifier and may contain confidential information such as the name of the visitor, authentication information like an account and password, credit card numbers, and online shopping habits.

These information containers are also known as persistent cookies because they can remain on a person's hard disk for a long time. Although they are not executable and do not pose a security threat to the operation of a computer, they can provide Web site owners, and sometimes hackers, with this information.

Unknown Cookies

User profile databases usually place cookies on a person's hard disk without their knowledge. Unless a person turns on the cookie alert feature in their browser, cookies deposit automatically on the local hard drive in total secrecy.

The information in a cookie updates from a user profile database each time a Web site is revisited. It often contains the last date and time a site was visited, the browser and OS they used, and more. This collection of data also allows for the customization of pages for visitors based on their interests and preferences.

The information is also used to display advertisements that match a person's interests by tracking what they see and do. It further provides the marketing and sales departments with data to improve the focus and effectiveness of the Web site.

Client-Side Cookies

Each time a visitor returns to a site, the browser sends its site-specific cookie from the hard disk to the user profile database on the server that originally created it and placed it. This allows the cookie to update. It also means administrators from other sites cannot review cookies other than the ones their system placed on a local hard drive. From that aspect, it provides a person with a degree of privacy.

Tracking Internet User Actions

The movements and activities of each visitor to a Web site are frequently captured in cookies. Actions such as clicking on particular pages or links are recorded in that visitor's cookie and stored in the user profile database. This information is placed in the user profile database along with a unique site-specific user identifier. This allows for personal customization of a person's visit to a Web site. If they have visited the pages or links to news, sports, or stock market stories, then the next time that person visits the Web site, that kind of information can be automatically displayed and waiting for them to read.

This customization is made possible when a person's browser enters a Web site that has a user profile database. Visitors often provide detailed information about themselves when they sign up as a member of a Web site. Visitors often reveal their names, e-mail addresses, and other personal information but may not realize that the information is saved in the user profile database and that a copy of their unique identifier is saved in the cookie. Then the cookie is placed on their hard disk where it is stored for comparison against the user profile database at a later time. The next time the visitor goes to the same Web site, the browser sends the cookie to the Web server where it is compared, updated by the database, and then saved back to the local hard disk.

Cookies for Security and Privacy

Cookies can also provide some security and privacy to visitors to a Web site because each cookie contains a unique identifier used for authentication. This reduces the chances that a hacker can access a user's profile because they do not possess the authentication token. This can be useful for online banking purposes or making online purchases. The cookie can be used by the database on a server to identify, authenticate, and provide access to a secure area on the site to allow the visitor to conduct confidential financial transactions.

Internet Viruses

A virus is a small program that acts similarly to a biological virus. They insert themselves into computer systems by being copied from contaminated disks, delivered in e-mail messages, or downloaded from Web sites by unsuspecting users. Once a system is contaminated, a virus can execute some immediate action, wait a specified time, or execute when a user hits a specific key or command.

Identifying a Virus

Workstation users and network administrators need to pay attention to unusual activity on a computer or network. Indications of a potential virus, or other threat, may include strange increases in file sizes, missing data, incorrect macro behavior, corrupted files, or a monitor that unexpectedly goes blank.

The National Computer Security Association (NCSA) and the Computer Security Institute organizations classify threats like these into two broad categories: viruses and other security threats.

Viruses

Viruses and similar programs can attack application files, macros, activity monitor logs, and more. Following are several types of viruses:

- File-infecting viruses usually infect or replace an executable file.

- A polymorphic virus changes itself each time it contaminates something to avoid detection by anti-virus software

- Boot Sector viruses overwrite the master boot record

- Macro viruses are executable programs that usually attach themselves to productivity files, such as Microsoft Excel spreadsheet files or Microsoft Word documents

- Multipart viruses infect executable files and boot sectors and use polymorphic and stealth techniques to prevent detection

- Stealth viruses hide in memory, hide changes to file sizes, and thwart attempts to use the operating system

Other Threats

Some viruses are harmless and simply display a message or animation. Others can corrupt vital data. There are also extremely destructive viruses that wipe all the information from a hard disk or rewrite the commands in the BIOS chip so the computer will not start after it is turned off.

Following are several types of security threats that you should be aware of:

- Trojan Horses are programs that appear to be harmless although they are either destructive or just gather information and e-mail the data to another location

- Worms are destructive programs that cannot replicate themselves like a virus

- Logic bombs are Trojan horses with a timing device

Virus Protection

Viruses are a threat to any computer or network. They can easily spread to other systems and infect entire organizations or companies. One of the best virus protections is anti-virus software that looks for virus signatures, then automatically isolates and disables them before removing them from a system. Even after detection and cleanup, a virus can remain on floppy disks or in other files, ready to re-infect a system. Good data backup practices and network anti-virus programs are important hedges against an all-out system disaster.

Fortunately, most anti-virus software products today can identify a virus by its signature or behavior and isolate it. Anti-virus software is an inexpensive form of protection for all computers and network systems. Installing anti-virus software on all workstations and servers and running it continuously helps to identify, intercept, isolate, and destroy all viruses.

Another essential practice is to regularly back up files and programs. The more valuable the data, the more frequently it should be saved to an archive. This practice can save a company or organization thousands, or even millions, of dollars in recovery or re-keying costs. An uncontaminated back-up archive is another inexpensive form of data insurance.

If your anti-virus software captures an unknown virus activity or suspected virus, send it to your network administrator with a note about your discovery. The administrator can send it to an anti-virus identification organization for analysis and creation of an antidote, which may be included in a virus signature file update.

Virus signature files require frequent updating because thousands of computer viruses are released into the Internet every month. This proliferation may require system administrators to download and update the virus signature files to their anti-virus software as often as every few days.

Two well-known anti-virus software makers are McAfee and the Symantec Corporation. Both companies offer network server anti-virus software products.

Workstations Virus Attacks

Workstation users need to use anti-virus software to inspect all removable media before copying files to a hard drive or server. Updates to workstation anti-virus protection software are also necessary every few days or, at most, weekly.

Anti-virus software needs to run each time a workstation is turned on and continue to run so it can monitor all files for viral signatures or activity. Enable the anti-virus software to intercept files that are downloading, scan e-mail and all attachments, and inspect all files before saving them to the hard disk

Constant reminders to workstation users about the potential damage a virus can inflict should be part of any comprehensive security plan.

If possible, make back-up copies of valuable data files and store them in a safe place. Do not use any media without subjecting it to an anti-virus scan.

Vocabulary

Review the following terms in preparation for the certification exam.

Term	Description
access controls	Methods used to control access to the Internet and internal networks.
ACL	Access Control Lists are databases of permissions assigned to users and groups
asymmetric key system	Encryption system where key pairs (a public and a private key) are generated. The public key encrypts and the private key decrypts the messages.
auditing	Keeping track of activity both from the outside (Internet/extranet) and from inside (a company intranet) to reveal potential security risks.
authentication	The process of determining if someone is who he or she claims to be before granting or denying network access. Usernames and passwords are forms of authentication.
cookies	Text files of which one part is loaded onto the hard disk of a client computer and another part resides on the visited server in a user profile database. Each cookie contains a unique identifier and may contain confidential information such as the name of the visitor, authentication, credit card numbers, and online shopping habits.
denial of service	Deliberate attacks to breach security by disabling a network rather than stealing critical data.

Term	Description
firewall	A security system that protects an organization's network against internal and external threats.
intrusion detection	Tracking and recording any suspicious activity on a network.
multiple logon failures	A number of unsuccessful attempts to access a network, which can indicate a possible hacker attack.
one-way hash function	An algorithm that converts text into a fixed-length string of digits which, in turn, is encrypted with a private key to create a digital signature that authenticates the sender.
packet filtering	Inspecting packets to determine whether or not to grant or deny access to a network.
PCT	Private Communication Technology is a protocol that separates authentication from encryption.
PGP	Pretty Good Privacy is an encryption method based on the asymmetric key system.
PING flood	Echo requests to an IP address (PINGs) transmit to a system in overwhelming numbers. The system under attack cannot handle the bombardment and crashes.
private key system	A symmetric encryption system that uses a single key which both the sender and the recipient use to encrypt and decrypt messages.
proxy server cache	A quickly accessible storage area for Web pages that are frequently viewed with a Web browser.
public key system	See asymmetric key system

Term	Description
screening router	Programmable routers that follow a set of rules to inspect packets and permit or deny access to a network based on those rules.
SET	Secure Electronic Transaction protocol provides strong encryption and direct data transfers to financial institutions.
S-HTTP	Secure HyperText Transfer Protocol encrypts individual messages for transmission across the unsecured Internet.
signature file	Anti-virus software programs rely on virus signature files to identify new and existing computer viruses. Makers of the anti-virus software frequently update virus signature files.
smurf	Another name for a PING flood attack.
spamming floods	An e-mail attack that transmits unsolicited data in quantities that can overwhelm a mail server and disable it.
spoofing	A technique used by hackers to trick their way through a firewall into a network by changing the information in a packet to look like a friendly packet.
SSL	Secure Sockets Layer is a protocol that creates a secure connection, or channel, over which all data between a Web client and a secure Web server are encrypted.

Term	Description
TLS	Transport Layer Security is a Microsoft security protocol that incorporates both SSL and PCT into one standard that supports both certificates and password authentication.
viruses	Viruses are small, often destructive, programs that may be disguised as part of a harmless file, game, utility, or e-mail attachment.
VPNs	A Virtual Private Network creates encrypted private communication channels over the public Internet.

In Brief

If you want to...	Then do this...
Connect to your corporate network using the public Internet	Use a VPN connection to a PPTP server to create an encrypted communications channel.
Protect your workstations and servers from a computer virus	Implement anti-virus software on all computers and follow procedures for checking all media and files for contamination.
Make certain a public-key encrypted message came from a certain individual	Check the digital signature using your private key.
Save frequently accessed Web pages to reduce the load on the connection to the Internet	Set up a proxy server cache directory on the proxy server computer.
Prevent specific IP Addressed packets from accessing a network	Install and program a screening router at the entrance point to the network you want to protect.
Track and analyze suspicious network activity	Install and use auditing software to log all access activity on networks and directories where important or sensitive data are located.
Allow authorized remote employees to access the company networks from long distance locations	Establish a VPN to create an encrypted data channel using the public Internet as the long distance medium.

If you want to...	Then do this...
Protect an e-mail message to a particular party from being read by unauthorized people	Encrypt the data using the intended recipient's public encryption key.
Send an encrypted e-mail message with attachments	Use an S/MIME e-mail client that can support the encryption of messages.
Prevent information from a particular host on a network from using the Internet	Install and program a packet filter on the outgoing side of the proxy server to dump packets that contain the source IP address of the computer you want to block.

Lesson 9 Activities

Complete the following activities to prepare for the certification exam.

1. Describe the function of a proxy server cache.

2. Explain the difference between SSL and S-HTTP.

3. Define spam attack.

4. Explain the purpose of S/MIME.

5. Describe the function of a digital signature.

6. Describe the benefits of using a VPN.

7. Explain the purpose of a SYN attack.

8. Describe the purpose of PPTP.

9. Explain the purpose of developing the SET protocol.

10. Explain why the public key system is preferred over the private key system.

Answers to Lesson 9 Activities

1. The function of a proxy server cache is to store frequently viewed Web pages on a network hard disk to reduce traffic on the connection to the Internet.

2. SSL is a protocol used to create a secure connection, or channel, over which all data between a Web client and a secure Web server are encrypted.

    S-HTTP is designed to encrypt only individual messages for transmission across the unsecured Internet.

3. A spam attack occurs when an e-mail server is bombarded with unsolicited e-mail messages with the intention of overloading the system.

4. The purpose of S/MIME is to support the encryption of e-mail messages and enable secure e-mail exchanges.

5. The function of a digital signature is to guarantee that a person who sent an electronic message is the person, company, or organization they claim to be or represent.

6. The benefits of using a VPN are that the data are protected by using an encrypted channel over the public Internet and the costs associated with using or leasing long-distance telephone lines are reduced.

7. The purpose of a SYN attack is not to steal information but to create a denial of service condition on the victim's Web server and cause it to crash.

8. PPTP creates an encrypted channel from one PPTP server to another PPTP server to enable data to be safely exchanged over the unsecured public Internet.

9. The SET protocol is in development to provide strong encryption and direct data transfers to financial institutions in connection with E-commerce.

10. The public key (asymmetric) system is preferred because public keys are easy to distribute to people who want to send encrypted messages to the holder of the private key. The private key system (symmetric) requires either an in-person hand-off of the private key to the intended recipient or use of another encryption and delivery method to get it to the authorized recipient.

Lesson 9 Quiz

These questions test your knowledge of features, vocabulary, procedures, and syntax.

1. Choose the correct standard for creating digital certificates.

    A. X.400

    B. CA

    C. S/MIME

    D. X.509

2. Select the answers that best describe a denial of service attack.

    A. An ICMP echo request PING flood

    B. An intrusion into a network designed to steal or destroy information

    C. Lots of unsolicited electronic mail that overwhelms a mail server

    D. Thousands of open port requests that contain false source IP-addresses that are aimed at a particular Web server

3. Which of these protocols can perform the transmission of encrypted electronic mail messages?
    A. SSL

    B. SET

    C. S-HTTP

    D. S/MIME

4. Which of the following are secure protocols?

    A. PPTP

    B. SYN

    C. S-HTTP

    D. Smurf

5. Which of the following are computer virus categories?

    A. Logic bomb

    B. File infecting

    C. Worm

    D. Stealth

6. Choose the most common methods of contracting computer viruses.

    A. Using floppy disks without checking them first with an anti-virus program

    B. Downloading files from un-trusted public Web sites

    C. Receiving e-mail attachments

    D. Opening a word processor file sent to you by a co-worker

7. Choose the answer that best describes the role of a firewall.

    A. A type of protocol dedicated to passing electronic mail among Internet e-mail systems

    B. A server configured only to store temporary Web page information for quick retrieval

    C. A program designed to keep unauthorized people from gaining access to an internal network

    D. A program that dials into a remote computer network

8. Which of the following actions do packet filters, or screening routers, perform?

    A. Decrypt data before it enters a network

    B. Inspect packet headers for source and destination IP addresses

    C. Grant or deny access to a network based on the contents of the IP addresses in packet headers

    D. Act as a proxy server

9. Which of the following describes an extranet? Select all that apply.

    A. The public Internet

    B. An internal Internet used to share information among people in a company or organization

    C. An Internet connection that allows authorized people to have limited access to an Intranet

D. A standalone public Web server

10. Which of the following is true about cookies? Select all that apply.

A. A cookie is used to control a computer by remote control

B. Cookies are used to collect information about visitors to a Web site

C. Once a cookie is placed on a hard disk, it never changes

D. Cookies are a network protocol used to Smurf remote Web servers

Answers to Lesson 9 Quiz

1. Answer D is correct. X.509 is the standard that sets the criteria for the creation of digital certificates.

    Answer A is incorrect because it is the specification for the X.400 Message Handling System. This is an electronic mail system primarily used by government bodies and companies for its built-in security.

    Answer B is incorrect because a CA is a company that issues Certificates of Authority that are used to verify that a person, company, or organization is the entity he or she claims to be or represent.

    Answer C is incorrect. S/MIME is the acronym for Secure/Multipurpose Internet Mail Extensions. It is the primary protocol for mailing encrypted electronic mail over the Internet.

2. Answers A, C, and D are correct. All of these are attacks designed to deny service by deliberately overwhelming a server with messages or requests to make it crash.

    Answer B is incorrect. An intrusion is designed to steal or destroy information and is not targeted specifically to deny service or crash a system.

3. Answer D is the correct answer. S/MIME is the e-mail protocol that can perform the transmission of encrypted e-mail messages.

    Answer A is incorrect. SSL creates an encrypted channel between an SSL-enabled client and an SSL-enabled server so that all information passing through is secure.

    Answer B is incorrect. SET is a new protocol that is being designed to use digital signatures to authenticate credit card holders, merchants, and financial institutions.

    Answer C is incorrect. S-HTTP is a secure application level protocol designed to transmit individual encrypted documents or messages using HTTP over the Internet.

4. Answer A is correct. PPTP uses PPTP servers to create VPNs. These servers create encrypted data transmission channels over the public Internet.

    Answer C is correct. S-HTTP is an application level protocol designed to encrypt individual messages and parts of documents for transmission using HTTP.

    Answer B is incorrect. SYN is a flag in a packet header used to make open port requests to a Web server. SYN requests can be deliberately used to flood a server with open port requests to disable the target server.

Answer D is incorrect. Smurf is another name for a PING-type of denial of service attack that is deliberately used to crash a network.

5.   Answer B is correct. It is classified as a computer virus. File-infecting viruses often target executable files and either infect them or replace them.

Answer D is correct. Stealth viruses hide in memory, try to hide changes to file sizes, and thwart attempts to use the operating system.

Answer A is incorrect. A Logic Bomb is a Trojan horse with a timing device.

Answer C is incorrect. A Worm is a threat similar to a virus, but it does not replicate itself as a virus does.

6.   Answer A is correct. Floppy disks are well known for being infected with computer viruses. Unwary people often save infected files or programs to floppy disks and pass them on to others to use. Always check floppy disks with an anti-virus program before using them.

Answer B is correct. Unsuspecting people often download infected files from untrusted public Web sites. Always have anti-virus software running on a server or workstation so it can identify, intercept, isolate, and remove a virus before it contaminates your hard disk.

Answer C is correct. E-mail attachments are a common method for spreading all viruses and similar threats like Worms and Trojan horses.

Answer D is correct. It is common for macro viruses to attach to word processor and spreadsheet files. They can damage or destroy data, making them unusable. As always, the best protection is to use anti-virus software to inspect all files and have the virus disabled or the threat from the file removed.

7.   Answer C is correct. A firewall is a program designed to keep unauthorized people from gaining access to a network.

Answer A is incorrect. The protocol that is dedicated to passing electronic mail among Internet mail servers is SMTP, the Simple Mail Transfer Protocol.

Answer B is incorrect. A server configured only to store temporary Web page information for quick retrieval is a cache server. However, you can configure a proxy server to also store frequently accessed Web pages in a proxy cache.

Answer D is incorrect. A program that dials up a remote computer network is a remote dial-up application.

8. Answer B is correct. Packet filters and screening routers inspect packet headers to identify the IP source and destination addresses of each packet.

    Answer C is correct. Packet routers and screening filters are programmed to grant or deny access to a network based on the contents of the IP address in packet headers.

    Answer A is incorrect. Packet filters and screening routers do not decrypt data. PPTP servers, private keys, and many other methods are used to decrypt data.

    Answer D is incorrect. Packet filters and screening routers are used in conjunction with proxy servers to boost network security as an added firewall measure.

9. Answer C is correct. An extranet is an Internet connection that allows authorized people to have limited access to a private Intranet. A challenge-response method is normally employed to ask for a username and password to an existing account.

    Answer A is incorrect. The public Internet is used for disseminating and sharing information worldwide. Some servers may have a public Web server configured as an extranet to allow certain people to access a private network.

    Answer B is incorrect. An internal Internet is called an intranet. It is used to share information among people in a company or organization. An intranet may have a connection to the public Internet.

    Answer D is incorrect. A standalone public Web server does not have physical or virtual connections to any network.

10. Answer B is correct. Cookies are used to collect information about visitors to a Web site. The data is saved to a user profile database and is often used by analysts in the company or organization that owns the Web site to determine the effectiveness of their site, its focus, and customer satisfaction.

    Answer A is incorrect. A cookie cannot take remote control of a computer.

    Answer C is incorrect. Information placed in a cookie often changes each time a person visits the same Web site or any of its segments. The new information is stored in the user profile database and in the cookie that reloads to the visitor's hard disk.

    Answer D is incorrect. Cookies are not a network protocol nor can they access remote servers. Cookies are information collection text files used to identify Web site visitors; they are often used to tailor and personalize a person's Web surfing experience. A smurf is a type of denial of service attack using PINGs.

Lesson 10: E-Commerce

Businesses are increasing their Internet presence on a daily basis. Every major company has a Web site and a Web address is considered as important as a toll-free phone number. Although many Internet sites offer little more than a digital version of a company brochure, the number of companies enabling customers to purchase goods online is increasing rapidly. E-commerce is the method and practice of selling goods and services through a Web page. These sales may be to consumers or to other businesses. The number of people purchasing merchandise online continues to grow at a rapid pace, far surpassing the rate of new customers generated at traditional businesses.

After completing this lesson, you should have a better understanding of the following topics:

- E-Commerce Overview

- Online Business Strategies

- Internet Commerce Site Creation

- Global Marketing

- Copyrights and Trademarks

- New Customer Sales Strategies

E-Commerce Overview

E-commerce is a rapidly growing field. Once dominated by U.S. companies, E-commerce businesses located throughout the world are gaining strength. Competition among online businesses—like competition between traditional businesses—typically benefits customers as businesses strive to lower prices and offer unique services.

Along with the rapid rise of E-commerce businesses has come an increasing political interest in the way in which these companies do business. Where there is money being made, there are those who wish to tax that money and those who wish to regulate the business practices. When the businesses use a relatively unregulated and fully global medium like the Internet, laws governing the businesses must be international in scope. Multi-government agencies like the World Trade Organization (WTO) and the United Nations (UN) are addressing these issues, as are commercial interest groups.

Standardizing E-Commerce

The Computer Technology Industry Association (CompTIA) formed an advisory board and task force to address issues of business-to-business E-commerce. This board, called the Electronic Commerce Standards Board (ECSB), is composed of members from many of the larger international companies, including IBM, Hewlett Packard, Sun Microsystems, APC, and Lotus.

 Tip: For more information about the ECSB, see CompTIA's Web page at *www.comptia.org*. From the front page, choose the link for E-commerce.

Independent of CompTIA's ECSB, The Ziff-Davis Global Information Infrastructure (GII) group has proposed the Standard for Internet Commerce. The first release of this standard was made available in December 1999. The document is the culmination of years of work from many industry leaders who hope to define new Internet standards for conducting E-commerce. They liken their standard to the Transmission Control Protocol/Internet Protocol (TCP/IP), which standardized all communication on the Internet. Like the ECSB, GII members come from a wide range of Internet-based and traditional businesses. When the first version of the standard was released, there were over 300 committee members.

Tip: The GII standard can be downloaded from www.gii.com/standard. The list of founding members of GII is in the standards document and is also displayed at www.gii.com/standard/who.

Online Business Strategies

Customers are looking for two things when purchasing online: convenience and price. E-commerce allows a company to sell merchandise without the overhead of a physical storefront, reducing their margin and thus reducing the retail price. Selling over the Internet also allows companies to be "right next door" to consumers worldwide. There is nothing more convenient than to make a purchase without leaving one's house.

The actual creation of an Internet-based company is not difficult. You provide customers access to information about your product and information on how to order the product. You make this information available by creating Web pages. The Web server, which may be part of your company's intranet, is publicly accessible, and so is part of an extranet. Usually, this extranet is the Internet. Whenever you open up any portion of your intranet to the "real world," you must make sure you implement proper security (for example, using a firewall) to prevent unwanted access to your entire intranet.

Business-to-Business Transactions

There are two facets to E-commerce businesses: providing a product to a customer (business-to-customer transactions), and selling information and products between businesses (business-to-business transactions). Generally, when you hear mention of E-commerce, it is in respect to the business-to-customer transactions. However, many communication and business dealings occur electronically, with manufacturers selling resources, services, and products. In fact, it is estimated that the value of inter-business E-commerce will reach $2.7 trillion in 2004 (source: Forrester Research, Inc., Feb 7, 2000).

Tip: The latest statistics on E-commerce can often be found in the Forrester Reports. For more information, access the Forrester Web page at http://www.forrester.com.

As an example of business-to-business (sometimes referred to as B2B) E-commerce, an online retailer may find it beneficial to form a partnership with a shipping company so that products ordered can be shipped promptly. In a traditional business, once an order is placed, the retailer contacts the shipping company (usually by phone) and arranges a pickup for delivery. The shipping company and the retailer exchange paperwork, and the package is delivered to the customer. With business-to-business E-commerce, the shipping company is notified immediately of an order and the paperwork is sent electronically as the order is processed.

This is a rather simple business-to-business E-commerce scenario. A typical transaction requires not only communication between the retailer and the shipping company, but also immediate communication between the retailer and the credit card companies (for card verification), the retailer's Web site location and the warehouses, the retailer, and the product suppliers. Information about the sale may be sent simultaneously to several departments within the company, as well. Those in charge of inventory control, advertising, and demographics may want certain information regarding the purchase. You can see how, without using electronic methods, a lot of paperwork is needed for one simple business transaction.

Electronic Data Interchange (EDI)

The Data Interchange Standards Association (DISA) created the EDI as a standard method for exchanging information between businesses. Information exchanged using EDI is in an agreed-upon format by both parties, so that the data does not need to be re-keyed or reformatted at either end of the transmission. This information, which is typically the same information contained on a conventionally-printed document like an invoice or purchase order, can be transferred without human interaction, reducing costs and errors.

Note: The EDI standard began with the Transportation Data Coordinating Committee (TDCC) in the early 1970s, and was redefined and incorporated in to the EDI standard in the early 1990s by American National Standards Institute's (ANSI) Accredited Standards Committee X12. Often, the EDI standards are referred to as the X12 standard.

Unfortunately, there is more than one EDI standard. The United States uses the X12 standard, while the rest of the world uses the UN/EDIFACT standard. Companies using EDI to transfer information globally must implement both standards. Furthermore, each industry may define its own guidelines for EDI implementation.

Although this customization is one of the strengths of EDI, it also becomes a problem for companies that work with several different industries. For example, a company that prints computer forms may need EDI guidelines for the medical, educational, and shipping industries.

Another disadvantage to using EDI is that the standard is updated and the codes change frequently. Although the updates benefit users of EDI, each change requires an update to your company's EDI code.

The size and price of EDI has resulted in limiting use to the largest corporations. According to the XML/EDI Group, 95% of Fortune 1000 companies use EDI, whereas only 2% of smaller companies use the standard (source: http://www.geocities.com/WallStreet/Floor/5815/).

Extensible Markup Language (XML)

XML is a subset of the Standard Generalized Markup Language (SGML), which provides a foundation for Web page design. XML is similar to the HyperText Markup Language (HTML), but it allows you to create customized format tags. XML is being promoted as an inexpensive, flexible alternative to, or enhancement of, EDI. XML allows you to provide information from a wide variety of applications to a user's desktop. Many industry leaders believe that XML will eventually replace EDI entirely, and may replace HTML as the language of the World Wide Web (WWW).

The following benefits of XML include:

- Flexibility

- System-independence

- Vendor-independence

- Easy integration with existing EDI platforms

- UNICODE (multilingual) support

- Error-checking

- Multimedia support

- Extends HTML, the language of the Web

 Note: In a series of "e-Buzz" newsletters published by CompTIA, the future of EDI and XML are discussed in depth. These newsletters can be found at the following Web address: http://www.comptia.org/ecommerce/ebuzz.htm.

Business-to-Customer Transactions

Business-to-customer E-commerce transactions provide the link from your company to the customer over the Internet. From a company Web page, customers can view products and make purchases. The Web page may be on a server in the company's network or another company may host it. When implementing E-commerce for your business, you must consider customer concerns. The most common concerns people have about making purchases online are security, privacy, and name recognition.

Using Secure Servers

Although credit card purchases made over the Internet are as safe (or safer) than those made over a telephone, people are far more reluctant to give their credit card information to a computer than to a person. One way to make people more comfortable about making online purchases is to provide a secure Internet connection. Secure connections typically use certificates and the Secure Sockets Layer

(SSL) protocol. Certificates verify that you are who you claim to be (they are like digital passports), and the SSL protocol ensures that sensitive data is sent encrypted.

A competing method for secure transmission is the Secure Electronic Transaction (SET) protocol, developed by VISA and MasterCard. Like SSL, SET uses digital certificates to transfer financial information and to verify the identities of the customer and seller. SET can make use of the full 128-bit security for all transactions.

Privacy Concerns

As an E-commerce company, you can easily collect and use customer information for your benefit. When customers make purchases, you obtain their name, address, and phone number. You can also find out what other Internet sites they visit. Combined with the type of purchases made, this information could be very valuable to telemarketing companies and other E-commerce businesses.

Many users will not purchase goods online if they feel this private information will be shared. It is important that you have a clear privacy statement on your Web page, and that it is easily accessible to potential customers. If you are not in the business of selling your customer database, let your potential customers know your policy. Most customers accept that you will use the information internally for your own company's benefit but will not accept you selling it to other companies.

Push and Pull Technologies

Most Internet transactions are a result of pull technology. With pull technology, data is sent to a user only after the user requests (or pulls) the data from the Web server. However, an increasing number of E-commerce sites are using push technology to customize their pages.

Push technology sends information to a user even if that information is not directly requested. For example, an E-commerce bookstore may present you with a list of the best-selling books in the genre of your most recently purchased book. If you recently purchased a mystery novel, you may be presented with a list of other mystery novels, books by the same author, or associated merchandise.

Customization and filtering of information using push technologies personalizes the Internet shopping experience. Many people shop on the Internet for convenience and price but long for the personal approach of traditional stores.

Using simple procedures, you can make an E-commerce page that greets a customer by his or her name, presents a list of new items since the customer last visited the Web page, and even suggests items based on past purchases. Of course, nothing can replace the person-to-person interactions of a real store, but push technologies are a step forward.

Internet Commerce Site Creation

Creating an E-commerce site can be a monumental task, or it can be something you do over one or two days. The complexity of your Internet presence depends on your needs and budget. Some E-commerce businesses begin with nothing more than a simple HTML Web page. This page may describe the product, have pictures of the product, and provide contact information for ordering. A slightly more advanced Web page may also include an order form that can be printed, faxed, or e-mailed to your company.

Although E-commerce sites based on simple HTML code may provide a starting place for new small businesses, you must consider what you, as a customer, want when conducting business online. Most customers want a sense of security, the ease of ordering online directly, and product information that is detailed yet easy to sift through.

Creating a Web page using basic HTML will usually not provide your potential customers with enough information and security to encourage purchases. You should create an online catalog that provides detailed information about your products and prices. In addition, you should provide a secure way for customers to place orders directly using credit cards or other electronic forms of money.

For most business owners, the tasks of providing a secure server, programming order forms using CGI or ASP scripting, and processing credit card orders are beyond reach. Fortunately, you can out-source tasks through numerous companies.

Online Catalog

The online catalog for your business should provide customers with all the information they need to make a purchase. Like a printed catalog, you want to promote the product. Products rarely sell themselves, so the catalog becomes the primary means by which you sell.

Your online catalog should be, above all else, well organized. If a customer cannot find a particular item within your selection of products, they will not buy it. A useful tool with online catalogs is a side bar containing an overview of the products and the catalog structure.

Tip: A good E-commerce page cannot be over-organized.

Customer Self-Service Functionality

A basic online catalog permits customers to view your products but does not allow them to order the product directly. A sufficient E-commerce site may have a product catalog and a page with order information (like a telephone or fax number, or an e-mail address). A more refined page should have a method for customers to place an order directly through your site.

Your online catalog should have a direct link to that order page. Many E-commerce sites have implemented a "shopping cart" method, where customers place items in the cart while browsing the catalog. When the customer is ready to finalize the purchase, all the items they selected are collected on the order form and the prices are totaled (including shipping charges), so the customer only needs to enter the credit card (or other payment) information. This customer self-service approach simultaneously increases sales and reduces costs.

Tip: Take advantage of compulsive shopping habits. By placing an instant order link from the catalog, you increase the likelihood of a sale. Once the item is in the "shopping cart," it is more likely to be purchased.

Merchant Accounts

To accept credit card orders, your business must establish a working relationship with a bank. Obtaining a merchant account, which allows you to process credit card orders, is an important step in building a successful E-commerce business. If your business is small or has a bad credit history, it may be difficult to obtain a merchant account. Fortunately, there are merchant system companies. Merchant system companies provide a merchant account for your company if you cannot obtain one.

Merchant system companies are Internet companies that have established themselves as providers of E-commerce solutions. Most merchant systems not only provide the means for processing credit card transactions, but also sell the software needed to create online catalogs and ordering systems. Some of the merchant systems also provide the Web hosting services, "renting" space on their secure servers as a virtual store front for your business.

Global Marketing

The Internet permits us to advertise and sell to a global audience very easily. As soon as you create a Web page and post it, people from around the world can view it. If you are using that page to sell goods and services, people can theoretically make purchases from any country in the world.

The universal aspect of the Internet is both a boon and bane to E-commerce marketers. The Internet allows small companies to reach international clients, customers previously unreachable by all but the largest companies. However, with international commerce comes a new set of troubles. Translation problems (language and currency) arise, as do issues of tariffs, duties, and taxes. When conducting international business, you must be familiar with these issues and ways in which you overcome these hurdles.

Products and International Currencies

One difficulty in performing overseas business transactions is dealing with foreign currencies. It is not feasible for a small E-commerce business to open and maintain a bank account in every nation in which it does business. Fortunately, there are several resources available to you.

For business-to-business E-commerce, there are companies that have bank accounts in numerous countries and who provide electronic transfer of funds between currencies (for example, visit www.fx4business.com/psiw.html or www.imex-fx.com). These services are particularly useful when customers cannot pay by credit card, as is common in business-to-business transactions.

For business-to-consumer transactions, most credit card companies will handle the exchange of currency automatically. Although this service is automatic, you may wish to provide approximate exchange rates for your customers. For example, if you are located in Canada and regularly sell goods to U.S. residents, you may wish to post prices in both Canadian and U.S. dollars or post the current conversion.

Tip: You can find the most current exchange rates on several Internet sites, including: www.xe.net/ucc/ and www.rubicon.com/passport/currency/currency.html

Supporting International Languages

Most Web pages created in the U.S. and western Europe are written using American Standard Code for Information Interchange (ASCII) characters. ASCII uses 8 bits (1 byte) of information to define an alphanumeric character (like the letter W or the number 5). Using 8 bits of information, ASCII supports up to 128 characters, with each character assigned its own number from 0 to 127. The problem with ASCII is that it only supports the alphanumeric Latin characters used in English. Other languages based on the Latin alphabet—like French, Spanish, and German—are partially supported, but special characters like ç, ñ, and ö are not included in the standard ASCII set.

As E-commerce becomes more global in scope, the need to simultaneously support many languages increases. To meet this need, a new language set has emerged, named Unicode. Unicode uses exactly twice as many bits—16 bits or 2 bytes—for each character. This increases the number of characters supported from 128 in ASCII to 65,000 characters with Unicode. This increase means that all characters, from all world languages, can be represented by a number and can be incorporated into documents.

Note: In Unicode, like in ASCII, each character is assigned a unique number, and this number will always be converted to the same character, whether it is an English number, an Arabic letter, or a Chinese Han symbol.

Support for Unicode is growing rapidly. The major Internet browsers (Microsoft Internet Explorer and Netscape Communicator) support Unicode conversion. Microsoft Office 2000 fully supports Unicode and ships with some Unicode fonts. Within Office 2000 documents, you can enter Asian symbols, edit "right-to-left" languages (like Arabic), and insert both English and Asian language characters into the same document.

When designing and building an E-commerce Web site, it behooves you to use Unicode. Although you may be targeting an English-speaking audience, the Internet is global and so is your company. Take advantage of the global opportunity by using the computer language set that supports all world languages.

Global Laws and Regulations

The laws regarding taxation on goods transmitted electronically are in a state of flux. The U.S. and some European countries are asking international groups (like the WTO and the U.N.) to adopt a policy banning taxes on electronically transmitted materials. The main argument is that international telephone calls and fax transmissions—both of which rely on electronic transmission—are not taxed, and so computer data transmissions should also be tax-free.

If the member nations adopt such a policy, you may sell goods over the Internet tax free, as long as those goods can be transmitted electronically. If you are selling products that will be shipped to another country, the product will be subject to the same taxes and tariffs as any other product.

Note: Regardless of what the international groups decide, individual countries can impose their own restrictions and taxes on electronic trade and commerce. You need to be aware of the national trade laws before selling a product to that country.

Good sources for information regarding international trade regulations are the shipping carriers you may already be using to ship your products. The major shipping companies (like United Parcel Service (UPS) www.ups.com and Federal Express www.fedex.com) have been conducting international business for years and provide services and information to help you conduct business internationally.

Copyrights and Trademarks

Placing your words, ideas, and products online makes them available to people around the world. That is precisely the point of E-commerce. However, it can also be a problem if someone else uses those ideas, words, or products for profit. The Internet is loosely governed, and its international scope precludes easy oversight by any one government (or collection of governments). Copyrights are used to protect original artistic and literary work, including Web pages and their content. A trademark is a word, phrase, or symbol that identifies the source of goods and services.

Copyrights

Copyrights protect your Web page by marking it as your creation. Officially, you do not need to register a copyright for it to take effect. By simply placing a copyright notice (the © symbol followed by the year and your name) on your page, the page is protected. However, for more thorough legal protection, you should register your copyrights with the U.S. Copyright Office.

Tip: The copyright statement should appear at the bottom of each Web page on your site, and should be in the following form:
Copyright © 2000, Jane Doe, All Rights Reserved

If you do not register your copyright, you have little legal protection. If you can prove lost income from the theft of your Web page content, you may be reimbursed for that income and for the profits realized by the company that committed the infringement. Registering your copyright allows you to recover costs associated with the legal proceedings, and the issuance of a fine of up to 100,000 U.S. dollars. Registration of the copyright also allows you to record the registration with the U.S. Customs Service for protection against imported copies of your content.

Copyright Registration

To register your copyright, you must complete the copyright form. Unfortunately, the copyright office has not issued a form specifically for Web pages, and so you must determine whether your page contains primarily text, video, sounds, or software and then choose the proper form. In addition to completing the form, you will need to provide hard copies (printed pages) of your Web pages or the HTML source code, or both.

The process of registering Web content is so detailed and difficult that many Web-based companies simply do not go through the process. Some of the largest companies on the Internet have decided that the costs involved in registering copyrights and suing the people who infringe on them is not worth it. They would rather take the risk of having some of their original material used elsewhere on the Internet.

If your page contains original artwork, photographs, sounds, or software that you are selling, registration of the Web content is a good idea. If your site contains pictures of the products you are selling, it is probably not worth the hassle or cost of registering the copyright.

Copyright Infringement

Neglecting to respect others' copyrights can result in stiff penalties. Even if the copyrights are not registered, you can be sued and may have to pay damages equal to your profits from using the copyrighted material and to the copyright holder's lost income. If the copyright is registered, you may also be fined for legal costs incurred by the plaintiff and be issued a punitive fine of up to 100,000 U.S. dollars.

Copyright infringements include using any text, graphics, applets, software, or sounds from another Web page in your own page. Some authors may allow you to use their material if you give them proper credit. However, before you use any material from another page, make sure you receive permission, in writing, from the legal owner of the material.

Trademarks

Trademarks protect your company name, logo, and domain name. Like copyrights, trademarks do not need registration to use. However, registration of a trademark ensures certain legal rights. Suppose two parties are using the same company name, and each is unaware of the other's presence. Company A has a registered trademark on the company name. If a lawsuit arises between the two parties over the trademark, company A will win the case, since they hold the registered trademark.

 Note: Detailed information about the registration process in the U.S. can be obtained from the U.S. Patent and Trademark Office (PTO), at the following Web address: www.uspto.gov.

Global Copyrights and Trademarks

There are currently no international laws governing trademark and copyright infringements. You may own a trademark on your company name, but that does not prevent a person in another country from using your company name as a domain name. Likewise, a U.S.-registered copyright on your Web page content is valid only within the U.S. The World Intellectual Property Organization (WIPO), a U.N. agency, has been established to mediate and resolve such international conflicts. The WTO is also working on resolutions to help with intellectual property rights.

New Customer Sales Strategies

As with any business, E-commerce businesses must be concerned with constantly generating new customers. Traditional businesses attract new customers through advertising. On the Internet, advertising is only one of the methods you use to attract new customers to your site. More important than banner advertising is inclusion of your Web page in Internet search engines. E-mail marketing may also be used to generate new customers.

Search Engines

Many sites on the Internet make a business of helping Internet users find resources. These sites use search engines to scan the Internet for the keywords found on Web pages. Examples of search engines and Internet indexing services include:

- www.yahoo.com

- www.excite.com

- www.lycos.com

- www.msn.com

- www.hotbot.com

- www.infoseek.com

- www.altavista.com

- www.goto.com

- www.go2net.com

- www.dogpile.com

- www.google.com

According to many E-commerce analysts, inclusion of your E-commerce site in the major Internet search engines is fundamental to the success of your business. According to one E-commerce provider, 85% of all Web page visitors come through search engines (source: Verio, www.home.verio.com). However, registration with Internet search engines can be time consuming.

There are hundreds of search engines on the Internet and second-guessing which ones potential customers will use is risky. You can register your Web page with each search engine, or you can contract out to have it done. Some companies will register your Web page with hundreds of search engines and indexes for a one-time fee.

Tip: The time and money costs for registering your Web page on the Internet are minimal considering the potential volume of customers search engines generate.

Two methods for search engine success are using the <META> HTML tag and creating "gateway" pages. Unlike other HTML tags, the <META> tag does not change the way in which a browser views a Web page. The <META> tag provides hidden information that the user does not see but search engines use to compile their list of keywords.

When using the <META> tag, be sure to include all keywords appropriate for your Web page. Consider all possible words a new customer would use to find your product or service. There is no cost to adding keywords to your page, but the benefits are high and can easily determine whether your Web page will appear in a search results page.

Tip: Using several different search engines, search for your product or service and see what keywords your competitors are using to identify their pages.

Gateway pages are front pages which search engines scan for keywords. The creation of gateway pages is a science in and of itself and often involves second-guessing the search engine algorithms for the most effective keyword placements.

For successful gateway pages, it is often worth the added expense to contract out to a company that creates these pages. It is their business to learn the algorithms and to create pages that appear at the top of search engine lists. For a more economical approach, view the source code for Web sites that appear at the top of search lists and see how they did it.

E-Commerce Site Banner Ads

Advertising remains one of the most popular ways to generate new business. Ironically, many traditional businesses with little to no Internet presence advertise on the Internet, and many E-commerce businesses advertise in more traditional media (television, radio, and print). The typical Internet advertisement is a banner—a colorful image that links directly to your Web page.

 Note: A survey conducted in November 1999 shows that 36% of users made an online purchase after viewing an advertisement in one of the traditional media (television, radio, or print) outlets (source: Nua Internet Surveys, www.nua.ie).

Like advertising in the real world, advertising costs on the Internet depend on product placement. You want to make sure that your banner ads are placed on other pages that potential customers may visit. Clearly, advertising on the popular search engine pages will attract more people than advertising on your neighbor's home page (unless your neighbor is Microsoft). Like advertising on television during the Super Bowl, if you want a high-profile location, you will pay dearly for it.

It is often more beneficial to target your advertising. If you sell medical supplies to doctors' offices, your advertising money is best spent on other pages that the doctors or their staff will likely visit. You may look to advertise on the "Journal of the American Medical Association" page, or the Web pages of other medical suppliers, for example.

Unlike traditional media, you can advertise free on the Internet. Free advertising comes in the form of banner exchange services. These banner exchanges place your advertisement on other companies' Web pages in exchange for you hosting a certain number of other banners. For example, if you agree to host four banner ads from other Web sites, your banner displays on three other Web pages.

You can view the following banner exchange programs on the Internet, to understand how they operate, and their respective charges.

- www.bannerexchange.com
- www.smartclicks.com

■ www.impressionz.com

■ www.i-stores.com/bannerx/index2.shtml

Warning: Be careful when selecting a banner exchange program. You have no control over which banners are displayed on your page, and you have no control over which pages display your ads. People will associate your product with the other advertisements. Check the banner exchange policies before signing up.

E-Mail Marketing

A final method for attracting new customers is the use of e-mail marketing. This is often the least effective method, as unsolicited e-mail ("spam") is usually ignored. Many Internet Service Providers (ISPs) block mass-mailed e-mail messages due to ever-increasing customer frustration with spam. However, many companies still resort to this method to attract customers to their sites. Like telemarketing, these companies rely on reaching thousands of people to attract just one customer.

Customer Relationship Maintenance

Attracting new customers to your business helps your business grow. The process of finding new customers can become the primary focus of a business. However, no business can afford to lose its existing customers. While you strive to build a larger customer base, do not forget to maintain those customers you already have.

The customer service rules that apply to a traditional business also apply to an online business. You may not interact face-to-face with the customer, but the customer still needs to feel important. In fact, because your company lacks the human interaction we are used to in business dealings, you must concentrate more on customer service.

The following are goals you should strive to achieve with your E-commerce business:

■ Be personable

- Be professional

- Be prompt

- Be patient

If you have designed your E-commerce site well, there will be little—if any—personal contact between the customer and anyone in your business. However, the customers should feel like they can reach a representative of your business if they need to.

Few things are more unsettling than making a large purchase and then not knowing how to contact the company if something goes wrong. Although it raises costs, you should provide a phone number for customer support. A customer will not make another purchase from you if you are unavailable to help with a problem. Personal contact is still an important aspect of purchasing, even if the purchase is made over the Internet.

 Note: Although people are willing (and eager) to purchase goods online, they still want a way to contact a human if something goes wrong. The presence of a phone number on your Web page could make the difference between a sale and no sale.

Professionalism is also important in obtaining and maintaining customers. If a customer contacts your business by e-mail, respond quickly to their message, addressing their needs thoroughly. Remember that you are an unknown to the customer. You have an Internet presence, but the customer needs to trust you with their credit card number. A customer may send a pre-purchase e-mail just to test your company's tech support responsiveness. If it is not handled professionally, you will lose a sale.

The same holds true for phone calls. If you are running your E-commerce business out of your home (not an unlikely scenario), get a second phone line, and answer it professionally. Nothing is more disturbing to a potential client than your 4-year-old son answering the business line.

When a customer orders a product, make sure it is shipped promptly and packed carefully. If the product arrives damaged or behind schedule, you have lost a customer. One of the main reasons customers shop online is to get a product quickly. If you do not ship on time, the customer will go elsewhere.

Finally, be patient. If a customer contacts you with a problem, work with them. They are most likely upset, frustrated, and doubting their decision to buy online. Listen to the problem and let the customer vent. Although it is never easy, be pleasant, even if they are insulting you, your business, or your product. Customers respond well if you simply listen first and then offer a solution.

Vocabulary

Review the following terms in preparation for the certification exam.

Term	Description
ASCII	The American Standard Code for Information Interchange uses an 8-bit number to represent an English alphanumeric character.
B2B	An abbreviation often used for Business-To-Business E-commerce transactions.
banner	An advertisement, usually more wide than high, that links to another page.
banner exchange	The mutual sharing of Web space among E-commerce businesses that provides free advertising through banner advertisement.
business-to-consumer	E-commerce transactions between a business and the consumer.
certificates	A digital identification, verifying a secure server's identity to the client and verifying the client's identity to the server.
DISA	The Data Interchange Standards Association is a not-for-profit organization that concentrates on E-commerce related standards and issues (including EDI).
ECSB	The Electronic Commerce Standards Board is a CompTIA advisory board that addresses business-to-business E-commerce standards and issues.

Term	Description
EDI	The Electronic Data Interchange is a standard for exchanging information electronically between businesses.
e-mail marketing	A method of attracting customers by sending large-volume bulk e-mail messages to potential customers.
GII	The Global Information Infrastructure is a group started by the Ziff-Davis publishing company to create the Standard for Internet Commerce.
intranet	The portion of a network that is not accessible to the general public. The intranet is usually separated from the extranet and Internet by a firewall.
ISP	An Internet Service Provider provides dial-up access to the Internet and e-mail services to end users.
merchant account	An account with a banking institution needed to process credit card sales.
META	An HTML tag used to insert hidden keywords into a Web page, so search engines will display your page when one or more of the keywords is searched for.
pull	The technology usually used on the Internet, where the user requests data from a Web server.
push	A technology that sends data to a user, even if that data was not specifically requested. Used to customize and filter Web page content.
search engines	Web sites that perform keyword searches of Web pages and provide a convenient location for users to find products and services.

Term	Description
SET	The Secure Electronic Transaction protocol uses 128-bit security to transmit financial information (like credit card numbers).
spam	Another term for e-mail marketing, spam is often blocked by ISPs.
SSL	The Secure Sockets Layer protocol encrypts data sent between a Web server and Web client.
UN/EDIFACT	One of two EDI standards, UN/EDIFACT is used by businesses outside the United States.
Unicode	A standard that assigns numbers to language characters, Unicode uses 16 bits of code per character, thus supporting 65,000 characters. Due to its support for all languages (not just English), it is expected to replace ASCII code as the standard for displaying characters.
X12	The EDI standard used by businesses within the U.S.
XML	The Extensible Markup Language that is a subset of SGML, and allows customized format tags.

In Brief

If you want to...	Then do this...
Provide online security for processing orders	Use SSL or SET to encrypt sensitive information being sent to and from the client.
Generate interest in your Web page	Use the <META> tag and gateway pages to increase the likelihood that your page will be found using a search engine. Advertise using banner ads.
Provide multi-lingual support on your Web page	Implement Unicode characters instead of ASCII.
Obtain free advertising space for your Web page	Join a banner exchange.
Customize data exchange between your business and another	Use EDI, XML, or a combination of the two.
Sell products overseas	Check export and import regulations and obtain necessary permits.
Check import and export regulations	Contact one of the major shipping companies (like UPS and Federal Express).
Minimize the number of people needed to run your E-commerce business	Implement customer self-service methods, including online ordering and instant credit-card verification. Implement EDI or XML for communications between your business and other businesses who need to complete your order (like shipping companies and banking institutions).

Lesson 10 Activities

Complete the following activities to better prepare you for the certification exam.

1. Before taking the I-Net+ exam or starting your E-commerce business, read the e-buzz newsletters for the latest information from CompTIA on the world of E-commerce.

2. Learn basic HTML programming. If you are already familiar with HTML, learn how to implement XML.

3. Assume you are planning on selling a product overseas. Check the current exchange rate for several countries. Use a search engine to find exchange rate Web pages other than those listed in this lesson.

4. Perform a search for a product using five different search engines. List the top five sites presented by each search engine. Why are there differences?

5. View the source page for the top site listed from each search engine in Activity #4. Can you discover what techniques they used for such good results?

6. Go to several of the E-commerce businesses from the search you performed in Activity #4. Notice the self-service methods and security features they have implemented. From which pages are you most likely to make a purchase? Why?

7. Using a search engine, intentionally misspell the product name or type, and then perform the search. Are any pages listed? Why?

8. If you already have a Web page, copyright the contents.

9. Obtain a copyright form from the U.S. Copyright Office and familiarize yourself with the information needed to register a copyright for a Web page.

10. Build a simple HTML-based Web page that appears in the top 10 lists of several major search engines.

Answers to Lesson 10 Activities

1. E-buzz newsletters are available online at: www.comptia.org/ecommerce/ebuzz.htm

2. A good Web site that teaches HTML programming is www.tips-tricks.com/index.shtml. For XML information, the best site is www.xml.com.

3. Exchange rates can be found at several sites on the Internet. It is always a good idea to check several pages and compare rates. Good keywords to search for may include "currency exchange" or "money conversion."

4. Each search engine uses its own algorithm, or computational method, for counting keywords. The different algorithms can result in very different search results.

5. To view a Web page source, open the page in a Web browser. Each Web browser has a different method for viewing the source code. For example, if you are using Internet Explorer, from the menu bar, choose View, and then select Source. Most often, you will find that the keywords you used for the search appear at least once in the <META> tag and may also appear several times within the text of the page.

6. You will find that some pages offer little more than a catalog and a toll-free phone number. Other pages will offer the full suite of purchasing options, including online catalogs, online order forms, and secure payment pages. Most people find that they are more likely to purchase on pages that appear professional and secure.

7. Most likely, several pages will be listed even if you misspell the keyword. Clever Web page designers will add common variations on keywords, including misspellings and typographical errors.

8. The only step needed to copyright your Web page is a declaration of copyright. At the bottom of every page, place the copyright symbol, followed by your name and the year of creation (for example, Copyright © Jane Doe, 2000, All Rights Reserved). To make the copyright symbol in HTML, you can either type (c), or use the "©" command to insert the proper-looking symbol.

9. Go to the U.S. Copyright Office Web site (www.loc.gov/copyright/) and follow the link for registration procedures. The forms and instructions can be downloaded from this site.

10. This is the end goal of every E-commerce Web designer. By carefully studying the other top-listed pages, you can compete for those most lucrative sites.

Lesson 10 Quiz

These questions test your knowledge of features, vocabulary, procedures, and syntax.

1. How many characters does Unicode support?

    A. 16

    B. 128

    C. 65,000

    D. 650,000

2. How many characters does ASCII support?

    A. 8

    B. 127

    C. 128

    D. 12,800

3. Which of the following is most often used to transfer forms between businesses?

    A. IDE

    B. X15

    C. HTTP

    D. EDI

4. What should you do to legally protect the contents and design of your Web page?

    A. Register the contents with the U.S. Trademark office

    B. Put a copyright statement at the bottom of each page

    C. Keep anyone from viewing the page

    D. Prevent search engines from finding your page

5. How do you provide a secure channel for your customers to provide credit card information?

    A. Implement a secure server using SSL

    B. Use XML on your Order Form page

    C. Implement a secure server using STP

    D. Create a gateway page

6. What is needed for your company to accept credit card purchases?

    A. A merchant marine

    B. A merchant account

    C. An EDI page

    D. A search engine

7. If you wish to require 128-bit encryption to transfer all personal information a user provides, you should implement:

    A. SET

    B. SSL

    C. HTML

    D. X12

8. What do you use to customize a Web page for a returning customer?

    A. Shopping carts

    B. ASCII

    C. Pull technology

    D. Push technology

9. How can you prevent someone outside the United States from using your company name or logo?
    A. Register the trademark with the U.N.

    B. Register your trademark with the U.S. trademark office

    C. Put a copyright statement at the bottom of each page

    D. There is nothing you can do

10. If you infringe on a registered copyright, what are the possible consequences? (Choose all that apply)

   A. You can be sued for up to 100,000 U.S. dollars

   B. You have to pay the copyright holder's legal expenses

   C. You lose your Internet access for up to 7 years

   D. You may be imprisoned for life

Answers to Lesson 10 Quiz

1. Answer C is correct. Unicode uses 16 bits per character, allowing 65,000 characters to be supported.

    Answers A, B, and D are incorrect.

2. Answer C is correct. ASCII uses 8 bits to define each character, providing support for 2^8 characters, or 128.

    Answers A, B, and D are incorrect.

3. Answer D is correct. EDI is a standard used to electronically transmit forms (like invoices and purchase orders) between businesses.

    Answer A is incorrect. IDE (Integrated Drive Electronics) is a hard disk drive specification.

    Answer B is incorrect. X15 is not a standard. X12 is an EDI standard and would have been a valid choice.

    Answer C is incorrect. HTTP (The HyperText Transfer Protocol) is used to transfer HTML-based Web pages.

4. Answer B is correct. Web page contents and design are protected by copyrights. You can also register your Web page with the U.S. copyright office.

    Answer A is incorrect. Trademarks apply to company names, logos, and domain names, not to Web page content.

    Answers C and D are incorrect. Although both of these methods may help protect the contents of your page, neither is a good solution. You need people to access your page to generate business.

5. Answer A is correct. The Secure Sockets Layer (SSL) protocol provides a secure link between the server and the client.

    Answer B is incorrect. XML does not provide security.

    Answer C is incorrect. STP is not a network security protocol.

    Answer D is incorrect. Gateway pages are used to generate more interest from people using search engines.

6. Answer B is correct. A merchant account, which is set up by a financial institution, permits your business to accept credit cards as forms of payment.

Answer A is incorrect.

Answer C is incorrect. EDI is used for business-to-business form transmissions.

Answer D is incorrect. Search engines have nothing to do with credit card purchases.

7. Answer B is correct. Only SSL can be used to encrypt all information with 128-bit security.

Answer A is incorrect. SET provides 128-bit security, but only for financial information.

Answers C and D are incorrect. Neither HTML nor X12 concern encryption.

8. Answer D is correct. Push technology allows you to send personalized information to the user.

Answer A is incorrect. Shopping carts are used to simplify the ordering process.

Answer B is incorrect. ASCII is a standard that uses numbers to represent alphanumeric characters.

Answer C is incorrect. Pull technology sends the information a client requests.

9. Answer D is correct. Currently, there are no international laws protecting company names and logos.

Answer A is incorrect. You cannot register trademarks with the U.N..

Answer B is incorrect. Registering your trademark with the U.S. will protect your company name and logo from use by other U.S.-based companies and will help you in an international court, but it does not prevent a company outside the U.S. from using your name or logo.

Answer C is incorrect. Copyrights protect original works (like the contents of your Web page), but do not protect company names and logos.

10. Answers A and B are correct. If you are found guilty of copyright infringement, you can be held responsible for lost profits and legal expenses incurred by the copyright holder and fined up to 100,000 U.S. dollars.

Answer C is incorrect. You cannot be prevented from accessing the Internet, since Internet access is unregulated (in the U.S.).

Answer D is incorrect. Imprisonment is not part of the penalty for copyright infringement.

Glossary

Term	Description
access controls	Methods used to control access to the Internet and internal networks.
ACL	Access Control Lists are databases of permissions assigned to users and groups
animated image	A GIF file that moves on the screen is an animated image.
ASCII	The American Standard Code for Information Interchange uses an 8-bit number to represent an English alphanumeric character.
asymmetric system	Encryption system where key pairs (a public and a private key) are generated. The public key encrypts and the private key decrypts the messages.
auditing	Keeping track of activity both from the outside (Internet/extranet) and from inside (a company intranet) to reveal potential security risks.
authentication	The process of determining if someone is who he or she claims to be before granting or denying network access. Usernames and passwords are forms of access control.
B2B	An abbreviation often used for Business-To-Business E-commerce transactions.
banner	An advertisement, usually wider than high, placed on a Web page that links to another page.

Term	Description
banner exchange	The mutual sharing of Web space among E-commerce businesses for banner advertisements that provides free advertising.
binary	A mathematical system that has only 2 values (1 or 0) for each number. In computer terminology, each binary number is called a bit.
bit	The basic building block of data, usually described as a 0 or 1.
bookmark	An entry in a list of favorite sites that is maintained by your browser.
BPS	Bits Per Second. Used to measure the data rate of a transmission medium.
bridge	A network hardware device that connects network segments into one logical network. Bridges also have functions that control broadcast traffic on a network.
broadband	Type of data transmission in which a single medium (wire) can carry several channels at once.
broadcast storm	A self-perpetuating broadcast cycle on a network. Broadcast storms completely dominate network traffic and shut down a network. A bridge using the Spanning Tree Algorithm can prevent a broadcast storm.

Term	Description
browser	A software application used to locate and display Web pages. Netscape Communicator and Microsoft Internet Explorer are the most popular graphical browsers. They interpret HTML codes to display graphics as well as text and can support programming languages like JavaScript to create interactive Web pages. Many browsers can also present full multimedia sound and video using small applications called plug-ins.
buffer	Temporary memory space used for constantly changing data.
business-to-consumer	E-commerce transactions between a business and the consumer.
byte	A combination of 8 bits, used, among other things, to represent characters such as letters of the alphabet or numbers.
C++	An object-oriented superset of the C programming language.
CA	Certificate Authority is a trusted third party, which after exhaustive background checks, issues digital certificates.
cable modem	A device that enables you to access the Internet through your cable TV system.
cache	A special memory space used to store frequently accessed information.
cache server	Servers that store frequently used Web pages and their components to speed client Web page access.

Term	Description
certificates	A digital identification, verifying a secure server's identity to the client and verifying the client's identity to the server.
CGI	Common Gateway Interface is not a programming language, but an interface that defines how programs can interact on the Web.
checksum	A calculation result that is compared to an expected result. Computers use checksums for error control.
cladding	Reflective covering that surrounds the glass core of a fiber-optic cable.
class	In a style sheet, categories into which you can divide HTML elements in order to assign styles to them more selectively.
client	The requestor of server services.
coax	Same as coaxial.
coaxial	Cabling (also called coax) that consists of one solid copper core which is surrounded by insulation, a braided metal shielding, and a jacket. The inner insulation ensures that no signals can pass from the copper core and no signals from outside the insulation can pass into the copper core. There are thick and thin types of coaxial cable.
COM	Component Object Model is a Microsoft specification that defines standards for interaction among programs, including application software and operating systems.

Term	Description
compiled programming language	A programming language in which source code converts in one fell swoop into machine code to create an executable file.
cookies	Text files of which one part is loaded onto the hard disk of a client computer and another part resides on the visited server in a user profile database. each cookie contains a unique identifier and may contain confidential information such as the name of the visitor, authentication, credit card numbers, and online shopping habits.
denial of service	Deliberate attacks to breach security by disabling a network rather than stealing critical data.
digital signatures	An electronic means of verifying a user's identity.
DISA	The Data Interchange Standards Association is a not-for-profit organization that concentrates on E-commerce related standards and issues (including EDI).
ECSB	The Electronic Commerce Standards Board is a CompTIA advisory board that addresses business-to-business E-commerce standards and issues.
EDI	The Electronic Data Interchange is a standard for exchanging information electronically between businesses.
e-mail marketing	A method of attracting customers by sending large-volume bulk e-mail messages to potential customers.
EMI	Electromagnetic Interference is a byproduct of electricity moving through wire.

Term	Description
encryption	Transforms data into a form unreadable to everyone except those that have the correct algorithm or key to unlock the data.
Ethernet	Ethernet is a local area networkLAN system developed by the Xerox Corporation in 1976. The IEEE Ethernet/ 802.3 standard for the 10- or 100-Mbps transmission for hardware and data packet construction specifications was derived from Ethernet.
extranet	A collection of intranets.
fiber-optic cable	A cable that uses glass strands and light pulses instead of electrical signals to transmit data.
firewall	A security system that protects an organization's network against internal and external threats.
frame relay	Packet-switching technology based on X.25 with less error control and faster speeds.
FTP	File Transfer Protocol—an Internet protocol used for transferring files among diverse computers.
FTP server	Servers used for sending out and receiving FTP file transfers.
gateway	Hardware or software setup that translates between two dissimilar protocols and performs conversion service for data.
Gbps	The abbreviation for Gigabits Per Second. Gbps is a measurement of data transfer speed on a network, in multiples of 1,073,741,824 (2^{30}) bits.

Term	Description
gigabyte	Written in powers of 2, a gigabyte is (2^{30}) or 1,073,741,824 bytes.
GII	The Global Information Infrastructure is a group started by the Ziff-Davis publishing company to create the Standard for Internet Commerce.
Gopher	Once the most popular client/server search engine on the Internet, Gopher has been almost completely replaced by modern search engines like Yahoo and AltaVista.
Gopher server	Servers used to display distributed text files by listing them in menus.
graphical interface	A computer interface designed with a visual metaphor to help users intuitively know how to perform operations.
hacker	An intrusive individual who is interested in gaining knowledge about computer systems and possibly using this knowledge for pranks.
home page	The initial page that a user sees in a browser or a Web page that people create to publish information about themselves.
hop	The path that data travel from one router to the next.
HPC	Handheld Personal Computer. A computer that fits in the palm of your hand.
HTML	HyperText Markup Language. A protocol used to package and transfer Web pages.

Term	Description
HTTP	HyperText Transfer Protocol. A computer language used for creating Web pages.
hub	Hardware that splits a network signal and connects networks together.
ICANN	Internet Corporation for Assigned Names and Numbers. A non-profit corporation that has responsibility for the accreditation of new domain registrars for the top-level domains of .com, .net, and .org.
IIS	Internet Information Server is a popular Web server made by Microsoft.
IMAP	Internet Message Access Protocol retrieves e-mail messages from an e-mail server. The latest version is IMAP4, which is similar to POP3 except that it supports several enhancements.
Internet	A network of networks connecting millions of computers in local, regional, national networks.
internetwork	A collection of LANs connected via routers.
InterNIC	A cooperative activity between the U.S. Government and Network Solutions, Inc. For many years, it was the sole provider of domain name registration services for .com, .net, and .org top-level domains.
intranet	The portion of a network that is not accessible to the general public. The intranet is usually separated from the extranet and Internet by a firewall and is used for internal communications within a business.

Term	Description
intrusion detection	Tracking and recording any suspicious activity on a network.
IP address	A 32-bit number represented as four decimal numbers separated by periods. The first 1, 2, or 3 bytes of the IP address identify the network to which the host is connected; the remaining bits identify the host itself.
ISDN	Integrated Services Digital Network is a high-speed digital communications network, which evolved from existing telephone services.
ISDN terminal adapter	Integrated Services Digital Network terminal adapters are devices that accept digital signals from a telephone line and translate them into digital data that is recognizable to a computer.
ISP	Internet Service Provider is a company or organization that provides Internet access to businesses, large and small organizations, and individual users.
jitter	Jitter is an annoying and perceptible variation in the time it takes various workstations to respond to messages.
K	A kilo or kilobyte is 1,024 bytes of data storage.
Kbps	Kilobits Per Second.
LAN	Local Area Network is a small network that covers a small area such as an office, one floor of a building, or one department of a large organization.
LDAP	Lightweight Directory Access Protocol is a client server service for search databases using ordinary text queries.

Term	Description
line protocol	Enables a local computer to connect to a modem on a remote computer and connect the two devices.
link	A spot in a Web page that transfers you to another Web page.
local computer	The computer that can be accessed directly rather than by means of a communications line.
local loop	Connects the subscriber wiring at a business or residence to the telephone company's local central office.
loop-back	This special IP address (127.0.0.1) will cause the PING utility to detect a host computer's own NIC.
LPR	Line Printer is a client/server protocol for sending and receiving print documents across a TCP/IP network.
M	Mega or megabyte is 1,048,576 bytes of data storage.
MAC	Media Access Control manages access to the physical network, delimits datagrams, and handles error control.
mail server	Servers that manage e-mail.
mailing list	A list of users who all wish to receive a common set of mail.
MAN	Metropolitan Area Network is a small WAN that covers a city or metropolitan area.
Mb	Abbreviation for Megabit (1,048,576 bits (2^{30})) and sometimes referred to as 1 million bits.

Term	Description
Mbps	Abbreviation for Megabits Per Second.
Megabit	A Megabit is a measurement of storage capacity equal to about 1 million bits or 1,048,576 bits (2^{30}).
merchant account	An account with a banking institution needed to process credit card sales.
META	An HTML tag used to insert hidden keywords into a Web page, so search engines will display your page when one or more of the keywords is searched for.
MIME	Multipurpose Internet Mail Extensions is a specification for formatting non-ASCII messages for transmission over the Internet. Many e-mail client applications support MIME because it enables them to send and receive graphics, video, and audio files through the Internet mail system.
modem	Originally referred to a device that MOdulated and DEModulated digital information across telephone lines. Now used to describe a wide variety of data interfaces for computers.
multiple logon failures	A number of unsuccessful attempts to access a network, which can indicate a possible hacker attack.
multiplexer	A device that can divide a single T1 or E1 connection into data lines and voice lines.
NAP	Network Access Point is a large exchange point for Internet traffic. Established by the NSF.
Navigator	Netscape's first browser.

Term	Description
NetBEUI	NetBIOS Enhanced User Interface is a simple fast network protocol that is not routable.
Netscape Enterprise Server	A popular Web server made by Netscape.
NETSTAT	A command line utility that generates datagram statistics sorted by protocols used.
network adapter	Another name for network interface card (NIC).
network protocol	TCP/IP, IPX/SPX, NetBEUI, AsyNetBEUI, are the usual network communications protocols used to access remote Internet network servers.
news server	A server that maintains a database of newsgroups.
newsgroup	A collection of messages with a related theme, located on a news server.
NIC	A Network Interface Card is an expansion card or other device that provides network access to a computer or other device, such as a printer. NICs mediate between the computer and the physical media, such as cabling over which transmissions travel.
NNTP	Network News Transfer Protocol provides services for special interest group forums to organize posted discussions in hierarchical threads.
NOC	Network Operations Center—the main operations center for DirecPC.

Term	Description
node	A device, such as a client computer, server, or shared printer that connects to the network and communicates with other network devices.
NSFNet	Funded by the National Science Foundation, this network's main constituents were universities, government agencies, and organizations involved in research. ARPANet was its foundation and it later evolved into the Internet.
NSP	Network Service Providers are companies such as PSINet and UUNET which maintain the nationwide communications links that make up the Internet backbone.
octet	A group of eight. In binary language an octet is 8 bits of information. Another term for 8 bits is a byte. In decimal format, a byte has a value range of 0 to 255.
one-way hash function	An algorithm that converts text into a fixed-length string of digits which, in turn, is encrypted with a private key to create a digital signature that authenticates the sender.
OSPF	Open Shortest Path First is a routing protocol that minimizes broadcast transmissions between routers supports variable-length subnetting.
packet	A unit of transmission data with fixed size and header information about source, destination, and data assembly.
packet filtering	Inspecting packets to determine whether or not to grant or deny access to a network.

Term	Description
packet switching	A networking technology that divides a message into packets, each labeled with a destination address. The packets travel through a network and are reassembled at the destination.
parameters	Properties represented by user-settable variables.
PCT	Private Communication Technology is a protocol that separates authentication from encryption and allows applications to use authentication that is stronger than the 40-bit key limit for encryption allowed by the U.S. Government for export.
PGP	Pretty Good Privacy is an encryption method based on the asymmetric key system.
physical address	The hexadecimal number associated with a Network Interface Card (NIC).
PING	A command line utility used to check network connections.
PING flood	Echo requests to an IP address (PINGs) transmit to a system in overwhelming numbers. The system under attack cannot handle the bombardment and crashes.
POP	Post Office Protocol is a protocol used for incoming messages.
port	An interface through which data are transferred between a computer and other devices, such as a network or another computer. It appears to the processing computer as an address in memory to send and receive data.
port number	The number associated with an application.

Term	Description
portal	An all-purpose link to the Web. It contains news, sports, weather, electronic mail and more.
POTS	Plain Old Telephone System refers to the public telephone system. Public phone lines are used to connect a local computer to a network computer using the DUN feature in Windows.
PPP	Point-to-Point Protocol is a protocol that controls communications from a user's residence over telephone lines to an ISP.
PPTP	Point-to-Point Tunneling Protocol is a more secure version of PPP. This connection supports the encryption and compression of all transmitted data. To use PPTP requires connection to a remote tunnel server. Once connected PPTP supports all the same network protocols as PPP (TCP/IP, IPX/SPX, NetBEUI, etc.) to access the network.
private key system	A symmetric encryption system that uses a single key which both the sender and the recipient use to encrypt and decrypt messages.
proxy server	A server located between a client application and remote servers which provides, among other things, security into and out of your network.
proxy server cache	A quickly accessible storage area for Web pages that are frequently viewed with a Web browser.
PSTN	Public Switched Telephone Network is the telephone system that carries analog voice data.
public key system	See asymmetric key system

Term	Description
pull	The technology usually used on the Internet, where the user requests data from a Web server.
push	A technology that sends data to a user, even if that data was not specifically requested. Used to customize and filter Web page content.
PWS	Personal Web Server is a popular Web server made by the Microsoft for PCs running Windows 95/98.
query	An inquiry for information from a database.
RAS	Remote Access Server. A Microsoft communications server.
remote	Any files, devices, or other resources not connected directly to your workstation. Resources connected directly to a workstation are local.
Remote Access Server	A network server that enables you to log into a Windows NT-based LAN using a modem.
remote computer	The computer that an operator accesses by way of a modem.
repeater	Repeaters are simple hardware devices that receive digital information, regenerate the signal, and pass it along.
RIP	Routing Information Protocol is a common service provided by routers that use broadcasts to communicate with other routers, gathering path and host ID information.
root servers	Primary servers at the foundation of DNS.

Term	Description
router	Any device having multiple NICs that filter, forward, and redirect network traffic.
S/MIME	Secure Multipurpose Internet Mail Extensions is a protocol used in secure e-mail exchanges.
screening router	Programmable routers that follow a set of rules to inspect packets and permit or deny access to a network based on those rules.
screening router	Programmable routers that follow a set of rules to inspect packets and permit or deny access to a network based on those rules.
SDSL	Symmetric Digital Subscriber Line. A European DSL standard that supports symmetric traffic, equivalent data transmission rates in each direction, of up to 3 Mbps
search engines	Web sites that perform keyword searches of Web pages and provide a convenient location for users to find products and services.
segment	Connected devices not separated by a bridge or a router.
server	A computer or program on the Internet or other network that responds to commands from a client.
SET	Secure Electronic Transaction protocol provides strong encryption and direct data transfers to financial institutions.
S-HTTP	Secure HyperText Transfer Protocol encrypts individual messages for transmission across the unsecured Internet.

Term	Description
SIG	Special Interest Group is any group of people that meet in person or via discussion groups over the Internet to exchange ideas and information about a single topic.
signature file	Anti-virus software programs rely on virus signature files to identify new and existing computer viruses. Makers of the anti-virus software frequently update virus signature files.
SLIP	Serial Line Internet Protocol is a UNIX protocol.
SMTP	Simple Mail Transport Protocol is a protocol used for outgoing messages and communications between mail servers.
smurf	Another name for a PING flood attack.
sockets	A software object that connects applications to a network protocol for sending and receiving TCP/IP messages.
source-route bridge	Connect token-ring networks, a network technology developed by IBM.
spam	Another term for e-mail marketing, spam is often blocked by ISPs.
spamming floods	An e-mail attack that transmits unsolicited data in quantities that can overwhelm a mail server and disable it.
Spanning Tree Algorithm	A standard that establishes protocols for network bridges and is responsible for controlling broadcast storms.

Term	Description
spoofing	A technique used by hackers to trick their way through a firewall into a network by changing the information in a packet to look like a friendly packet.
SQL Server	A Microsoft database management system.
SSL	Secure Sockets Layer is a protocol that creates a secure connection, or channel, over which all data between a Web client and a secure Web server are encrypted.
STP	Shielded Twisted-Pair cable.
streaming media	A data transfer system that allows the media to be accessed while it is still being transferred.
subnet	A local area network (LAN) that has been divided into separate network segments. Routers can divide LANs into subnets and transfer data among subnets. All devices on a subnet can communicate without routing datagrams.
subnet mask	The subnet mask, or address mask, determines which part of the 32-bit binary IP address is the network ID information and which part is the host ID information.
supernet	A process where bits are borrowed from network ID bits and used to combine networks. This process is used to combine multiple Class C networks into virtual class B networks.
switch	A hub with bridge functionality for each port.

Term	Description
SYN flood	A SYN is a flag in a packet header. The SYN flag is a request to open a port in a firewall. When a hacker sends hundreds or thousands of these to a firewall in a few minutes or seconds, it is a SYN flood attack designed to create a denial of service and bring down the target network.
T1	High-speed carrier with 24 64-Kbps channels combined into one 1.5-Mbps connection.
T3	High-speed carrier that transmits at 45 45-Mbps connections.
Telnet	A command-line utility for remote connectivity across TCP/IP.
Telnet server	Servers which permit a computer to act as a terminal for another computer.
terminal emulation	Software designed to make a PC mimic the behavior of a particular monitor/keyboard model associated with mainframe computers.
thicknet	A thick type of coaxial cable that is somewhat rigid and measures about 0.5 inch in diameter with a thick copper core.
thinnet	A thin type of coaxial cable that is flexible and measures about 0.25 inch thick in diameter.
throughput	The rate at which data are transferred on a network and measured as the number of transmitted bits per second (bps).

Term	Description
TLS	Transport Layer Security is a Microsoft security protocol that incorporates both SSL and PCT into one standard that supports both certificates and password authentication.
top-level servers	The second tier of DNS, these computers store registration data about domain names.
TRACERT	A command line utility that generates datagram path information on an internetwork.
translational bridge	Connect different types of networks, such as TCP/IP and token-ring networks.
UDP	User Datagram Protocol is available as an alternative protocol to TCP. UDP is fast but contains no error checking or delivery confirmation services.
UN/EDIFACT	One of two EDI standards, UN/EDIFACT is used by businesses outside the United States.
Unicode	A standard that assigns numbers to language characters, Unicode uses 16 bits of code per character, thus supporting 65,000 characters. Due to its support for all languages (not just English), it is expected to replace ASCII code as the standard for displaying characters.
up-link	Usually refers to sending data to a satellite receiver.
URL	Uniform Resource Locator is an address that points to a document on the World Wide Web.
Usenet	The most popular newsgroup system.
UTP	Unshielded Twisted-Pair cable.

Term	Description
variable-length subnetting	A system for creating internal IP addressing that allows use of any class address while registering a single subnet with InterNIC.
viruses	Viruses are small, often destructive, programs that may be disguised as part of a harmless file, game, utility, or e-mail attachment.
VPNs	A Virtual Private Network creates encrypted private communication channels over the public Internet.
WAN	Wide Area Network is a collection of LANs or internetworks that covers a large geographic area such as multiple branches of a large company.
Web browser	A program used to display Web pages.
Web page	A page displayable in a Web browser, containing hot links, text, graphics, video, audio and more.
Web server	A server that provides data in the form of Web pages.
WebTV	A system that displays Internet content on your TV screen.
WINS	Windows Internet Naming Service is a Microsoft solution for NetBIOS/IP address name resolution.
Winsock	This API enables Windows programs to communicate with other computers by using the TCP/IP protocol. Winsock is designed upon the socket's API in UNIX. Windows 98 and Windows NT use the Dynamic Link Library (DLL) called WINSOCK.DLL to read and write data to and from TCP/IP-supported applications.

Term	Description
WWW	World Wide Web is a subset of the Internet characterized by easy-to-navigate Web pages.
X.25	Packet-switching technology with robust error control and maximum connection speeds of 64 Kbps.
X12	The EDI standard used by businesses within the U.S.
XML	Extensible Markup Language is a new markup language similar to HTML but with a richer feature set.

Index

www.ingramcontent.com/pod-product-compliance
Lightning Source LLC
Chambersburg PA
CBHW080131060326
40689CB00018B/3750